By the Same Authors

The Lone and Level Sands

For Carolyn, the ocean supporting my ark.
~MPM

For my brother.
~ADL

SOME NEW KIND OF SLAUGHTER

~or~Lost in the Flood (and How We Found Home Again)

Diluvian Myths from Around the World

BY MPMANN & A. DAVID LEWIS

ARCHAIA

SOME NEW KIND OF SLAUGHTER

Written by mpMann and A. David Lewis
Illustrated by mpMann

Published by Archaia

PJ Bickett, President
Mark Smylie, Publisher
Stephen Christy III, Development Director
Brian Torney, Associate Creative Director
Mel Caylo, Marketing Manager

Archaia Entertainment, LLC
A Kunoichi Company
3759 N. Ravenswood Ave, Suite 230
Chicago IL 60613

www.Archaia.com

Printed in China.

ISBN: 1-932386-53-X
ISBN-13: 978-1-932386-53-0

10 9 8 7 6 5 4 3 2 1
First Edition

Foreword

For me, it all began with the 2004 Asian tsunami. Horrified by the huge loss of life, I was also fascinated by the imagery, by the idea that life-giving water could bring such epic death and destruction. I remember trolling the Internet for video from the tsunami, watching YouTube clips over and over again. What was most mesmerizing about what I saw was not that the water came in crashing waves, but rather that it seemed to surge from below, to inexorably grow deeper and deeper, like some nightmare from which you couldn't wake. And that was exactly it — the tsunami, the flooding, the very themes of water and drowning, were like dreams, a nightmare millions of helpless people shared that late-December night in 2004.

Less than a year later, when Hurricane Katrina struck the U.S. Gulf Coast, I experienced the same morbid fascination with the storm surge and the flooding of New Orleans. This time, however, I was moved to action. For whatever reason, I woke from my waterlogged reverie and volunteered with the Red Cross. Almost before I knew it, I was in the Gulf Coast, providing emergency relief to those left behind. Walking through the rubble of Biloxi, Mississippi, and listening to the clients' survival stories made the experience all too real, but the rising waters still haunted my dreams. Perhaps they always will.

So for me at least, mpMann and A. David Lewis's *Some New Kind of Slaughter* is especially resonant. Mainly through the visions of the ancient Sumerian king Ziusudra, adrift on his great ark, Mann and Lewis take the reader on a dreamlike tour through the world's great flood myths. From Babylonia to the Nile Delta, from the Chinese tales of Da Yu to the Native American Menomines, and from modern-day eco-warriors to the Old Testament, we see how these disparate creation and destruction myths share themes of divine punishment, visionary pariahs, and… turtles? Even the familiar story of Noah comes to life in unexpected ways.

Humor leavens the tales. The ancient stories, cultures, and names go down easy via Lewis's characters' naturalistic, witty dialogue. And Mann's beautiful, painterly art completely meshes with the story. The expert weaving of word and image is augmented by the landscape-style alignment of the pages, a device that would seem gimmicky in other contexts, but here reinforces the hallucinatory narrative.

Reading this book reminded me of my youthful backpacking days. Traveling through Southeast Asia and Central Europe, I read author Gore Vidal's series of historical novels tracing the exploits of one family through American history. Completely captivated by Vidal's unique vision and his gleeful assault on our cultural myths, when I returned home I sought out the primary sources, reading up on events I hadn't thought about since high school. I thoroughly enjoyed that journey, and will always be grateful to Vidal for his expert use of the art of fiction to teach fact. *Some New Kind of Slaughter* does the exact same thing.

The human instinct to tell stories — to make sense of the senseless, to impose order on what seems like the capricious whims of nature — is timeless. What began with poems around a fire, or ancient symbols on cracked parchment, comes to us now in the form of viral video and the pages of the graphic novel. Like a dream shared across cultures and history, *Some New Kind of Slaughter* ties our modern present to the ancient and/or biblical past. It is a triumphant demonstration that the graphic novel may be the future's best teaching tool.

— Josh Neufeld
  Brooklyn, March 2009

Josh Neufeld is the author of *A.D.: New Orleans After the Deluge*, a true story of Hurricane Katrina told in comics form. *A.D.* debuts from Pantheon in summer 2009. www.smithmag.net/afterthedeluge

An Introduction

Some New Kind of Slaughter
~or~ Lost in the Flood (and How We Found Home Again):
Diluvian Myths from Around The World
by mpMann and A. David Lewis

Wow. That's a mouthful of a title, no question. The working title was *High Waters*, which wasn't bad, just a bit…compact. (Also, should we really follow *The Lone and Level **Sands*** with *Waters?* A bit too gimmicky.) *Lost in the Flood* came next, but it seemed prosaic, too literal, or maybe just too Springsteen. Dave found *Some New Kind of Slaughter* from a line in Robert Frost's poem *"The Flood"* (about the 1927 Mississippi Flood), and it struck Marv as about as attention-getting a title as one could wish. But it also suggested a crime or horror book – sure, flood myths are about genocide on a godly scale, but they are also about the survivors. And so is this book.

Since this is a book largely about ancient stories or, at least, connections to the past, we felt that a more antique style of name, complete with subtitles and alternate headings was appropriate. Hence, *Some New Kind Of Slaughter,* the attention-grabber, followed by *~or~ Lost in the Flood (and How We Found Home Again)* cozy and hobbit-like, and finally, *Diluvian Myths from Around the World,* utilitarian and almost scholarly.

And don't overlook our gallows-humor punning, either. The acronym for *Some New Kind of Slaughter* – sinks! All things for all people. The same way we approach these stories of antiquity as well.

Structuring a project like this posed its own challenges. We researched myths, songs, jokes, and even resorted to pure invention. Flood myths are usually about the destruction of humanity because we've offended the gods for some reason. The Sumerians claimed we made too much noise. The parallel to modern ocean rising or mankind as stewards of the Earth seemed immediately apparent.

But after that, and despite a few recurring motifs such as giants, snakes and turtles, the stories vary so much as to resist a syncretic approach. They do not come together in a single coherent story. But they do echo each other in their themes and leitmotifs, and they can be strung together and play off each other. They're, very appropriately, fluid. And universal.

We developed four movements, Warnings, Preparations, Deluge, and Aftermath, and we selected the earliest known flood figure, Ziusudra, from the Sumerian version of the *Epic of Gilgamesh* as our narrator. Standing alone at the prow of his ark, hallucinating after a week of wakeful watchfulness, Ziusudra provides a slim narrative course, piloting us through the oceans of story yoked together as much by theme as by event.

For, as Ziusudra learns, stories have the power to guide us through the dangers of the world to a fuller understanding of our place in it.

MPM & ADL, El Sobrante and East Boston, April 2008.

W a r n i n g s

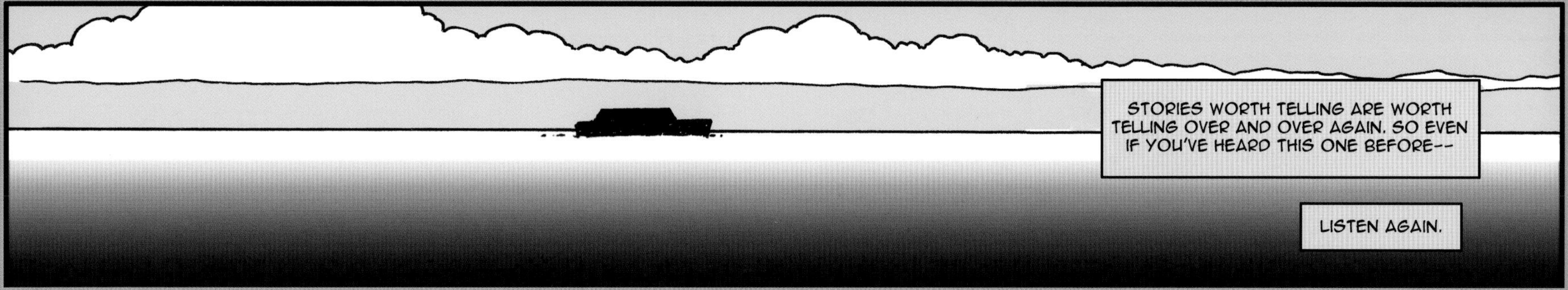
STORIES WORTH TELLING ARE WORTH TELLING OVER AND OVER AGAIN. SO EVEN IF YOU'VE HEARD THIS ONE BEFORE--
LISTEN AGAIN.

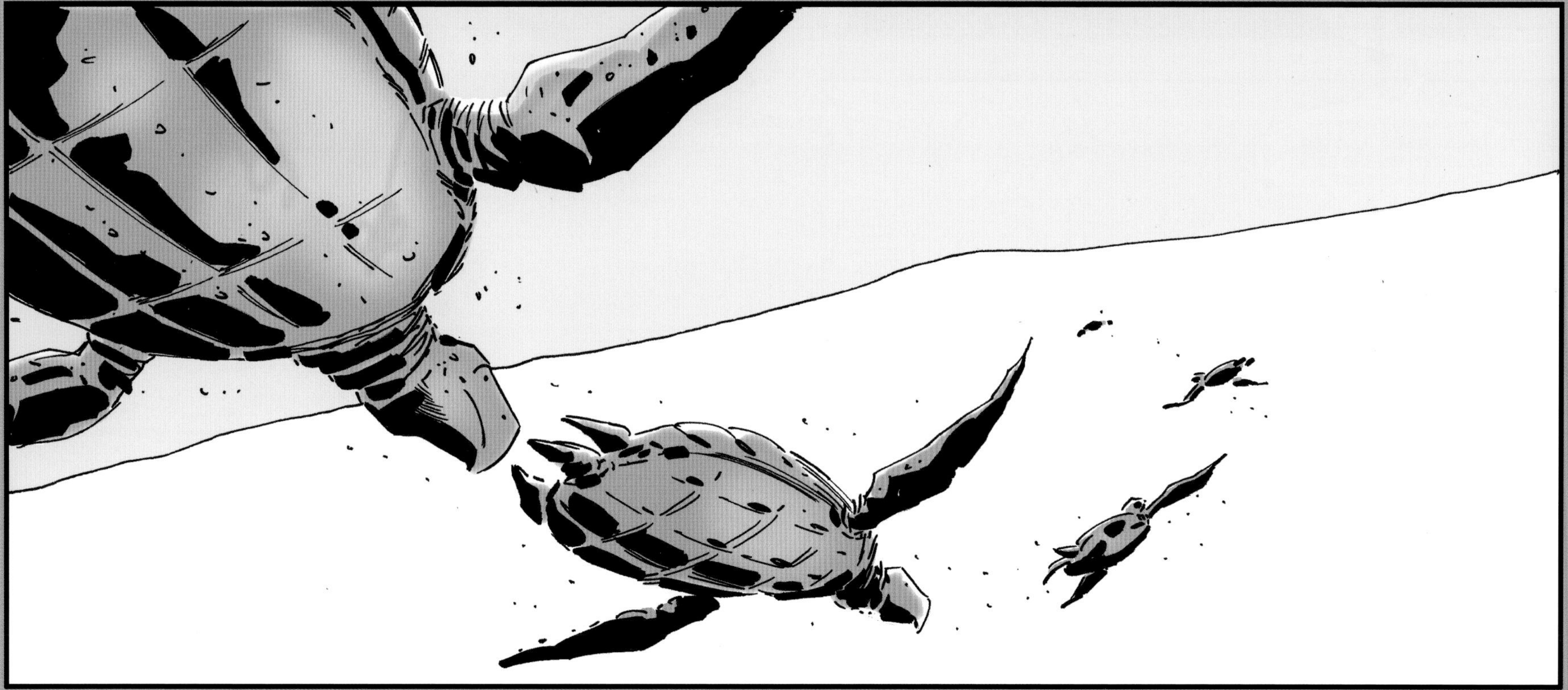

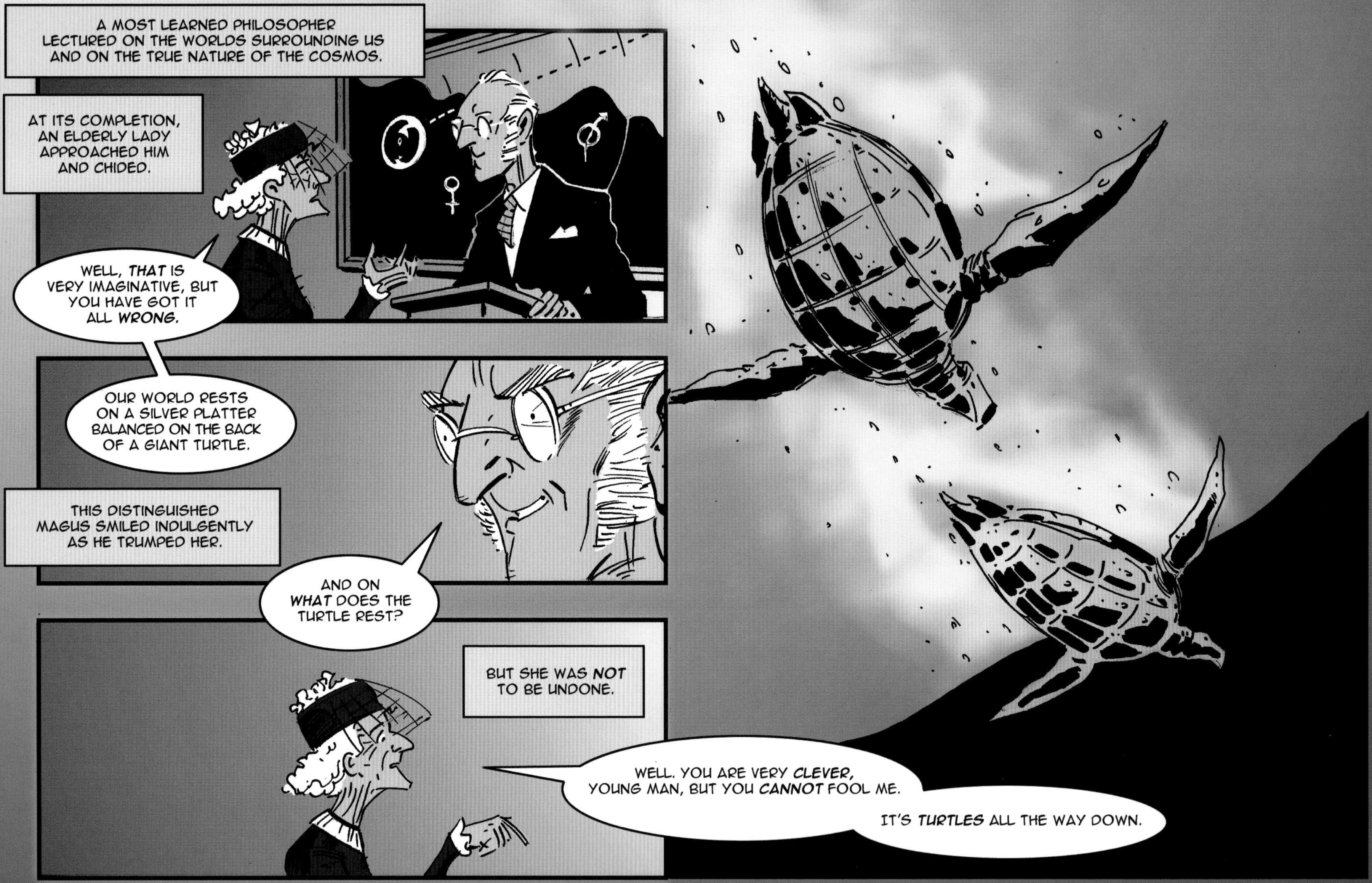
A MOST LEARNED PHILOSOPHER LECTURED ON THE WORLDS SURROUNDING US AND ON THE TRUE NATURE OF THE COSMOS.
AT ITS COMPLETION, AN ELDERLY LADY APPROACHED HIM AND CHIDED.
WELL, *THAT* IS VERY IMAGINATIVE, BUT YOU HAVE GOT IT ALL *WRONG.*
OUR WORLD RESTS ON A SILVER PLATTER BALANCED ON THE BACK OF A GIANT TURTLE.
THIS DISTINGUISHED MAGUS SMILED INDULGENTLY AS HE TRUMPED HER.
AND ON *WHAT* DOES THE TURTLE REST?
BUT SHE WAS *NOT* TO BE UNDONE.
WELL. YOU ARE VERY *CLEVER,* YOUNG MAN, BUT YOU *CANNOT* FOOL ME.
IT'S *TURTLES* ALL THE WAY DOWN.

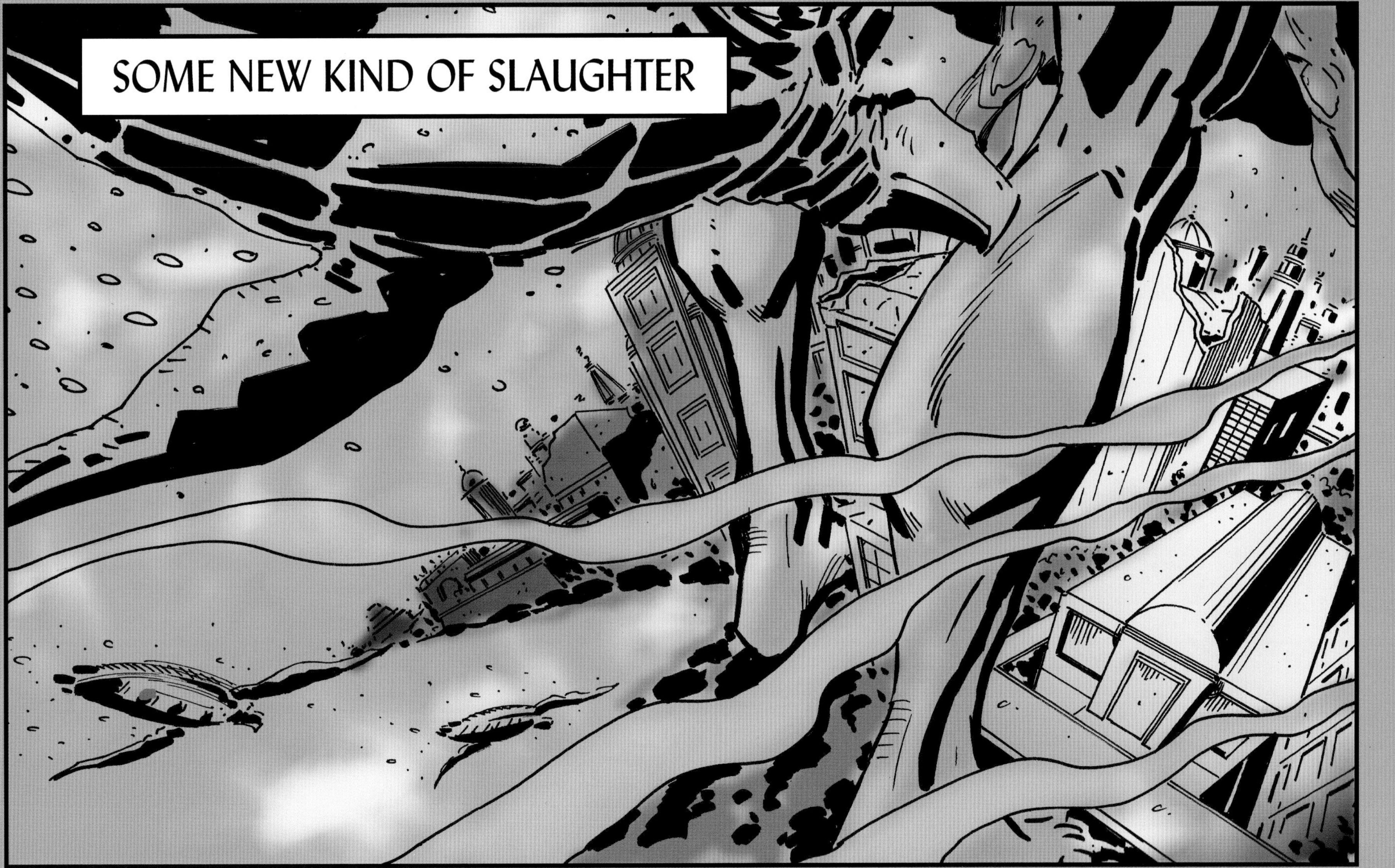
SOME NEW KIND OF SLAUGHTER

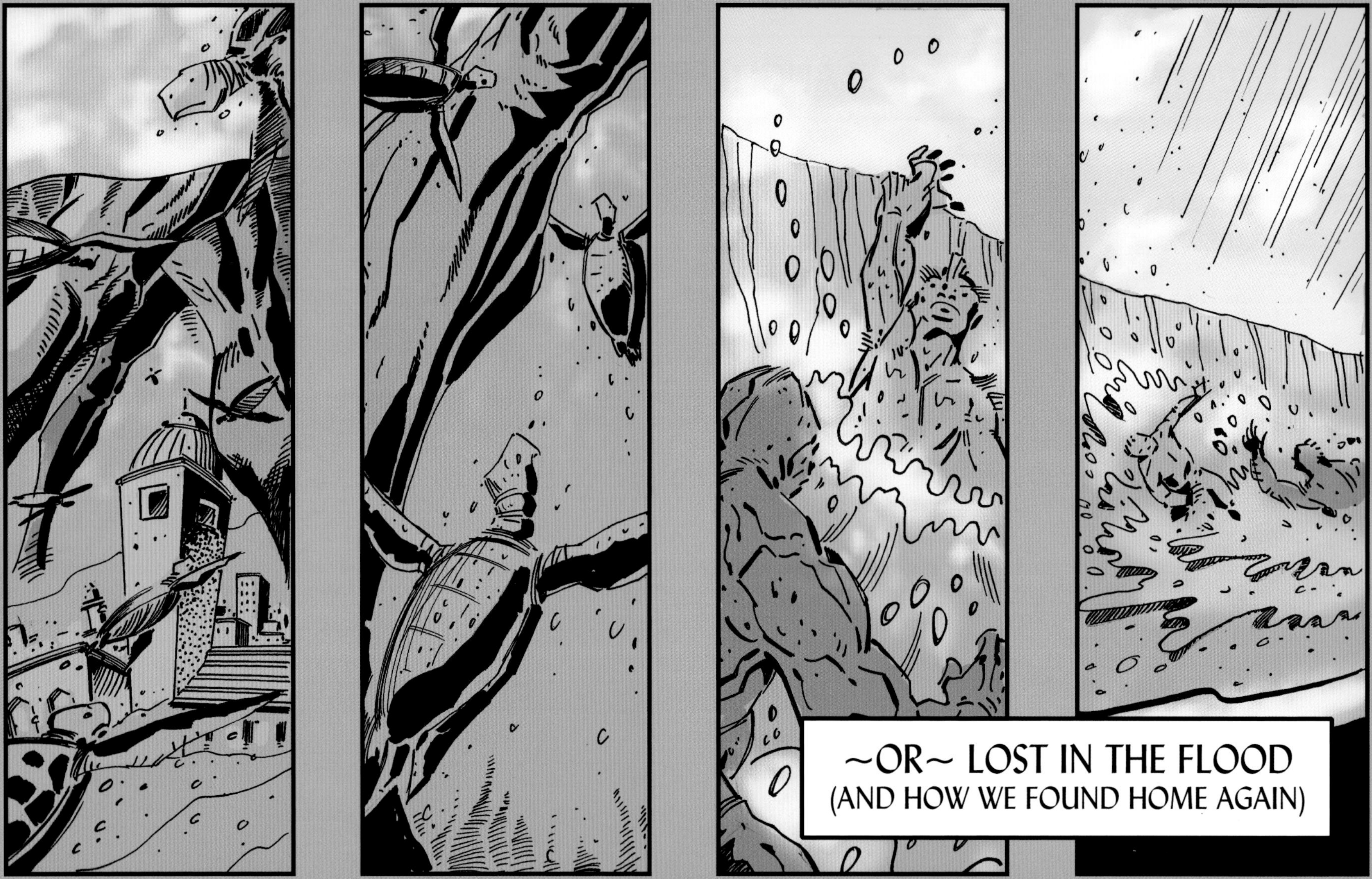
~OR~ LOST IN THE FLOOD
(AND HOW WE FOUND HOME AGAIN)

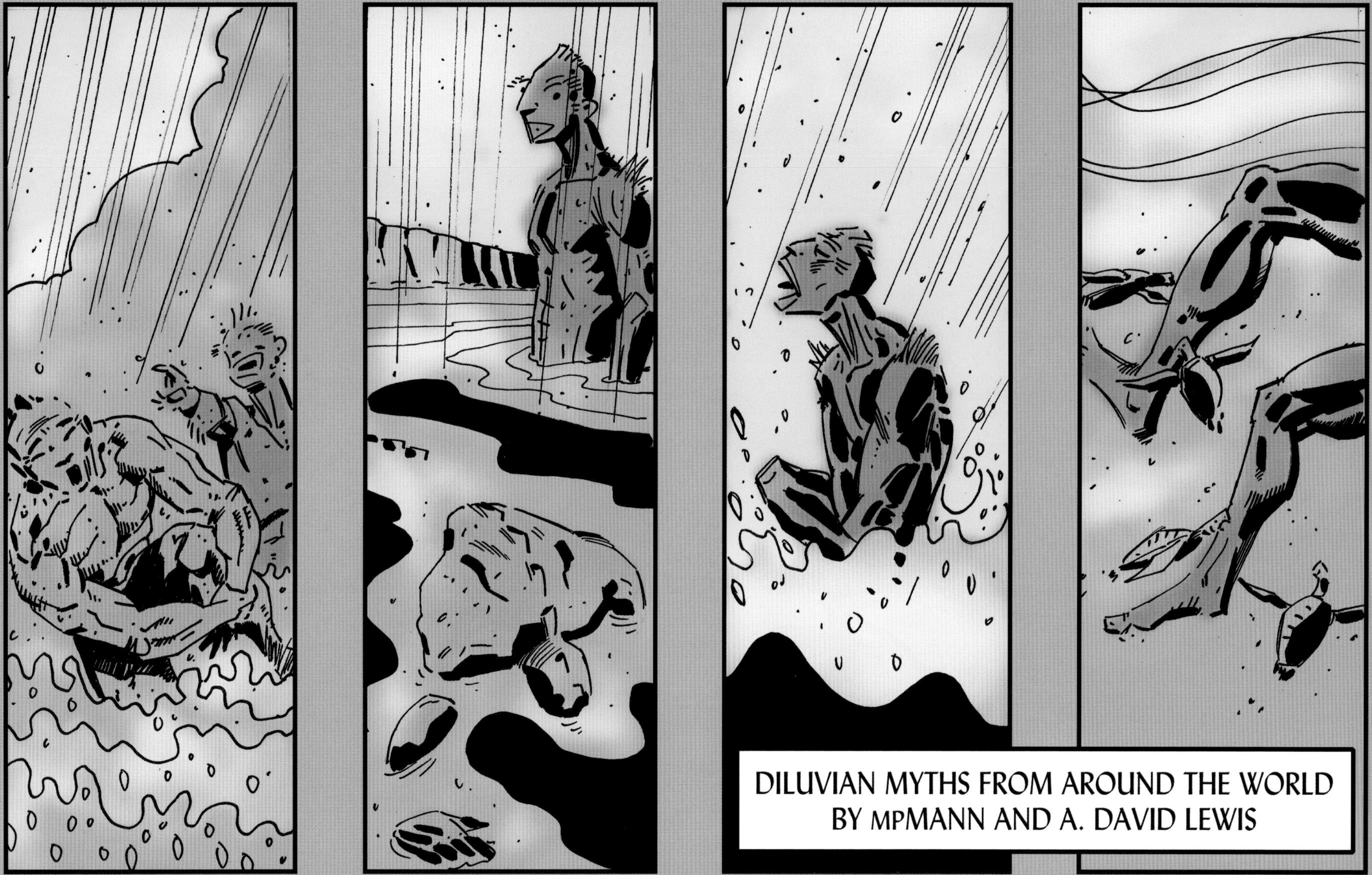
DILUVIAN MYTHS FROM AROUND THE WORLD
BY MPMANN AND A. DAVID LEWIS

ALL IS FLUID.

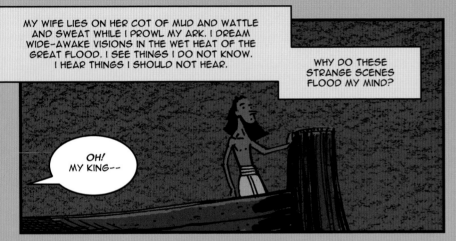

MY WIFE LIES ON HER COT OF MUD AND WATTLE AND SWEAT WHILE I PROWL MY ARK. I DREAM WIDE-AWAKE VISIONS IN THE WET HEAT OF THE GREAT FLOOD. I SEE THINGS I DO NOT KNOW. I HEAR THINGS I SHOULD NOT HEAR.

WHY DO THESE STRANGE SCENES FLOOD MY MIND?

OH! MY KING--

PARDON ME.

YOU DO NOT SLEEP?

NOR DO YOU, DAUGHTER. IT IS THE SEVENTH NIGHT OF THE SEVENTH DAY, AND I HAVE NOT SLEPT WHILE ALL OTHERS BARELY STIR.

WHAT THOUGHTS HAVE ROUSED YOU THIS NIGHT?

THE END OF THINGS. OF SHARRUPAK, OUR HOME, THE WORLD OF MEN. OF THIS WATER.

ENLIL DECREED TO US THE END OF SHARRUPAK AND SENT THIS WATER.

BUT ENKI HAS PROMISED ME AN END TO THIS FLOOD. IT *WILL* CEASE!

BUT WHAT WILL BE AT THE END OF THIS FLOOD? I WORRY, MY KING, THAT THE WORLD OF MEN IS GONE FOREVER.

SHARRUPAK IS GONE, AND WITH IT, MY KINGSHIP. I AM BUT MAN, BUT WHILE I AM A MAN, I REMAIN WAKEFUL FOR SIGNS BY WHICH TO DEFEND OUR PEOPLE.

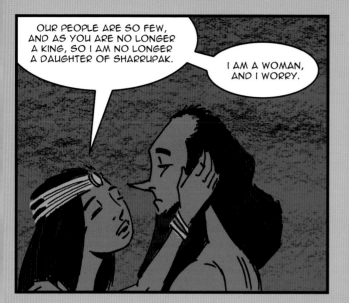

OUR PEOPLE ARE SO FEW, AND AS YOU ARE NO LONGER A KING, SO I AM NO LONGER A DAUGHTER OF SHARRUPAK.

I AM A WOMAN, AND I WORRY.

AT THE END OF THESE WATERS, WILL THERE BE A HUSBAND FOR ME?

...I HAVE A WIFE.

SHE IS YOUR KINSWOMAN.

BUT YOU ARE AWAKE, AND SHE IS ASLEEP.

YOU ARE AWAKE, AND SO AM I.

*

SO I WENT TO MY GOOD WIFE AND, EVEN AS SHE SLEPT THROUGH THE MOIST, TIRING HAZE, I SPOKE TO HER, AS I HAVE ALWAYS DONE.

BELOVED, I WILL TELL YOU OF A YOUNG WOMAN. SHE HAS NO HUSBAND. HER HUSBAND HAS LEFT HER.

AMONG HER PEOPLE, HER NAME IS "SHAR-EN BOE-TREIT."

SHE IS A SEER.

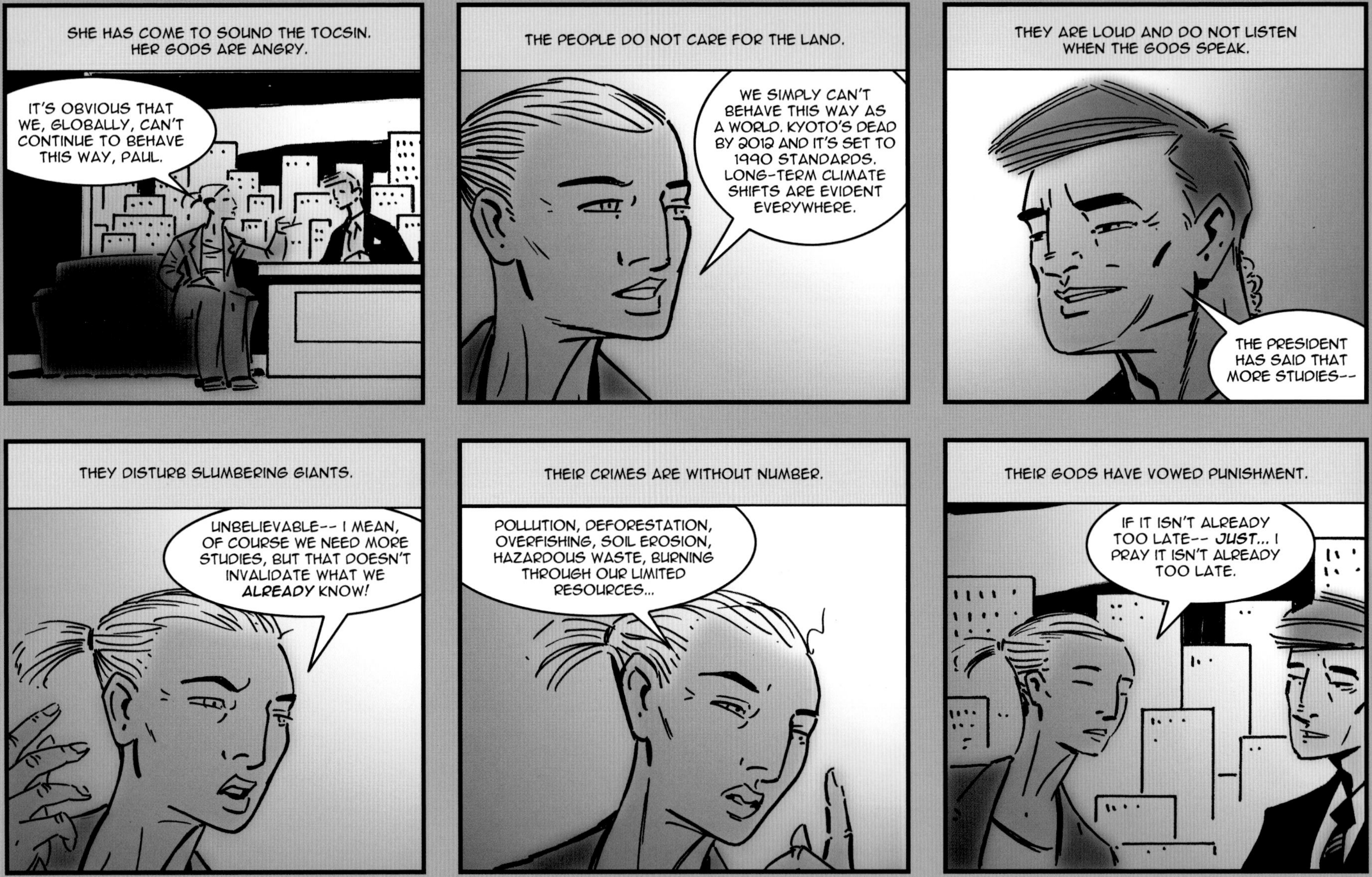
SHE HAS COME TO SOUND THE TOCSIN. HER GODS ARE ANGRY.
IT'S OBVIOUS THAT WE, GLOBALLY, CAN'T CONTINUE TO BEHAVE THIS WAY, PAUL.
THE PEOPLE DO NOT CARE FOR THE LAND.
WE SIMPLY CAN'T BEHAVE THIS WAY AS A WORLD. KYOTO'S DEAD BY 2012 AND IT'S SET TO 1990 STANDARDS. LONG-TERM CLIMATE SHIFTS ARE EVIDENT EVERYWHERE.
THEY ARE LOUD AND DO NOT LISTEN WHEN THE GODS SPEAK.
THE PRESIDENT HAS SAID THAT MORE STUDIES--
THEY DISTURB SLUMBERING GIANTS.
UNBELIEVABLE-- I MEAN, OF COURSE WE NEED MORE STUDIES, BUT THAT DOESN'T INVALIDATE WHAT WE *ALREADY* KNOW!
THEIR CRIMES ARE WITHOUT NUMBER.
POLLUTION, DEFORESTATION, OVERFISHING, SOIL EROSION, HAZARDOUS WASTE, BURNING THROUGH OUR LIMITED RESOURCES...
THEIR GODS HAVE VOWED PUNISHMENT.
IF IT ISN'T ALREADY TOO LATE-- *JUST*... I PRAY IT ISN'T ALREADY TOO LATE.

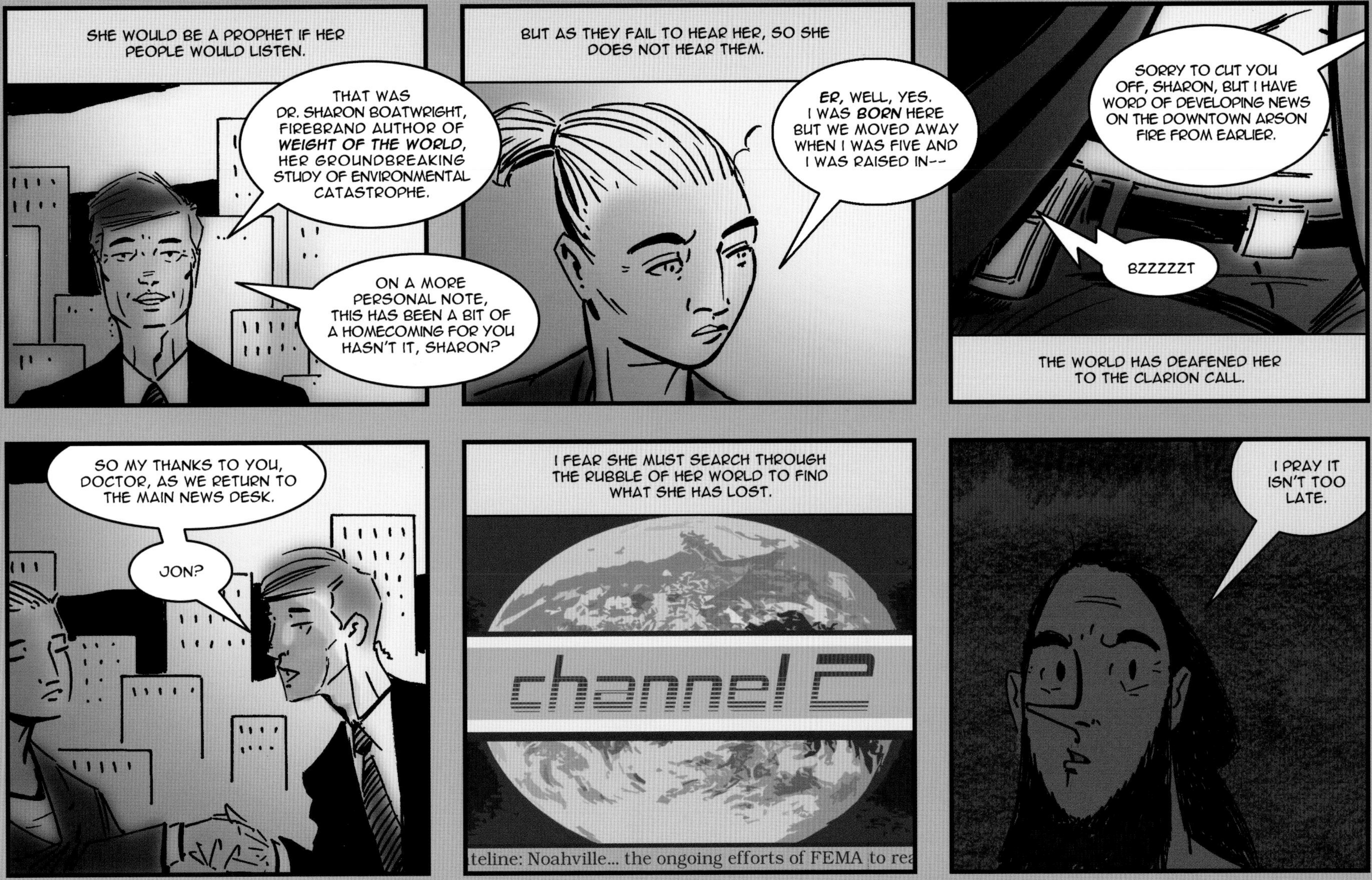
SHE WOULD BE A PROPHET IF HER PEOPLE WOULD LISTEN.
THAT WAS DR. SHARON BOATWRIGHT, FIREBRAND AUTHOR OF *WEIGHT OF THE WORLD*, HER GROUNDBREAKING STUDY OF ENVIRONMENTAL CATASTROPHE.
ON A MORE PERSONAL NOTE, THIS HAS BEEN A BIT OF A HOMECOMING FOR YOU HASN'T IT, SHARON?
BUT AS THEY FAIL TO HEAR HER, SO SHE DOES NOT HEAR THEM.
ER, WELL, YES. I WAS ***BORN*** HERE BUT WE MOVED AWAY WHEN I WAS FIVE AND I WAS RAISED IN--
SORRY TO CUT YOU OFF, SHARON, BUT I HAVE WORD OF DEVELOPING NEWS ON THE DOWNTOWN ARSON FIRE FROM EARLIER.
BZZZZZT
THE WORLD HAS DEAFENED HER TO THE CLARION CALL.
SO MY THANKS TO YOU, DOCTOR, AS WE RETURN TO THE MAIN NEWS DESK.
JON?
I FEAR SHE MUST SEARCH THROUGH THE RUBBLE OF HER WORLD TO FIND WHAT SHE HAS LOST.
channel 2
ateline: Noahville... the ongoing efforts of FEMA to rea
I PRAY IT ISN'T TOO LATE.

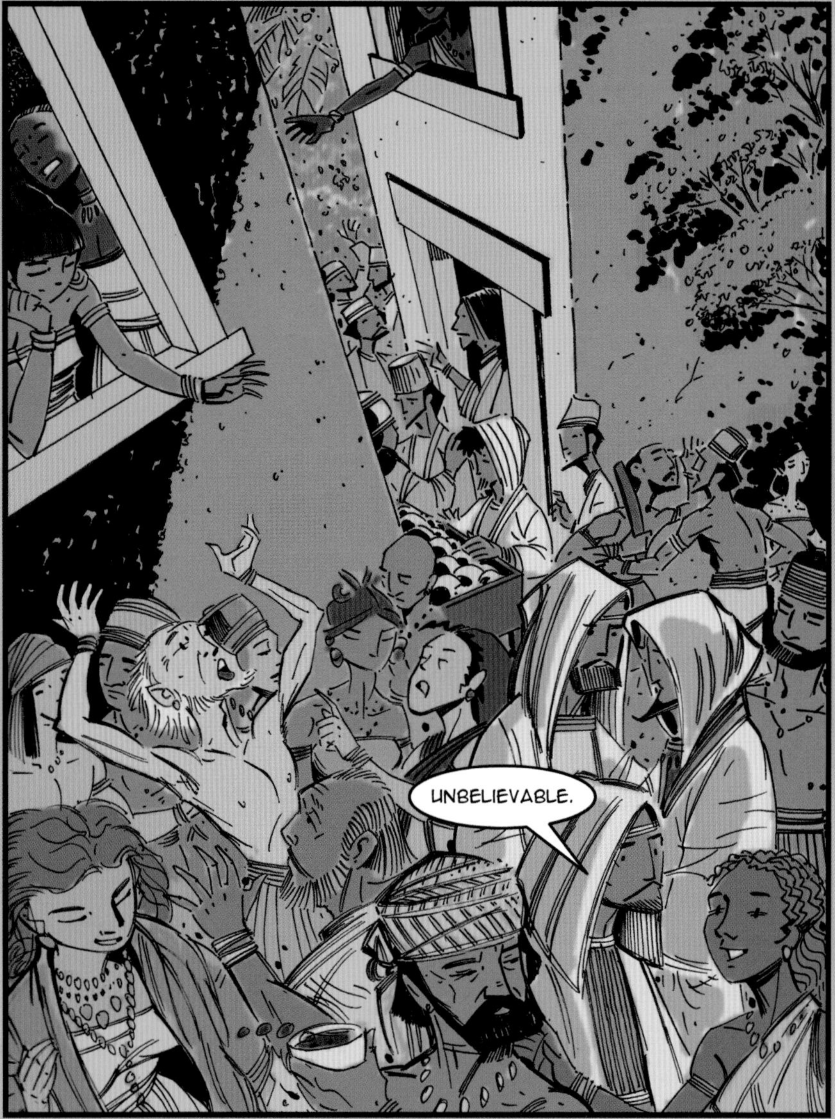
UNBELIEVABLE.

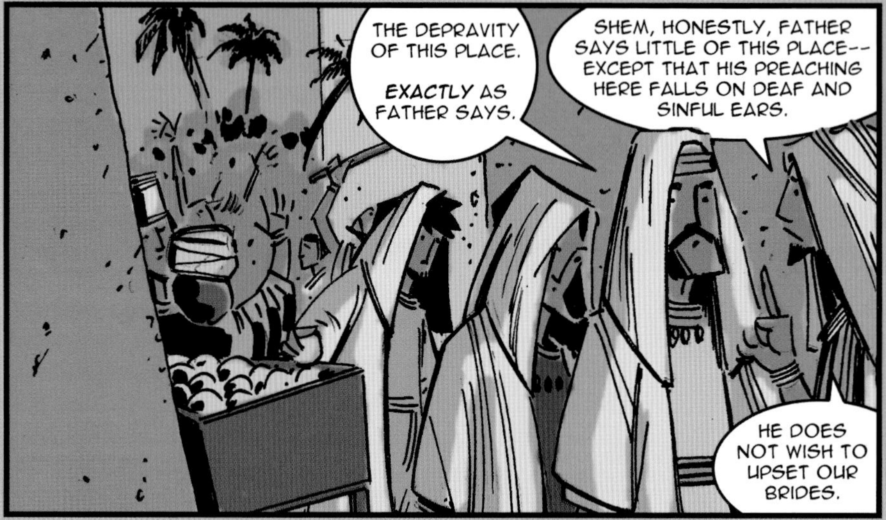
THE DEPRAVITY OF THIS PLACE.
EXACTLY AS FATHER SAYS.
SHEM, HONESTLY, FATHER SAYS LITTLE OF THIS PLACE-- EXCEPT THAT HIS PREACHING HERE FALLS ON DEAF AND SINFUL EARS.
HE DOES NOT WISH TO UPSET OUR BRIDES.

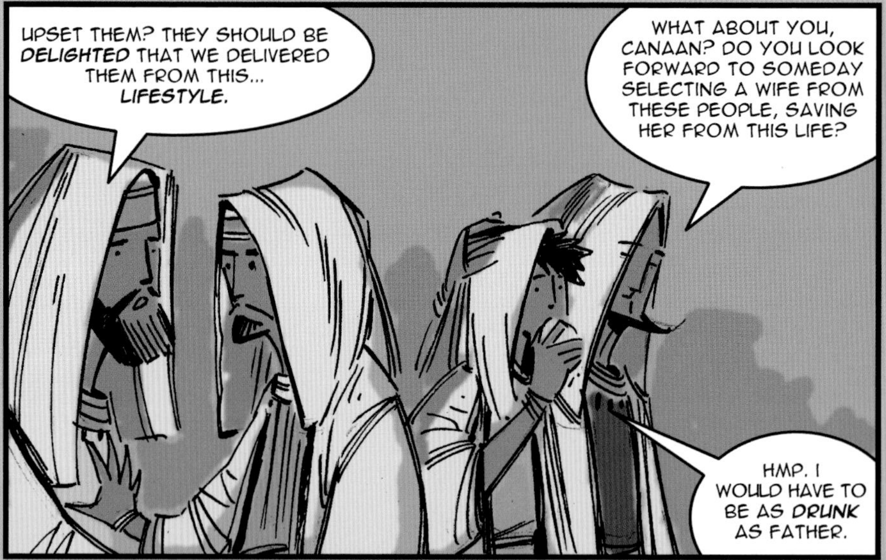
UPSET THEM? THEY SHOULD BE DELIGHTED THAT WE DELIVERED THEM FROM THIS... LIFESTYLE.
WHAT ABOUT YOU, CANAAN? DO YOU LOOK FORWARD TO SOMEDAY SELECTING A WIFE FROM THESE PEOPLE, SAVING HER FROM THIS LIFE?
HMP. I WOULD HAVE TO BE AS DRUNK AS FATHER.

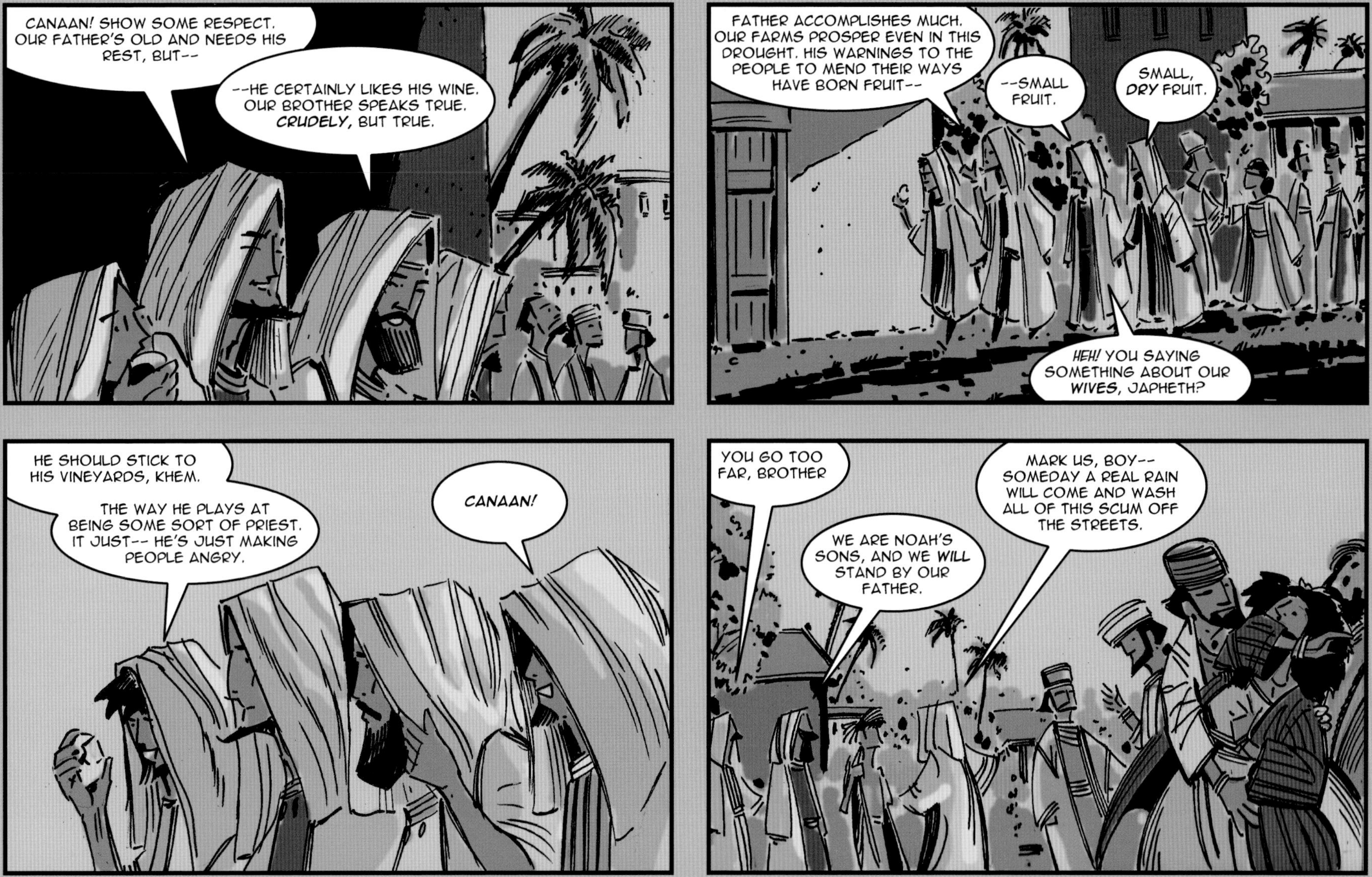
CANAAN! SHOW SOME RESPECT. OUR FATHER'S OLD AND NEEDS HIS REST, BUT--
--HE CERTAINLY LIKES HIS WINE. OUR BROTHER SPEAKS TRUE. *CRUDELY*, BUT TRUE.
FATHER ACCOMPLISHES MUCH. OUR FARMS PROSPER EVEN IN THIS DROUGHT. HIS WARNINGS TO THE PEOPLE TO MEND THEIR WAYS HAVE BORN FRUIT--
--SMALL FRUIT.
SMALL, *DRY* FRUIT.
HEH! YOU SAYING SOMETHING ABOUT OUR *WIVES*, JAPHETH?
HE SHOULD STICK TO HIS VINEYARDS, KHEM.
THE WAY HE PLAYS AT BEING SOME SORT OF PRIEST. IT JUST-- HE'S JUST MAKING PEOPLE ANGRY.
CANAAN!
YOU GO TOO FAR, BROTHER
WE ARE NOAH'S SONS, AND WE *WILL* STAND BY OUR FATHER.
MARK US, BOY-- SOMEDAY A REAL RAIN WILL COME AND WASH ALL OF THIS SCUM OFF THE STREETS.

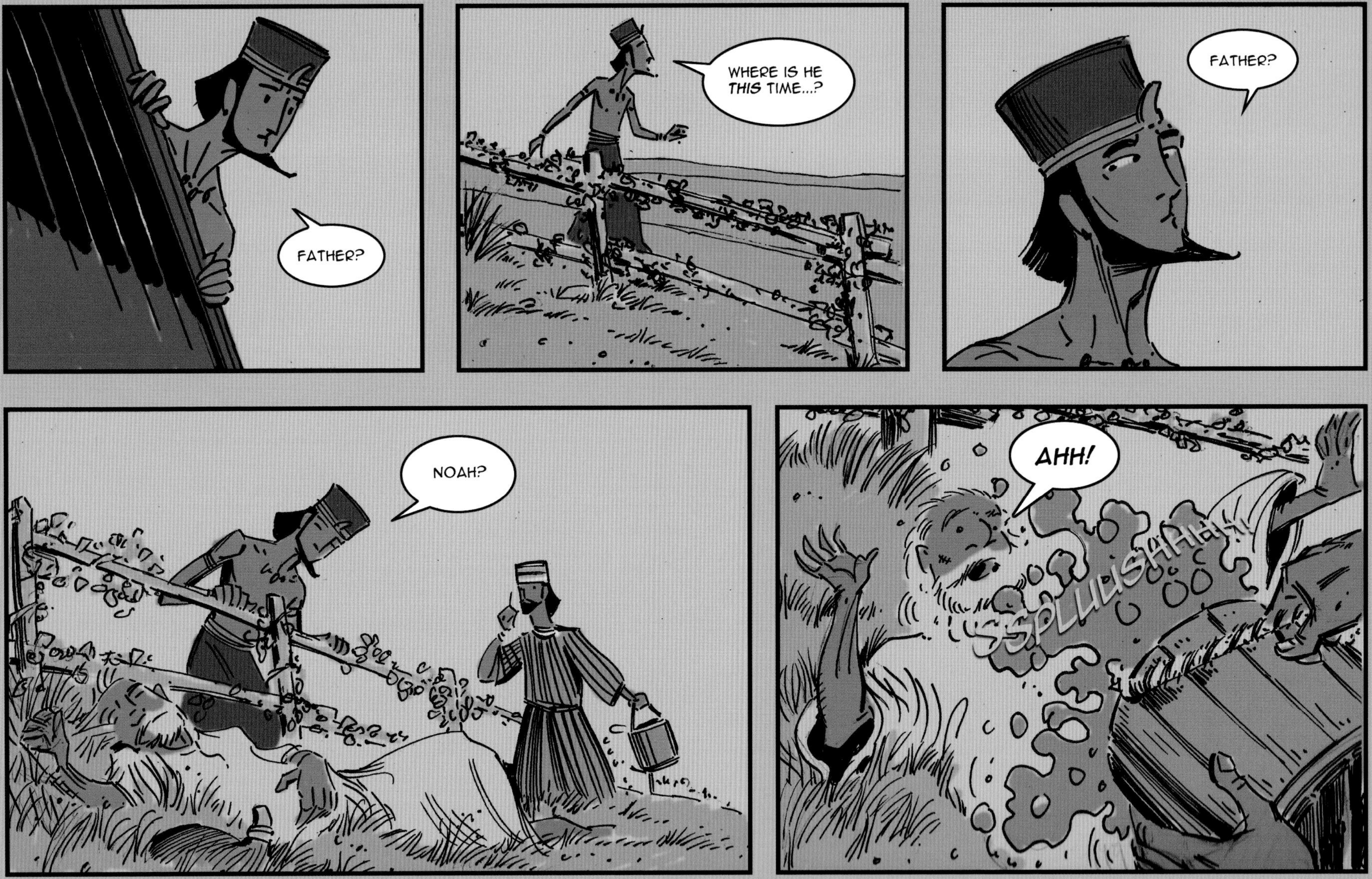
FATHER?
WHERE IS HE THIS TIME...?
FATHER?
NOAH?
AHH!
SSPLUUSHHH!!

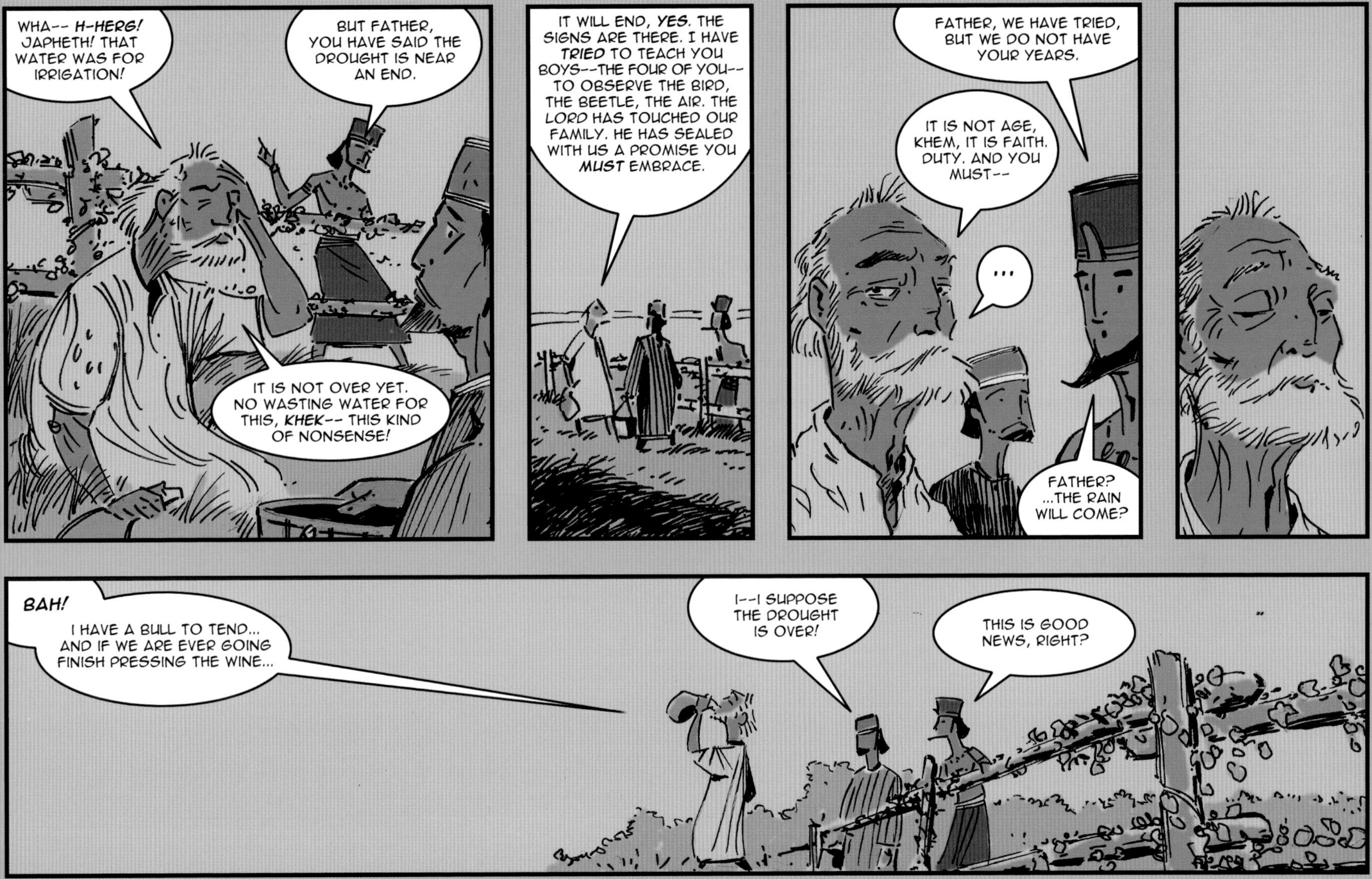

WHA-- H-HERG! JAPHETH! THAT WATER WAS FOR IRRIGATION!
BUT FATHER, YOU HAVE SAID THE DROUGHT IS NEAR AN END.
IT IS NOT OVER YET. NO WASTING WATER FOR THIS, KHEK-- THIS KIND OF NONSENSE!
IT WILL END, YES. THE SIGNS ARE THERE. I HAVE TRIED TO TEACH YOU BOYS--THE FOUR OF YOU-- TO OBSERVE THE BIRD, THE BEETLE, THE AIR. THE LORD HAS TOUCHED OUR FAMILY. HE HAS SEALED WITH US A PROMISE YOU MUST EMBRACE.
FATHER, WE HAVE TRIED, BUT WE DO NOT HAVE YOUR YEARS.
IT IS NOT AGE, KHEM, IT IS FAITH. DUTY. AND YOU MUST--
...
FATHER? ...THE RAIN WILL COME?
BAH!
I HAVE A BULL TO TEND... AND IF WE ARE EVER GOING FINISH PRESSING THE WINE...
I--I SUPPOSE THE DROUGHT IS OVER!
THIS IS GOOD NEWS, RIGHT?

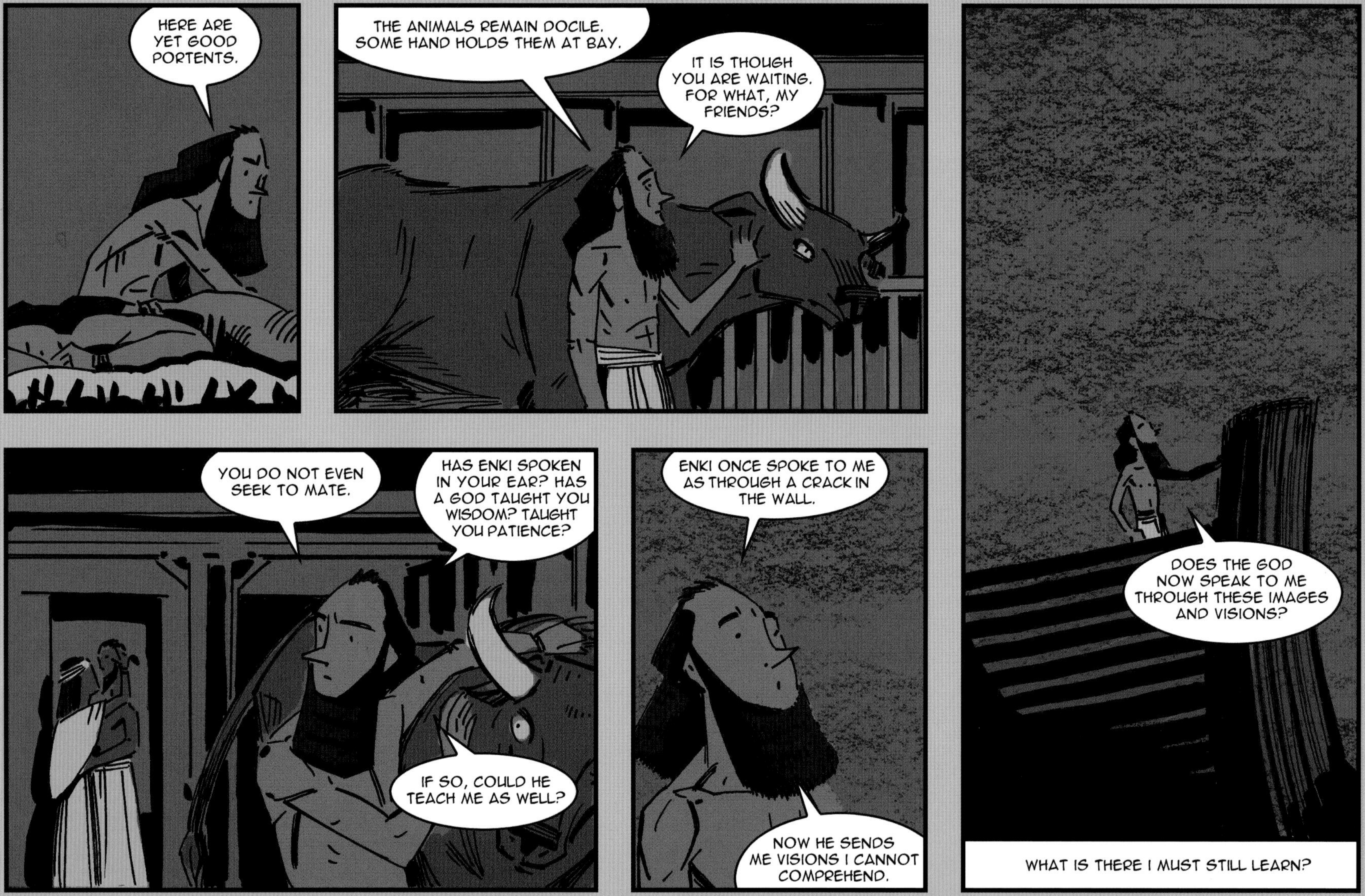
HERE ARE YET GOOD PORTENTS.
THE ANIMALS REMAIN DOCILE. SOME HAND HOLDS THEM AT BAY.
IT IS THOUGH YOU ARE WAITING. FOR WHAT, MY FRIENDS?
YOU DO NOT EVEN SEEK TO MATE.
HAS ENKI SPOKEN IN YOUR EAR? HAS A GOD TAUGHT YOU WISDOM? TAUGHT YOU PATIENCE?
IF SO, COULD HE TEACH ME AS WELL?
ENKI ONCE SPOKE TO ME AS THROUGH A CRACK IN THE WALL.
NOW HE SENDS ME VISIONS I CANNOT COMPREHEND.
DOES THE GOD NOW SPEAK TO ME THROUGH THESE IMAGES AND VISIONS?
WHAT IS THERE I MUST STILL LEARN?

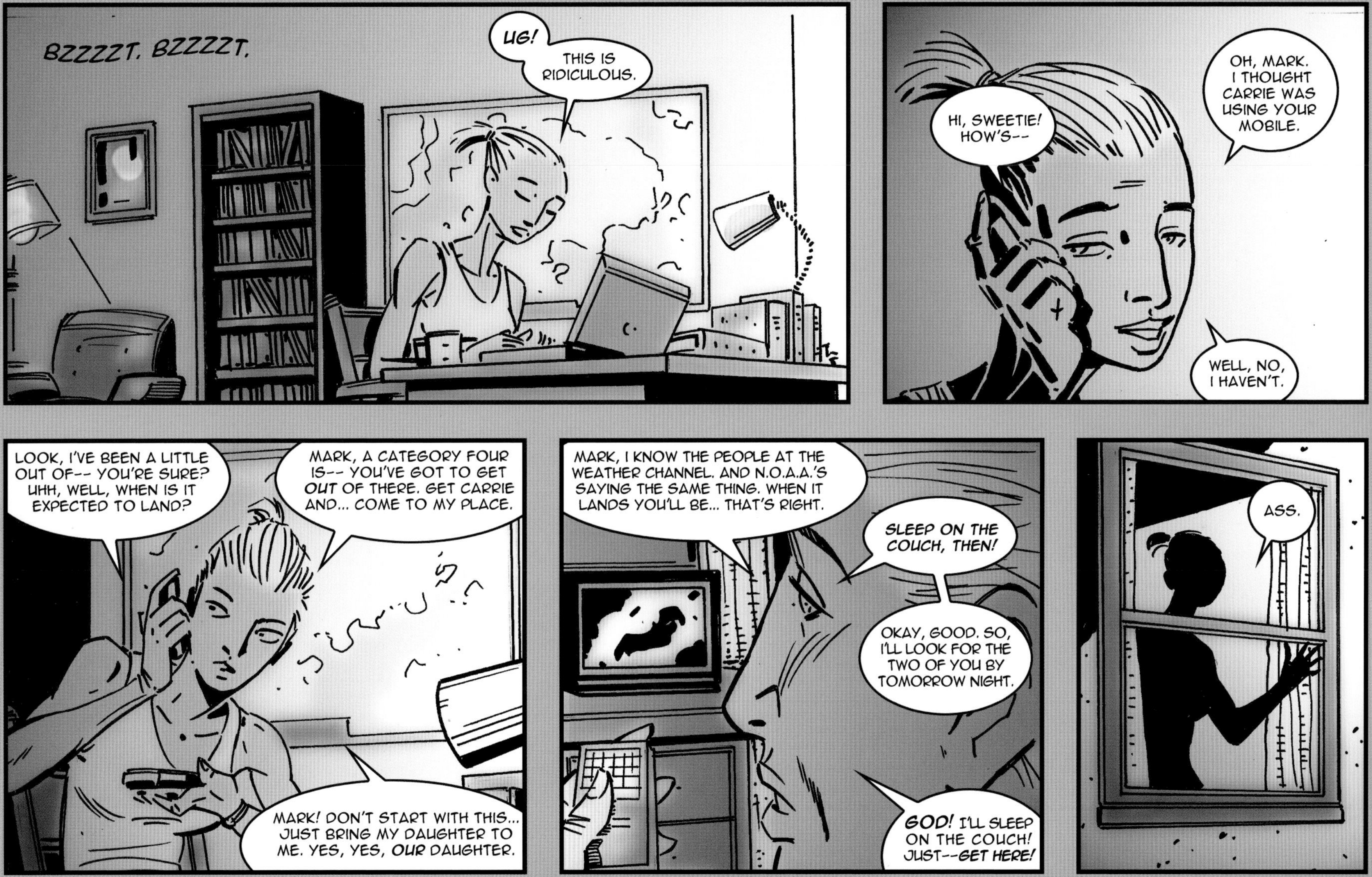
BZZZZT. BZZZZT.
UG!
THIS IS RIDICULOUS.
HI, SWEETIE! HOW'S--
OH, MARK. I THOUGHT CARRIE WAS USING YOUR MOBILE.
WELL, NO, I HAVEN'T.
LOOK, I'VE BEEN A LITTLE OUT OF-- YOU'RE SURE? UHH, WELL, WHEN IS IT EXPECTED TO LAND?
MARK, A CATEGORY FOUR IS-- YOU'VE GOT TO GET *OUT* OF THERE. GET CARRIE AND... COME TO MY PLACE.
MARK! DON'T START WITH THIS... JUST BRING MY DAUGHTER TO ME. YES, YES, *OUR* DAUGHTER.
MARK, I KNOW THE PEOPLE AT THE WEATHER CHANNEL. AND N.O.A.A.'S SAYING THE SAME THING. WHEN IT LANDS YOU'LL BE... THAT'S RIGHT.
SLEEP ON THE COUCH, THEN!
OKAY, GOOD. SO, I'LL LOOK FOR THE TWO OF YOU BY TOMORROW NIGHT.
GOD! I'LL SLEEP ON THE COUCH! JUST--*GET HERE!*
ASS.

THERE IS A PLACE: ARNHEM LAND. THERE, THE WAWALIK SISTERS AND THEIR INFANT CHILDREN CAMPED BY THE MIRRIRMINA WATERHOLE.

AT THE OLDER SISTER'S TIME, HER BLOOD FLOWED TOO FREELY, AND IT FELL INTO THE WELL.

THE RAINBOW SERPENT YURLANGGUR, HE SMELLED IT. HIS TONGUE LASHED.

DID HE SMELL THE BLOOD OR SMELL... FRUIT?

NO, NO, IT WAS BLOOD, RED AS RIPE BERRIES.

HIS SCALES BRISTLED. HE SPAT IN THE SKY AND HISSED A CALL FOR RAIN.

AND RAINS, SO DID THEY COME. THE WATER LEVEL ROSE EVER HIGHER.

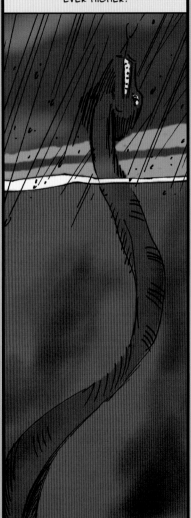

THE WOMEN WENT INSIDE THEIR HOUSE, BUT YURLANGGUR PUT SLEEP UPON THEM AND SWALLOWED THE SISTERS WHOLE.

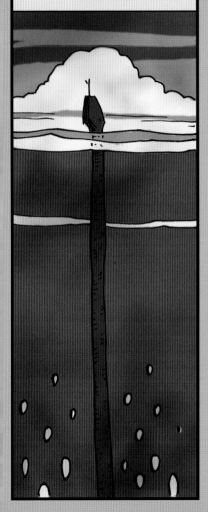

FROM HIS WELL, HE ROSE VERY STRAIGHT AND TALL, TO THE HEIGHT OF THE CLOUDS, AND THE FLOOD WATERS CAME UP TO HIS HEAD.

YURLANGGUR WAS ENVELOPED, HIS HISSING DROWNED OUT, AND HE SUNK TO THE OCEAN'S FLOOR. HE FELL, THE WATERS WITHDREW. THE GROUND DRIED.

THE TWO ORPHANED SONS, WITH NO MOTHERS TO SUCKLE, WERE LEFT IN THE CARE OF THE MAN WIRILI-UP. BUT HE SHIRKED THE RESPONSIBILITY. HE DRANK BY THE WELL INSTEAD.

THE CHILDREN WERE HUNGRY AND CRIED SO MUCH THAT YURLANGGUR ROSE AGAIN TO FLOOD THE LAND WITH WATER LIKE VENOM.

WIRILI-UP FLED AND--

GODS... HE LEFT THE BOYS TO DROWN.

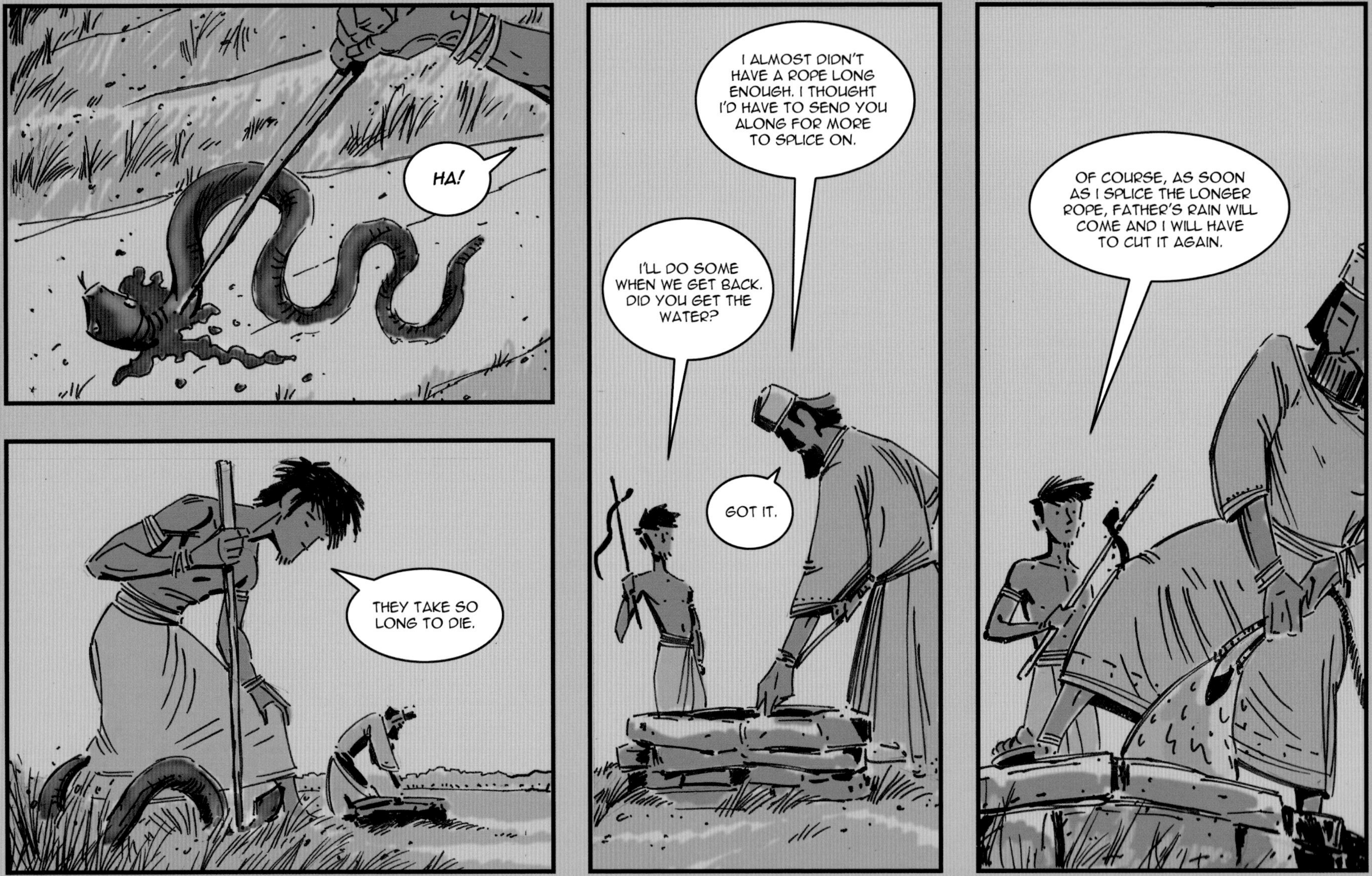
HA!
THEY TAKE SO LONG TO DIE.
I ALMOST DIDN'T HAVE A ROPE LONG ENOUGH. I THOUGHT I'D HAVE TO SEND YOU ALONG FOR MORE TO SPLICE ON.
I'LL DO SOME WHEN WE GET BACK. DID YOU GET THE WATER?
GOT IT.
OF COURSE, AS SOON AS I SPLICE THE LONGER ROPE, FATHER'S RAIN WILL COME AND I WILL HAVE TO CUT IT AGAIN.

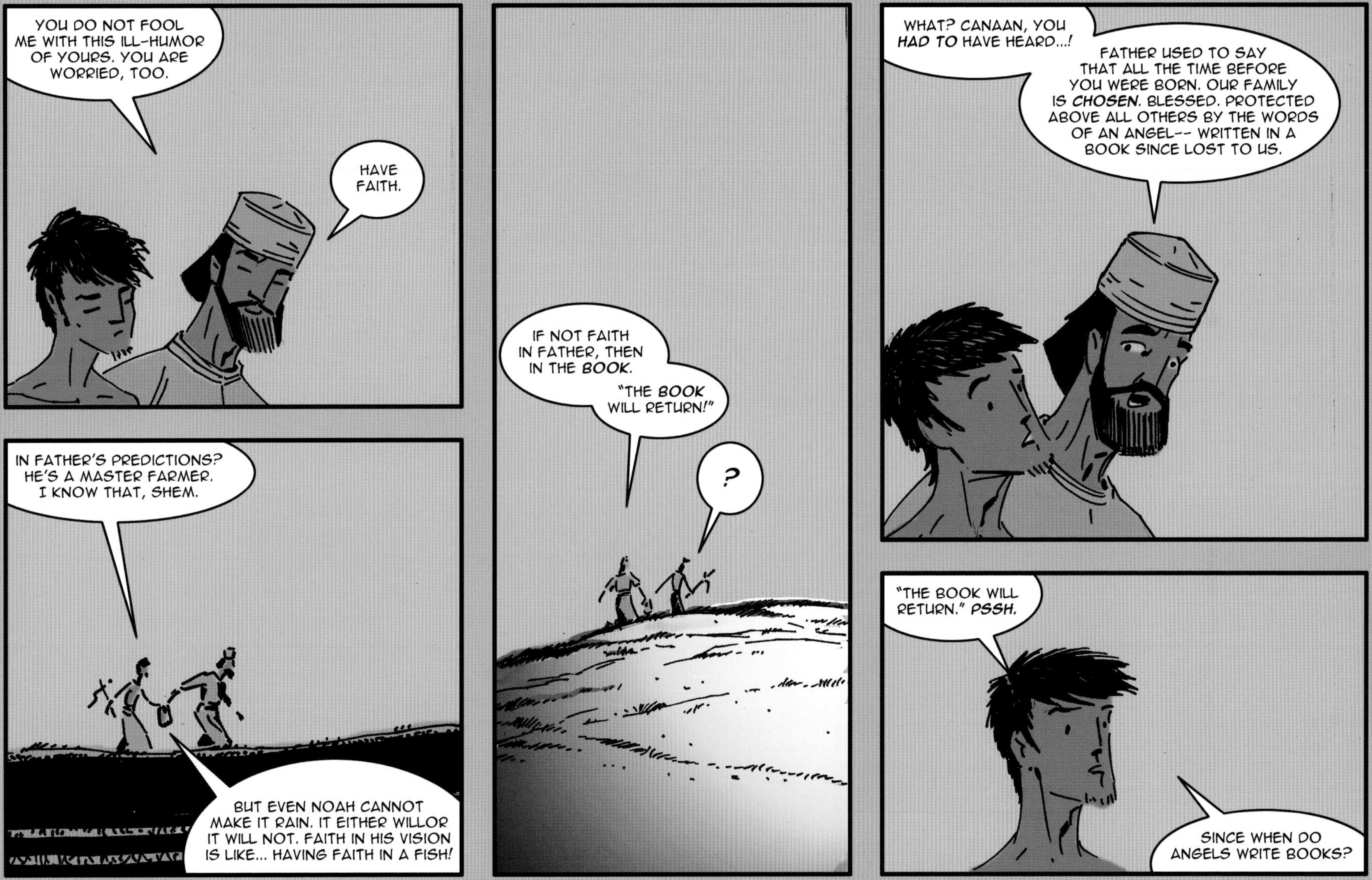

YOU DO NOT FOOL ME WITH THIS ILL-HUMOR OF YOURS. YOU ARE WORRIED, TOO.
HAVE FAITH.
IN FATHER'S PREDICTIONS? HE'S A MASTER FARMER. I KNOW THAT, SHEM.
BUT EVEN NOAH CANNOT MAKE IT RAIN. IT EITHER WILLOR IT WILL NOT. FAITH IN HIS VISION IS LIKE... HAVING FAITH IN A FISH!
IF NOT FAITH IN FATHER, THEN IN THE **BOOK**.
"THE **BOOK** WILL RETURN!"
?
WHAT? CANAAN, YOU **HAD TO** HAVE HEARD...!
FATHER USED TO SAY THAT ALL THE TIME BEFORE YOU WERE BORN. OUR FAMILY IS **CHOSEN**. BLESSED. PROTECTED ABOVE ALL OTHERS BY THE WORDS OF AN ANGEL-- WRITTEN IN A BOOK SINCE LOST TO US.
"THE BOOK WILL RETURN." **PSSH.**
SINCE WHEN DO ANGELS WRITE BOOKS?

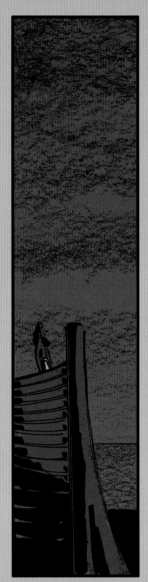

THE BOYS DROWN AND THE SISTERS DIE. BUT WE ARE PROTECTED BY ENKI. THE FAULT IS MINE IF I CANNOT GRASP HIS WISDOM. THE ANIMALS HEAR HIS VOICE AND ARE AT PEACE.

WHY THEN DO I STRUGGLE WITH THESE THOUGHTS?

MY PEOPLE SLEEP. NOT WELL, PERHAPS. THEY WRESTLE WITH THEIR DREAMS... BUT, THEY DO SLEEP. THEY HAVE FAITH.

THEY BELIEVED ME. "LEAVE YOUR HOMES! FOLLOW ME! THE GOD ENKI HAS SPOKEN."

HE STILL SPEAKS, BUT ONLY THROUGH THE PLIGHT OF OTHERS.

WHY SHOULD THEIR FAITH *REMAIN* WITH ME?

I KNOW YOURS REMAINS WITH ME, MY BRIDE. YOUR FAITH.

HAVE I TOLD YOU TODAY THAT I LOVE YOU?

YOU SAT AT MY SIDE IN THE GOOD DAYS OF SHARRUPAK, WHEN THE WINE WAS SWEET AND OUR LOVE WAS YOUNG.

020

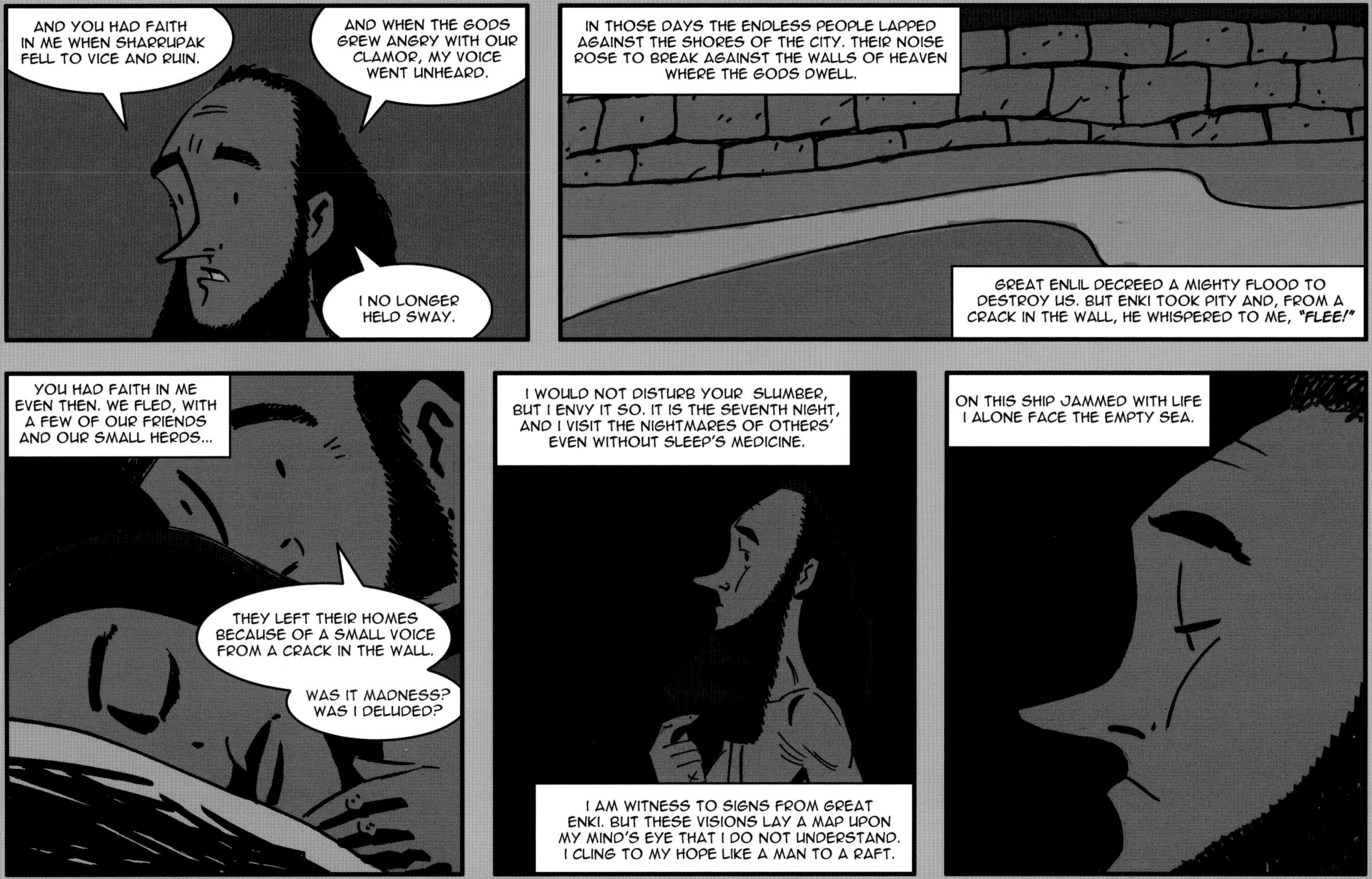
AND YOU HAD FAITH IN ME WHEN SHARRUPAK FELL TO VICE AND RUIN.
AND WHEN THE GODS GREW ANGRY WITH OUR CLAMOR, MY VOICE WENT UNHEARD.
I NO LONGER HELD SWAY.
IN THOSE DAYS THE ENDLESS PEOPLE LAPPED AGAINST THE SHORES OF THE CITY. THEIR NOISE ROSE TO BREAK AGAINST THE WALLS OF HEAVEN WHERE THE GODS DWELL.
GREAT ENLIL DECREED A MIGHTY FLOOD TO DESTROY US. BUT ENKI TOOK PITY AND, FROM A CRACK IN THE WALL, HE WHISPERED TO ME, *"FLEE!"*
YOU HAD FAITH IN ME EVEN THEN. WE FLED, WITH A FEW OF OUR FRIENDS AND OUR SMALL HERDS...
THEY LEFT THEIR HOMES BECAUSE OF A SMALL VOICE FROM A CRACK IN THE WALL.
WAS IT MADNESS? WAS I DELUDED?
I WOULD NOT DISTURB YOUR SLUMBER, BUT I ENVY IT SO. IT IS THE SEVENTH NIGHT, AND I VISIT THE NIGHTMARES OF OTHERS' EVEN WITHOUT SLEEP'S MEDICINE.
I AM WITNESS TO SIGNS FROM GREAT ENKI. BUT THESE VISIONS LAY A MAP UPON MY MIND'S EYE THAT I DO NOT UNDERSTAND. I CLING TO MY HOPE LIKE A MAN TO A RAFT.
ON THIS SHIP JAMMED WITH LIFE I ALONE FACE THE EMPTY SEA.

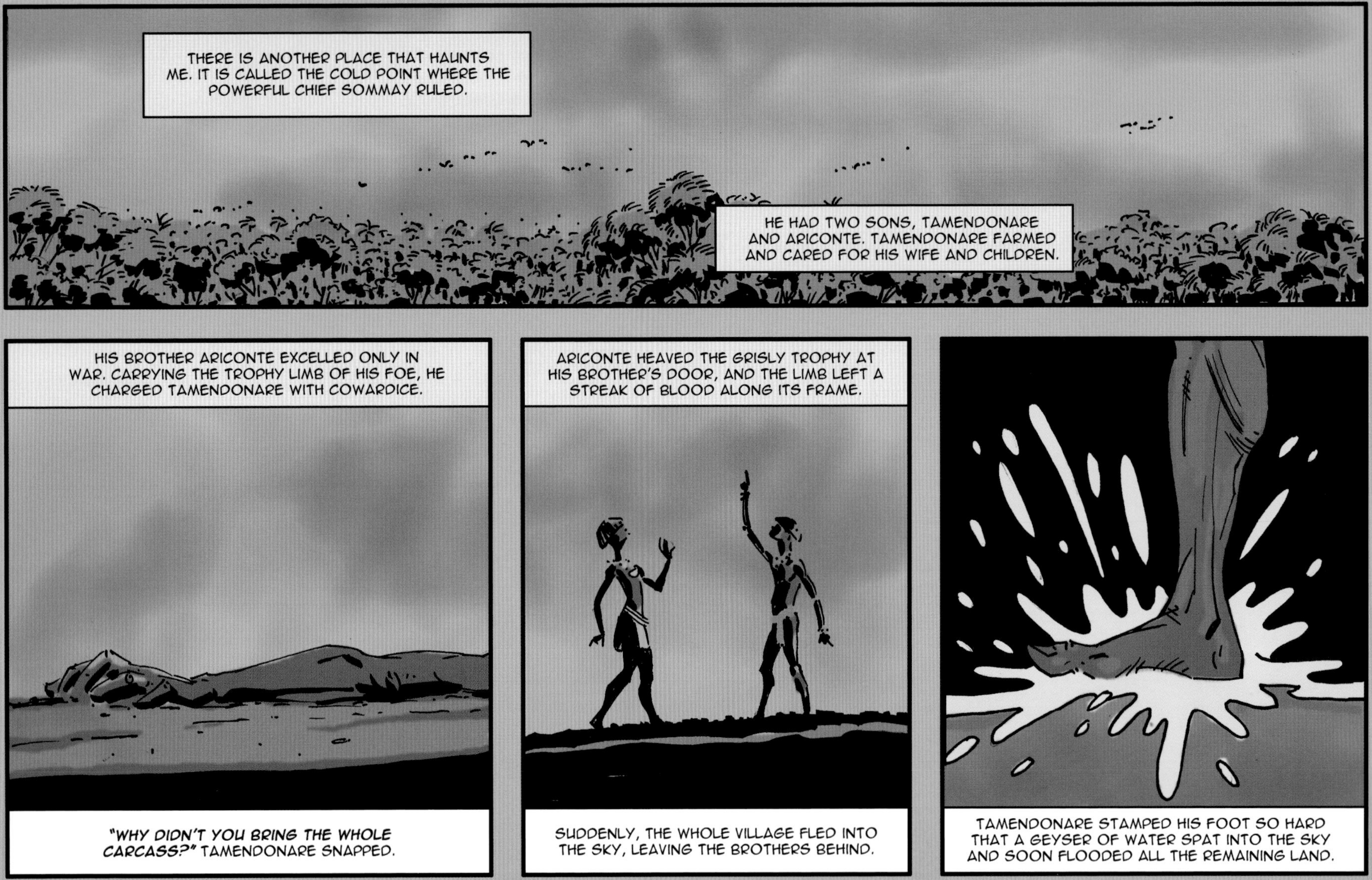

THERE IS ANOTHER PLACE THAT HAUNTS ME. IT IS CALLED THE COLD POINT WHERE THE POWERFUL CHIEF SOMMAY RULED.
HE HAD TWO SONS, TAMENDONARE AND ARICONTE. TAMENDONARE FARMED AND CARED FOR HIS WIFE AND CHILDREN.
HIS BROTHER ARICONTE EXCELLED ONLY IN WAR. CARRYING THE TROPHY LIMB OF HIS FOE, HE CHARGED TAMENDONARE WITH COWARDICE.
"WHY DIDN'T YOU BRING THE WHOLE CARCASS?" TAMENDONARE SNAPPED.
ARICONTE HEAVED THE GRISLY TROPHY AT HIS BROTHER'S DOOR, AND THE LIMB LEFT A STREAK OF BLOOD ALONG ITS FRAME.
SUDDENLY, THE WHOLE VILLAGE FLED INTO THE SKY, LEAVING THE BROTHERS BEHIND.
TAMENDONARE STAMPED HIS FOOT SO HARD THAT A GEYSER OF WATER SPAT INTO THE SKY AND SOON FLOODED ALL THE REMAINING LAND.

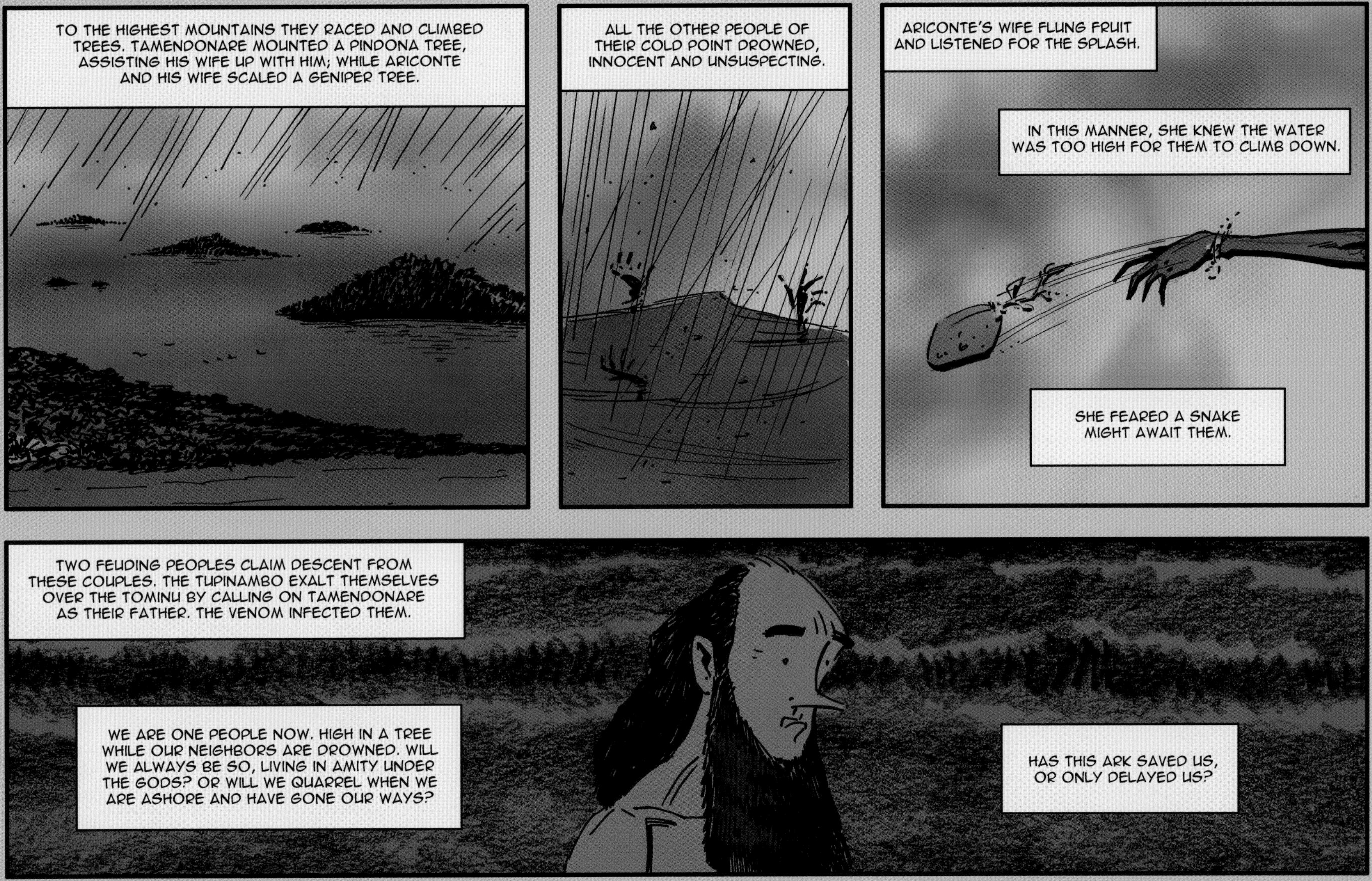
TO THE HIGHEST MOUNTAINS THEY RACED AND CLIMBED TREES. TAMENDONARE MOUNTED A PINDONA TREE, ASSISTING HIS WIFE UP WITH HIM; WHILE ARICONTE AND HIS WIFE SCALED A GENIPER TREE.
ALL THE OTHER PEOPLE OF THEIR COLD POINT DROWNED, INNOCENT AND UNSUSPECTING.
ARICONTE'S WIFE FLUNG FRUIT AND LISTENED FOR THE SPLASH.
IN THIS MANNER, SHE KNEW THE WATER WAS TOO HIGH FOR THEM TO CLIMB DOWN.
SHE FEARED A SNAKE MIGHT AWAIT THEM.
TWO FEUDING PEOPLES CLAIM DESCENT FROM THESE COUPLES. THE TUPINAMBO EXALT THEMSELVES OVER THE TOMINU BY CALLING ON TAMENDONARE AS THEIR FATHER. THE VENOM INFECTED THEM.
WE ARE ONE PEOPLE NOW. HIGH IN A TREE WHILE OUR NEIGHBORS ARE DROWNED. WILL WE ALWAYS BE SO, LIVING IN AMITY UNDER THE GODS? OR WILL WE QUARREL WHEN WE ARE ASHORE AND HAVE GONE OUR WAYS?
HAS THIS ARK SAVED US, OR ONLY DELAYED US?

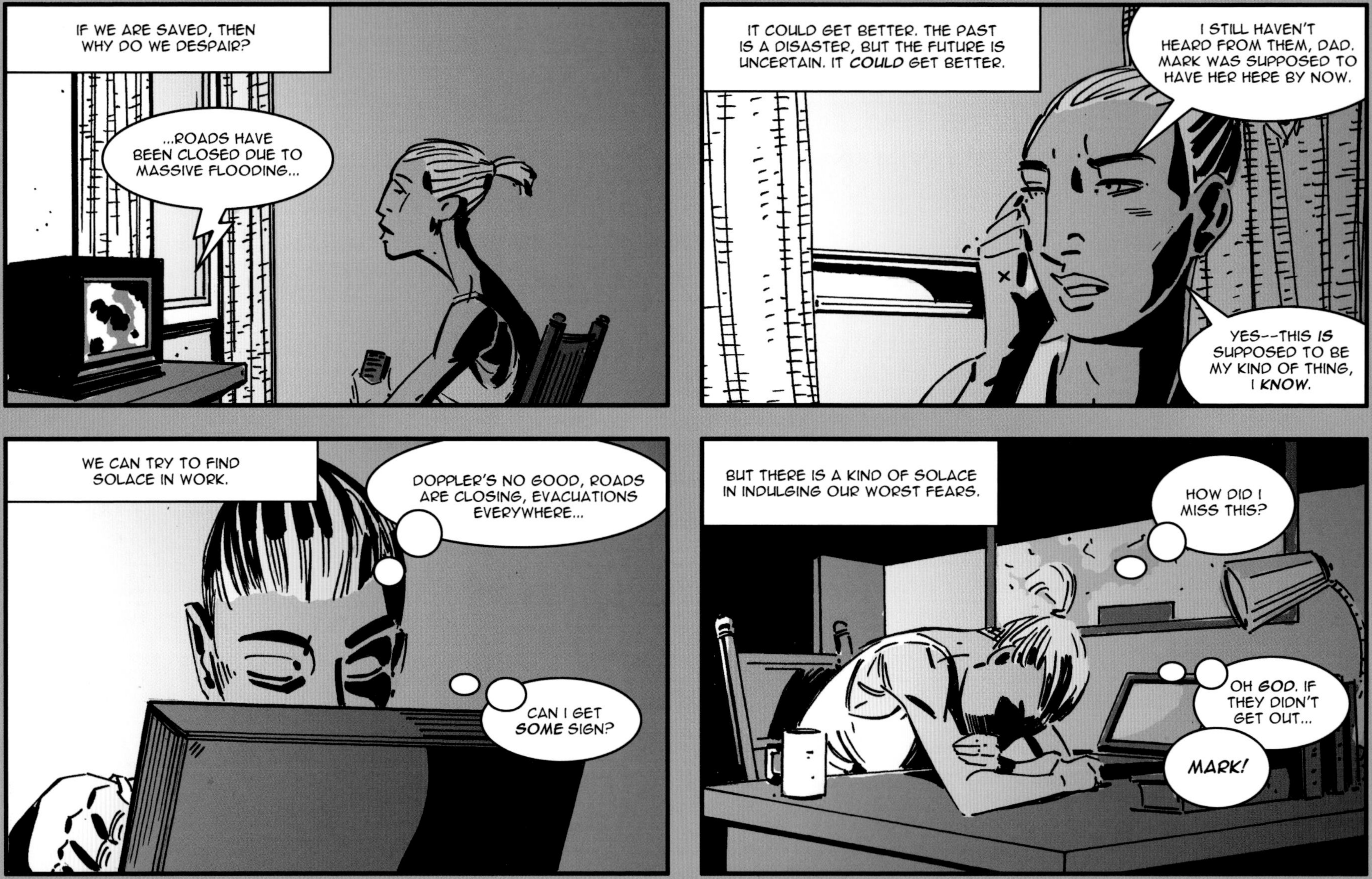
IF WE ARE SAVED, THEN WHY DO WE DESPAIR?
...ROADS HAVE BEEN CLOSED DUE TO MASSIVE FLOODING...
IT COULD GET BETTER. THE PAST IS A DISASTER, BUT THE FUTURE IS UNCERTAIN. IT COULD GET BETTER.
I STILL HAVEN'T HEARD FROM THEM, DAD. MARK WAS SUPPOSED TO HAVE HER HERE BY NOW.
YES--THIS IS SUPPOSED TO BE MY KIND OF THING, I KNOW.
WE CAN TRY TO FIND SOLACE IN WORK.
DOPPLER'S NO GOOD, ROADS ARE CLOSING, EVACUATIONS EVERYWHERE...
CAN I GET SOME SIGN?
BUT THERE IS A KIND OF SOLACE IN INDULGING OUR WORST FEARS.
HOW DID I MISS THIS?
OH GOD. IF THEY DIDN'T GET OUT...
MARK!

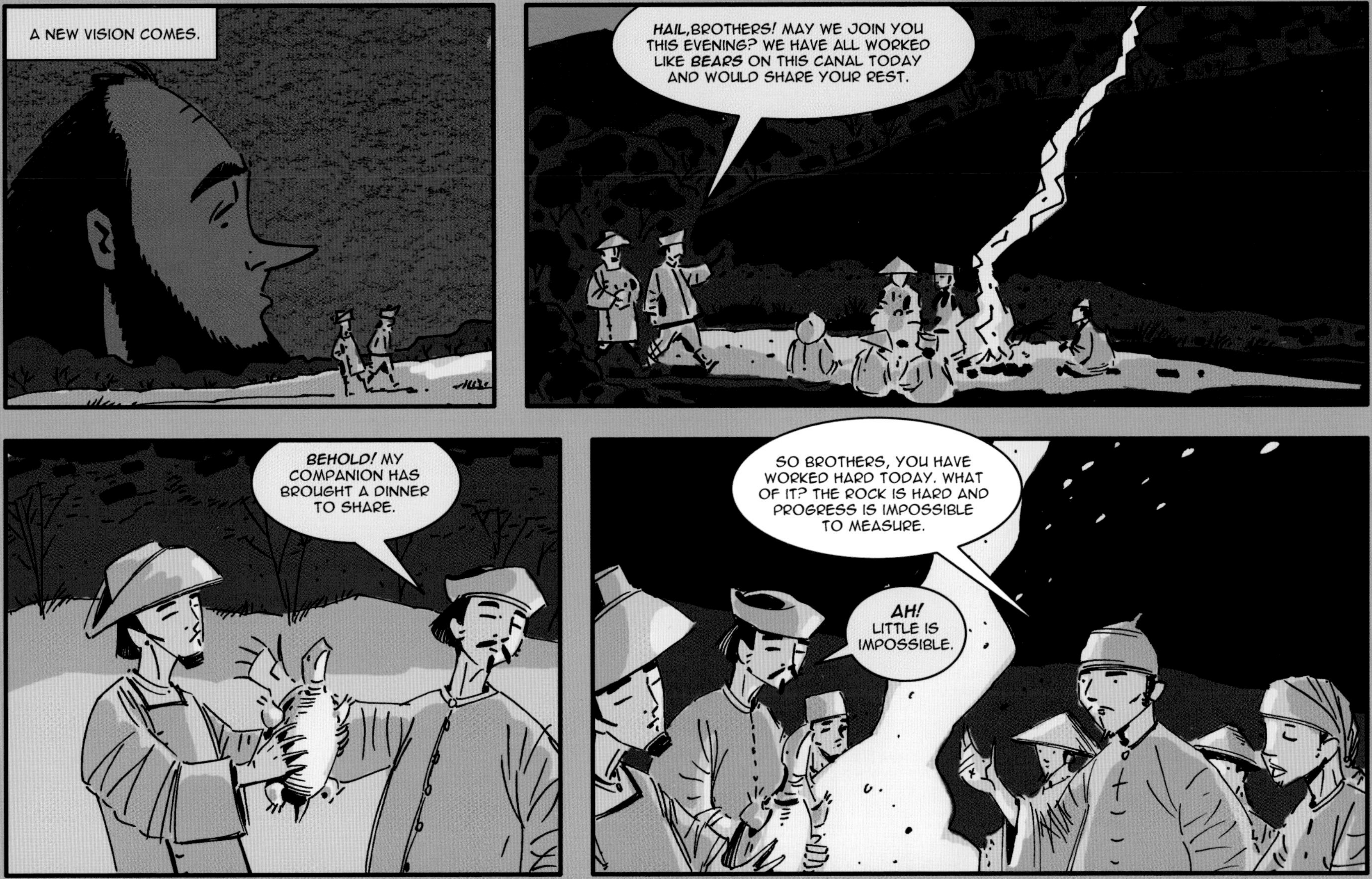
A NEW VISION COMES.
HAIL, BROTHERS! MAY WE JOIN YOU THIS EVENING? WE HAVE ALL WORKED LIKE BEARS ON THIS CANAL TODAY AND WOULD SHARE YOUR REST.
BEHOLD! MY COMPANION HAS BROUGHT A DINNER TO SHARE.
SO BROTHERS, YOU HAVE WORKED HARD TODAY. WHAT OF IT? THE ROCK IS HARD AND PROGRESS IS IMPOSSIBLE TO MEASURE.
AH! LITTLE IS IMPOSSIBLE.

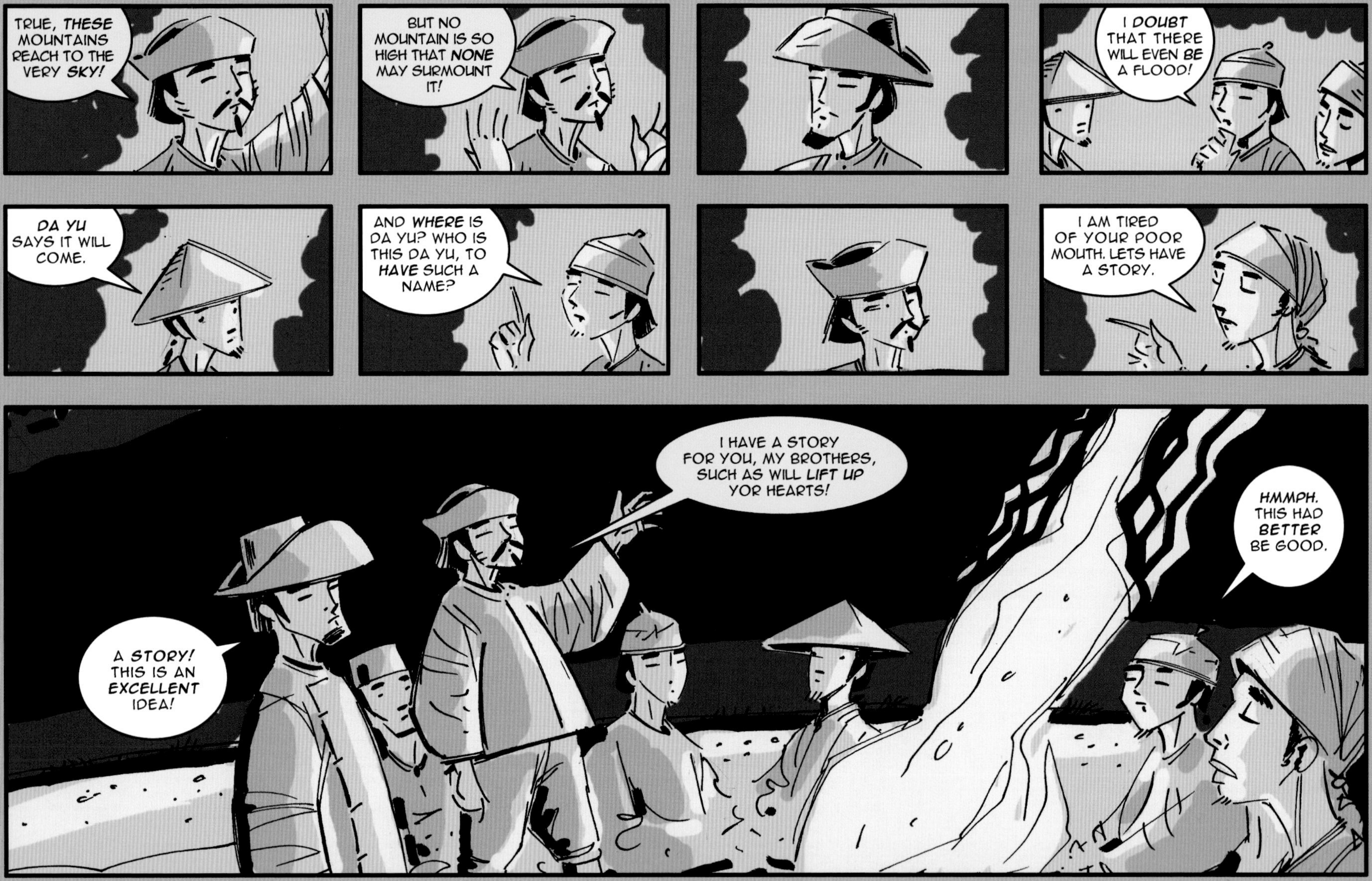
TRUE, *THESE* MOUNTAINS REACH TO THE VERY *SKY!*
BUT NO MOUNTAIN IS SO HIGH THAT *NONE* MAY SURMOUNT IT!
I *DOUBT* THAT THERE WILL EVEN *BE* A FLOOD!
DA YU SAYS IT WILL COME.
AND *WHERE* IS DA YU? WHO IS THIS DA YU, TO *HAVE* SUCH A NAME?
I AM TIRED OF YOUR POOR MOUTH. LETS HAVE A STORY.
I HAVE A STORY FOR YOU, MY BROTHERS, SUCH AS WILL *LIFT UP* YOR HEARTS!
HMMPH. THIS HAD *BETTER* BE GOOD.
A *STORY!* THIS IS AN *EXCELLENT* IDEA!

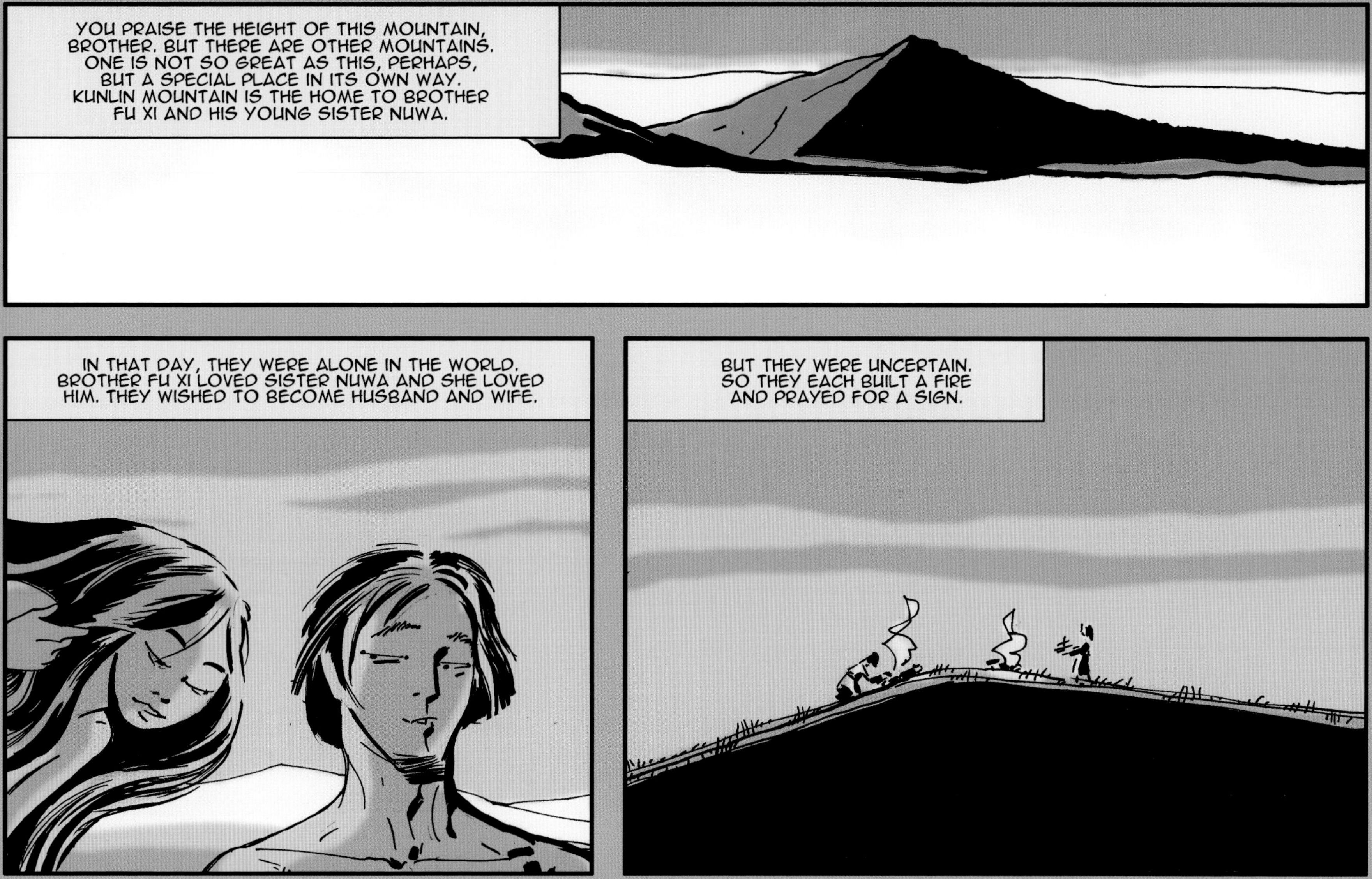
YOU PRAISE THE HEIGHT OF THIS MOUNTAIN, BROTHER. BUT THERE ARE OTHER MOUNTAINS. ONE IS NOT SO GREAT AS THIS, PERHAPS, BUT A SPECIAL PLACE IN ITS OWN WAY. KUNLIN MOUNTAIN IS THE HOME TO BROTHER FU XI AND HIS YOUNG SISTER NUWA.
IN THAT DAY, THEY WERE ALONE IN THE WORLD. BROTHER FU XI LOVED SISTER NUWA AND SHE LOVED HIM. THEY WISHED TO BECOME HUSBAND AND WIFE.
BUT THEY WERE UNCERTAIN. SO THEY EACH BUILT A FIRE AND PRAYED FOR A SIGN.

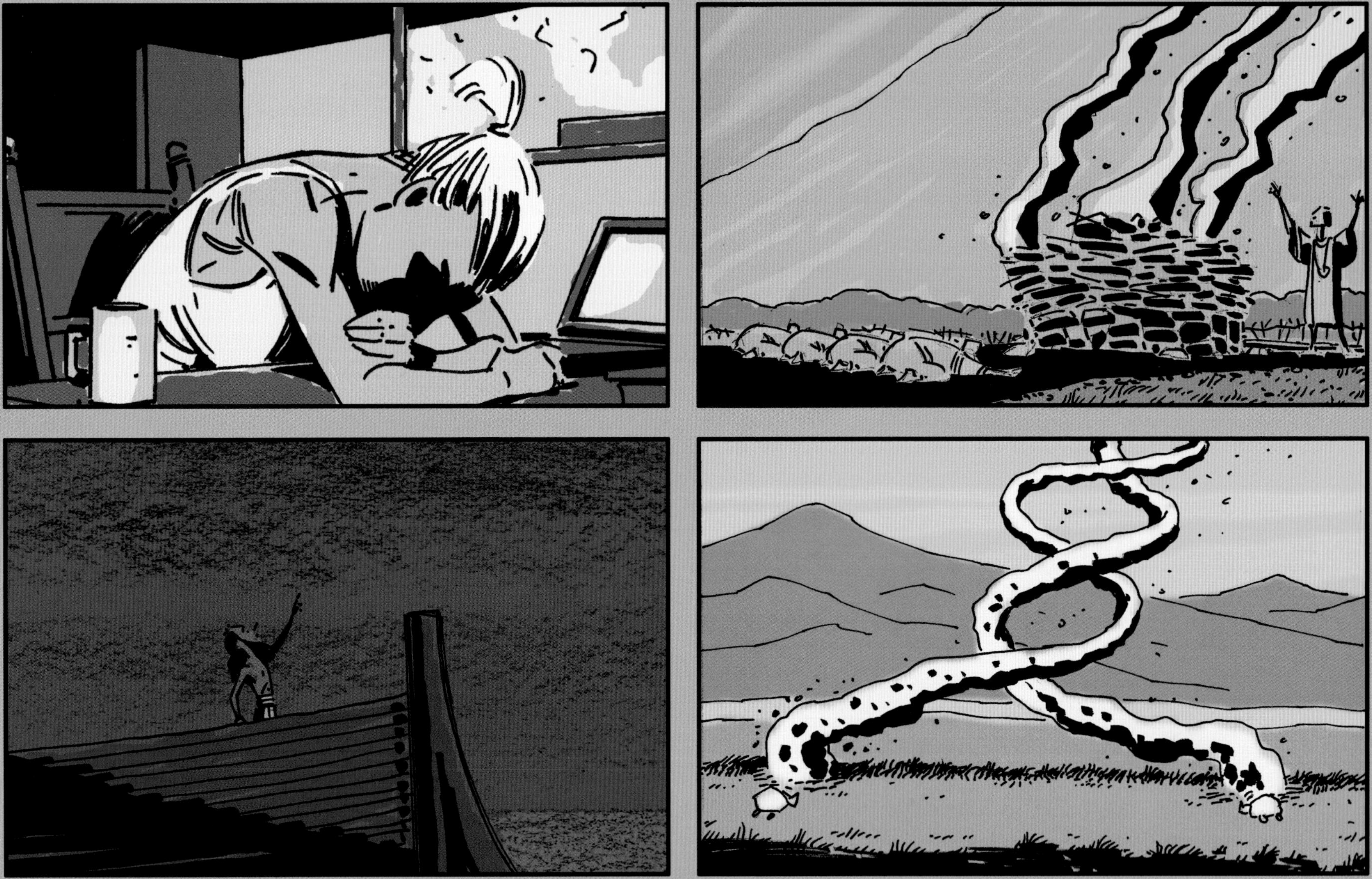

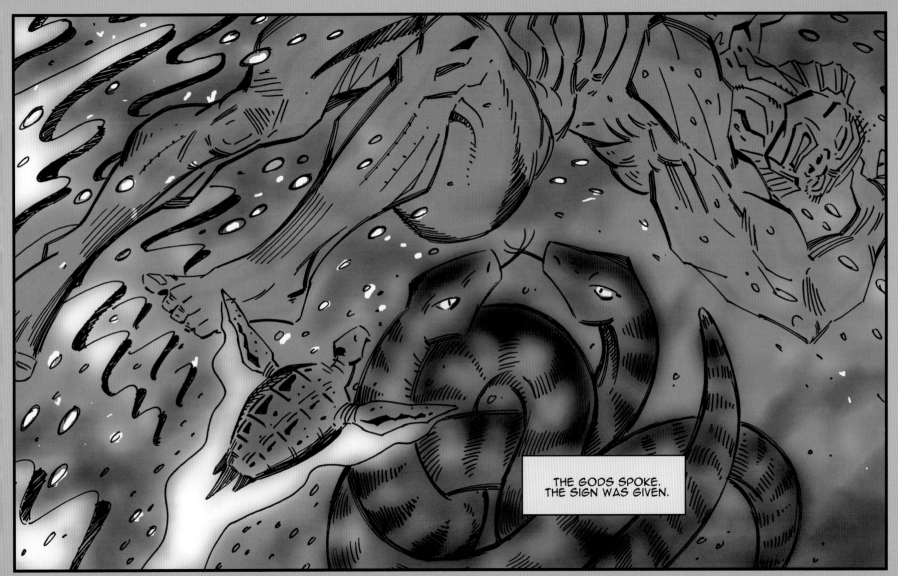

THE GODS SPOKE.
THE SIGN WAS GIVEN.

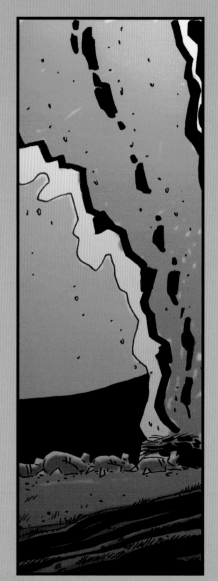

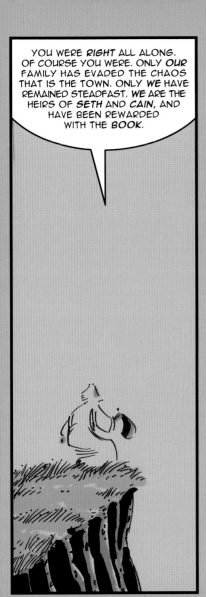

YOU WERE *RIGHT* ALL ALONG. OF COURSE YOU WERE. ONLY *OUR* FAMILY HAS EVADED THE CHAOS THAT IS THE TOWN. ONLY *WE* HAVE REMAINED STEADFAST. *WE* ARE THE HEIRS OF *SETH* AND *CAIN*, AND HAVE BEEN REWARDED WITH THE *BOOK*.

AND I-- HAVE *LOST* IT, FATHER. YET-- NO, *NO!* I HAVE *NOT* ABANDONED GOD--

AND GOD HAS *NOT* ABANDONED AN OLD FOOL AND HIS FOOLISH FAMILY. MERCIFUL GOD!

WE ARE FOOLISH AND STEADFAST. MORE FOOLS THAN THE TOWNFOLK. *CANAAN*, MAYBE, IS THE ONLY--

...*HUH?*

WHAT'S THAT? LOUDER PLEASE, I AM OLD AND CANNOT HEAR SO WELL ANYMORE.

FATHER? LAMECH? THAT IS NOT YOUR VOICE-- WHO *IS* THIS?

CAN YOU HEAR ME NOW!?

AH, GOOD... NOW, WHAT WERE YOU SAYING?

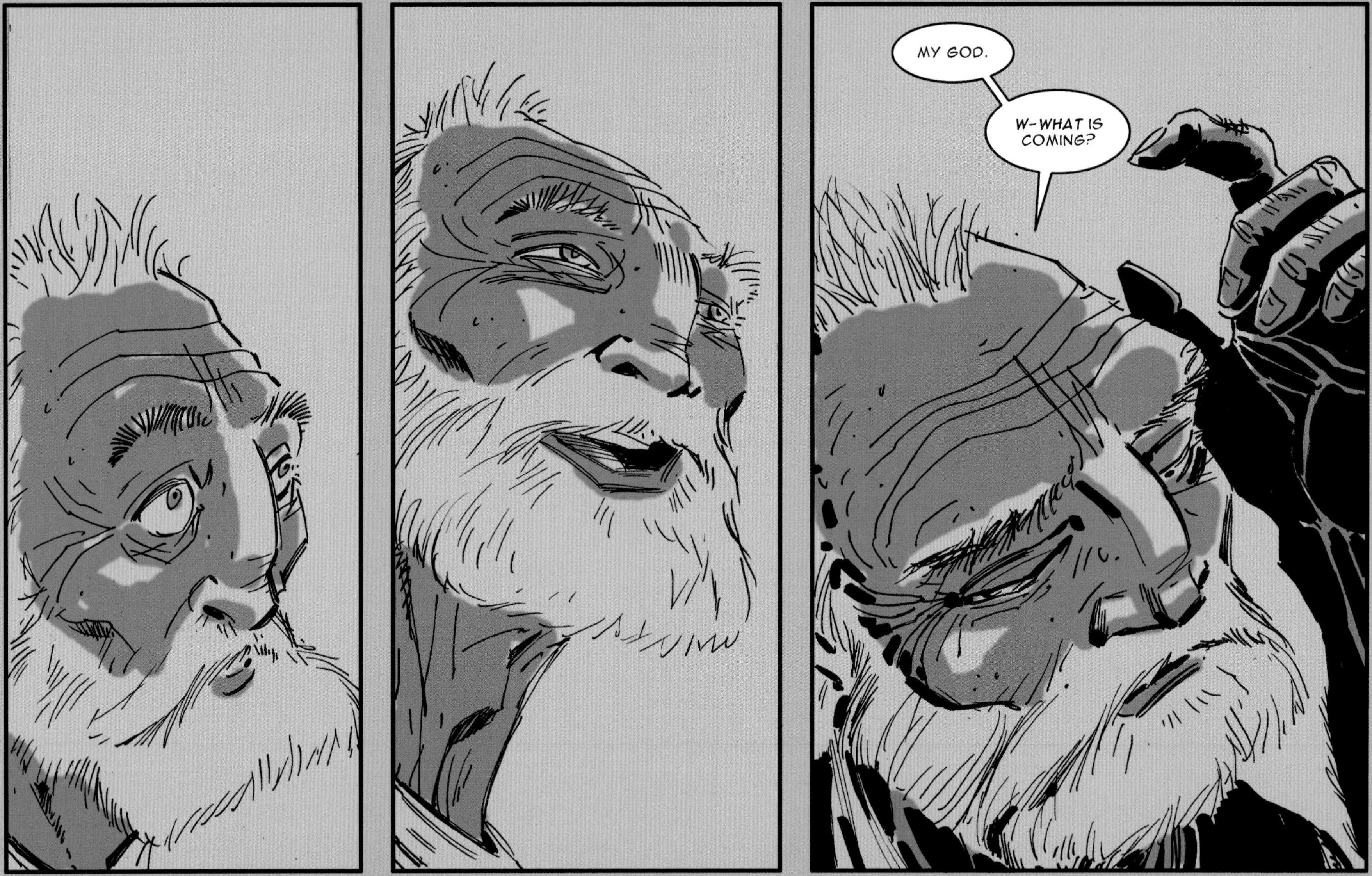
MY GOD.
W-WHAT IS COMING?

Preparations

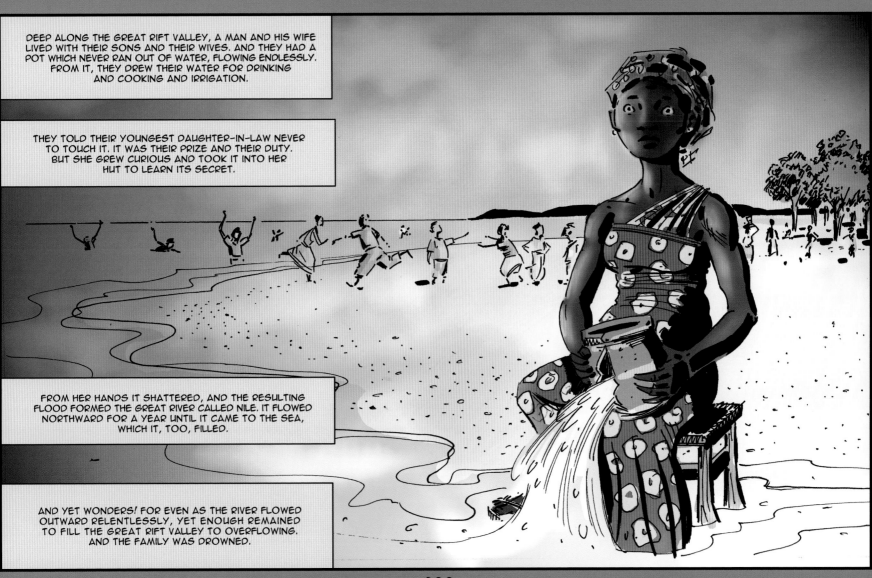

DEEP ALONG THE GREAT RIFT VALLEY, A MAN AND HIS WIFE LIVED WITH THEIR SONS AND THEIR WIVES. AND THEY HAD A POT WHICH NEVER RAN OUT OF WATER, FLOWING ENDLESSLY. FROM IT, THEY DREW THEIR WATER FOR DRINKING AND COOKING AND IRRIGATION.

THEY TOLD THEIR YOUNGEST DAUGHTER-IN-LAW NEVER TO TOUCH IT. IT WAS THEIR PRIZE AND THEIR DUTY. BUT SHE GREW CURIOUS AND TOOK IT INTO HER HUT TO LEARN ITS SECRET.

FROM HER HANDS IT SHATTERED, AND THE RESULTING FLOOD FORMED THE GREAT RIVER CALLED NILE. IT FLOWED NORTHWARD FOR A YEAR UNTIL IT CAME TO THE SEA, WHICH IT, TOO, FILLED.

AND YET WONDERS! FOR EVEN AS THE RIVER FLOWED OUTWARD RELENTLESSLY, YET ENOUGH REMAINED TO FILL THE GREAT RIFT VALLEY TO OVERFLOWING. AND THE FAMILY WAS DROWNED.

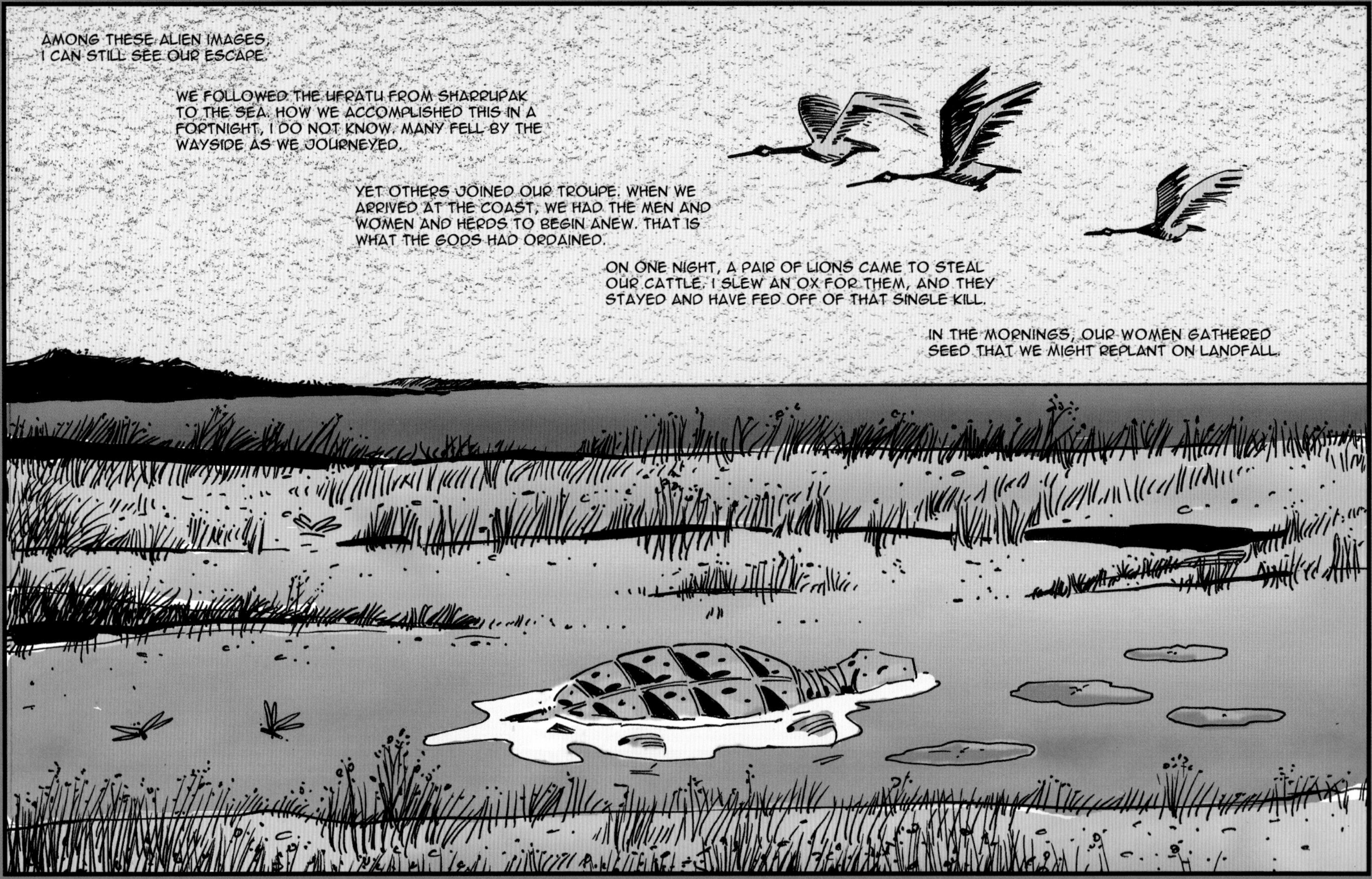
AMONG THESE ALIEN IMAGES, I CAN STILL SEE OUR ESCAPE.
WE FOLLOWED THE UFRATU FROM SHARRUPAK TO THE SEA. HOW WE ACCOMPLISHED THIS IN A FORTNIGHT, I DO NOT KNOW. MANY FELL BY THE WAYSIDE AS WE JOURNEYED.
YET OTHERS JOINED OUR TROUPE. WHEN WE ARRIVED AT THE COAST, WE HAD THE MEN AND WOMEN AND HERDS TO BEGIN ANEW. THAT IS WHAT THE GODS HAD ORDAINED.
ON ONE NIGHT, A PAIR OF LIONS CAME TO STEAL OUR CATTLE. I SLEW AN OX FOR THEM, AND THEY STAYED AND HAVE FED OFF OF THAT SINGLE KILL.
IN THE MORNINGS, OUR WOMEN GATHERED SEED THAT WE MIGHT REPLANT ON LANDFALL.

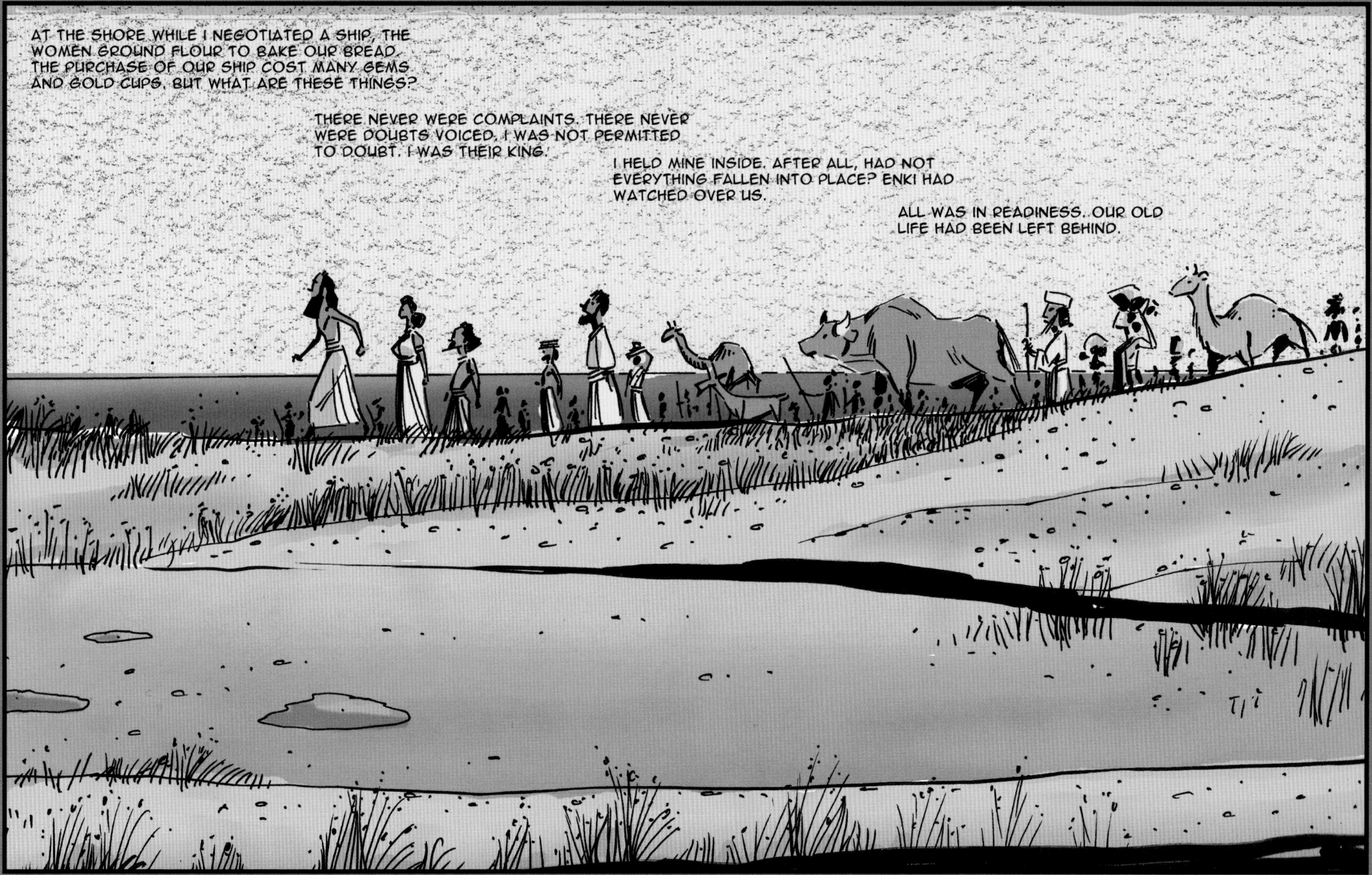
AT THE SHORE WHILE I NEGOTIATED A SHIP, THE WOMEN GROUND FLOUR TO BAKE OUR BREAD. THE PURCHASE OF OUR SHIP COST MANY GEMS AND GOLD CUPS. BUT WHAT ARE THESE THINGS?
THERE NEVER WERE COMPLAINTS. THERE NEVER WERE DOUBTS VOICED. I WAS NOT PERMITTED TO DOUBT. I WAS THEIR KING.
I HELD MINE INSIDE. AFTER ALL, HAD NOT EVERYTHING FALLEN INTO PLACE? ENKI HAD WATCHED OVER US.
ALL WAS IN READINESS. OUR OLD LIFE HAD BEEN LEFT BEHIND.

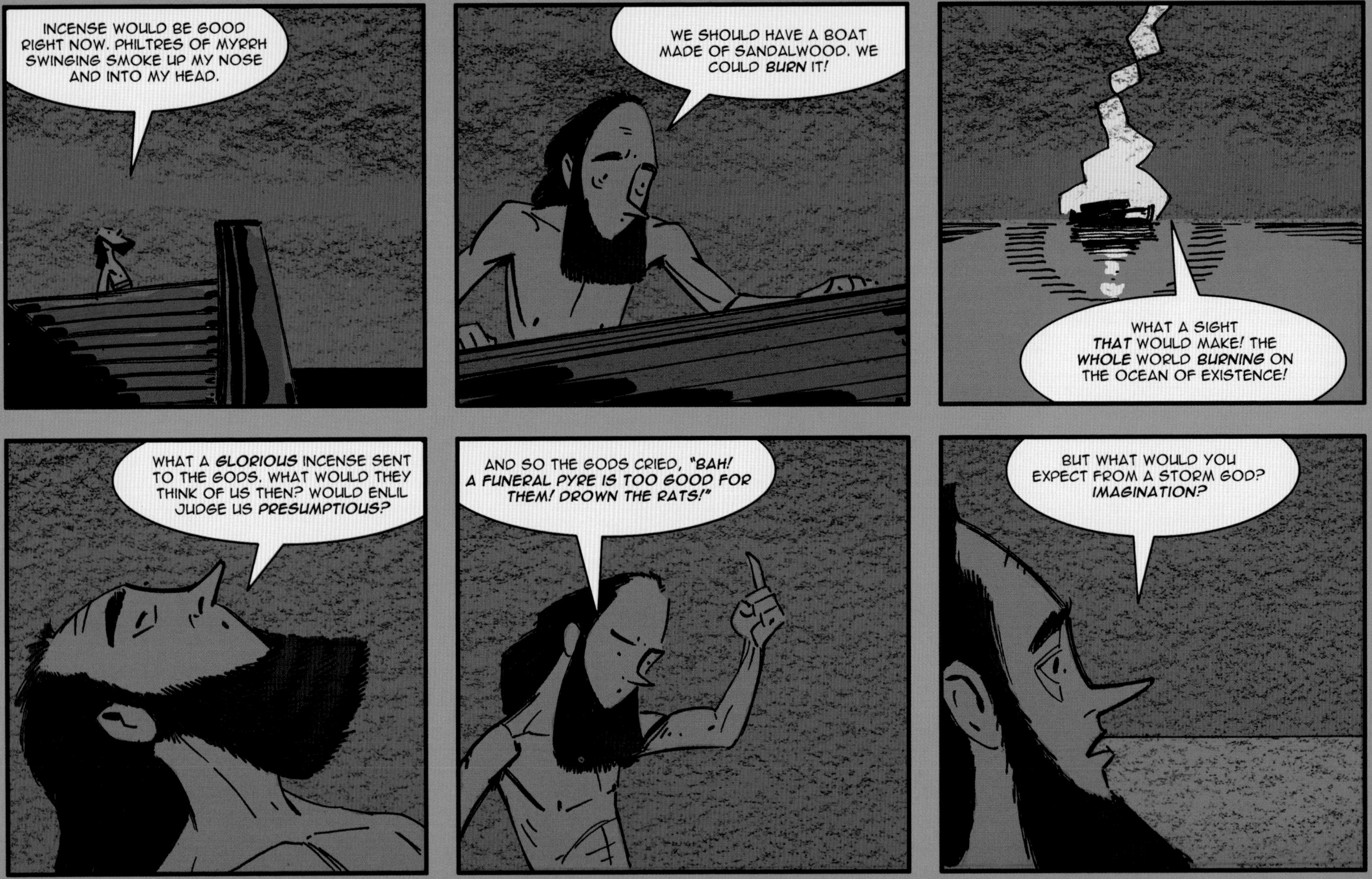
INCENSE WOULD BE GOOD RIGHT NOW. PHILTRES OF MYRRH SWINGING SMOKE UP MY NOSE AND INTO MY HEAD.
WE SHOULD HAVE A BOAT MADE OF SANDALWOOD. WE COULD *BURN* IT!
WHAT A SIGHT *THAT* WOULD MAKE! THE *WHOLE* WORLD *BURNING* ON THE OCEAN OF EXISTENCE!
WHAT A *GLORIOUS* INCENSE SENT TO THE GODS. WHAT WOULD THEY THINK OF US THEN? WOULD ENLIL JUDGE US *PRESUMPTIOUS?*
AND SO THE GODS CRIED, *"BAH! A FUNERAL PYRE IS TOO GOOD FOR THEM! DROWN THE RATS!"*
BUT WHAT WOULD YOU EXPECT FROM A STORM GOD? *IMAGINATION?*

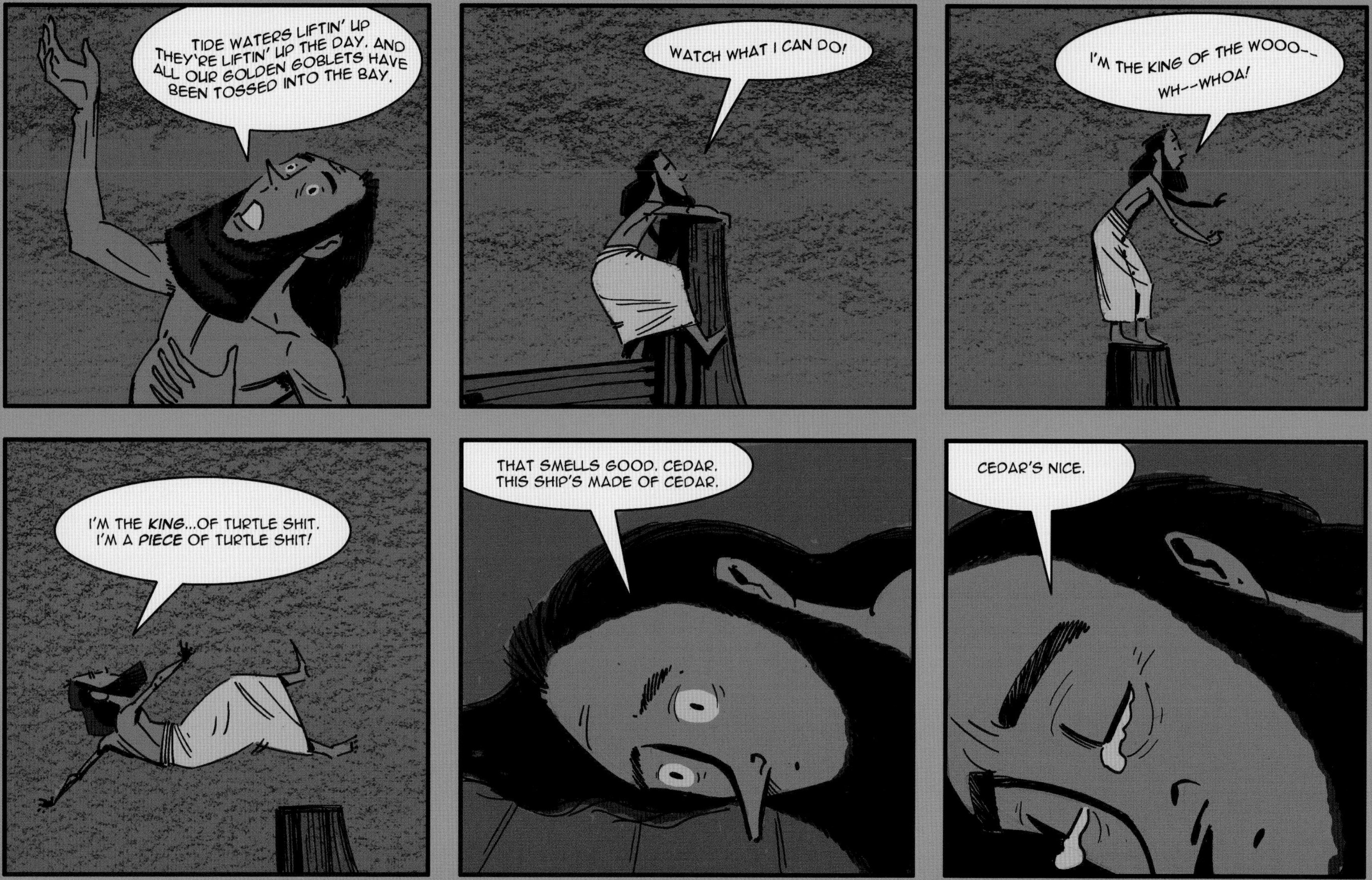
TIDE WATERS LIFTIN' UP THEY'RE LIFTIN' UP THE DAY. AND ALL OUR GOLDEN GOBLETS HAVE BEEN TOSSED INTO THE BAY.
WATCH WHAT I CAN DO!
I'M THE KING OF THE WOOO-- WH--WHOA!
I'M THE *KING*...OF TURTLE SHIT. I'M A *PIECE* OF TURTLE SHIT!
THAT SMELLS GOOD. CEDAR. THIS SHIP'S MADE OF CEDAR.
CEDAR'S NICE.

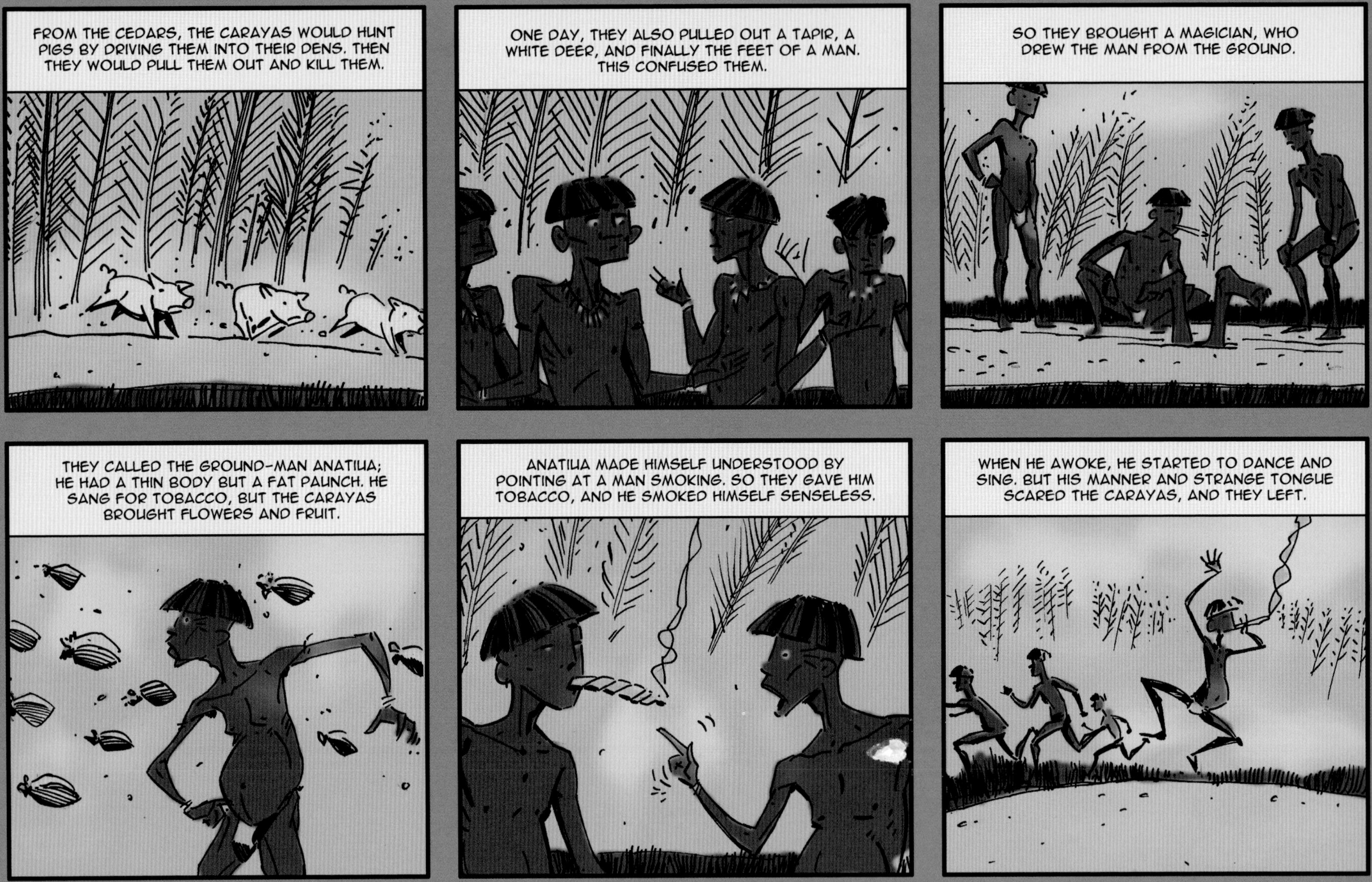
FROM THE CEDARS, THE CARAYAS WOULD HUNT PIGS BY DRIVING THEM INTO THEIR DENS. THEN THEY WOULD PULL THEM OUT AND KILL THEM.
ONE DAY, THEY ALSO PULLED OUT A TAPIR, A WHITE DEER, AND FINALLY THE FEET OF A MAN. THIS CONFUSED THEM.
SO THEY BROUGHT A MAGICIAN, WHO DREW THE MAN FROM THE GROUND.
THEY CALLED THE GROUND-MAN ANATIUA; HE HAD A THIN BODY BUT A FAT PAUNCH. HE SANG FOR TOBACCO, BUT THE CARAYAS BROUGHT FLOWERS AND FRUIT.
ANATIUA MADE HIMSELF UNDERSTOOD BY POINTING AT A MAN SMOKING. SO THEY GAVE HIM TOBACCO, AND HE SMOKED HIMSELF SENSELESS.
WHEN HE AWOKE, HE STARTED TO DANCE AND SING. BUT HIS MANNER AND STRANGE TONGUE SCARED THE CARAYAS, AND THEY LEFT.

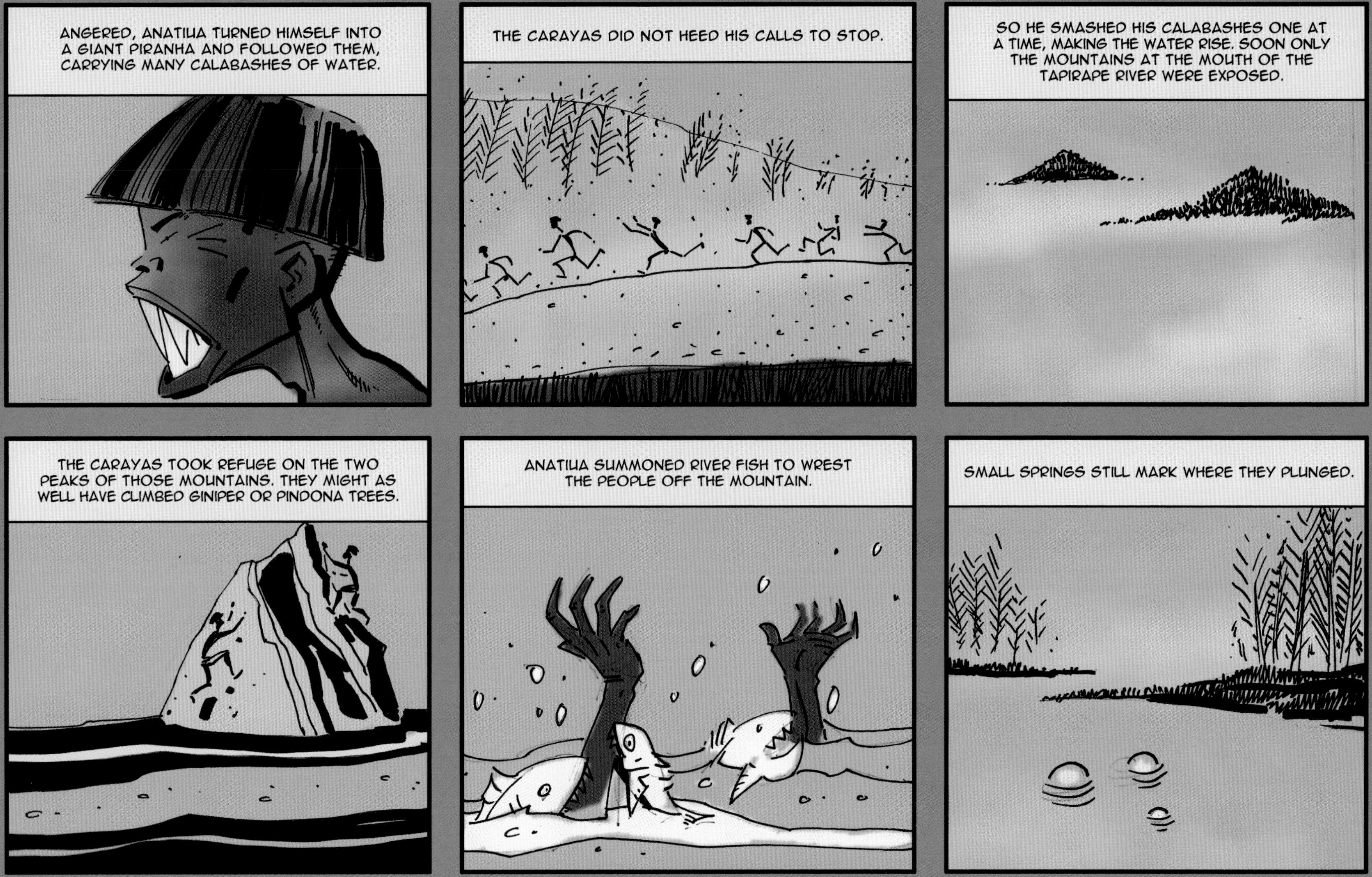
ANGERED, ANATIUA TURNED HIMSELF INTO A GIANT PIRANHA AND FOLLOWED THEM, CARRYING MANY CALABASHES OF WATER.
THE CARAYAS DID NOT HEED HIS CALLS TO STOP.
SO HE SMASHED HIS CALABASHES ONE AT A TIME, MAKING THE WATER RISE. SOON ONLY THE MOUNTAINS AT THE MOUTH OF THE TAPIRAPE RIVER WERE EXPOSED.
THE CARAYAS TOOK REFUGE ON THE TWO PEAKS OF THOSE MOUNTAINS. THEY MIGHT AS WELL HAVE CLIMBED GINIPER OR PINDONA TREES.
ANATIUA SUMMONED RIVER FISH TO WREST THE PEOPLE OFF THE MOUNTAIN.
SMALL SPRINGS STILL MARK WHERE THEY PLUNGED.

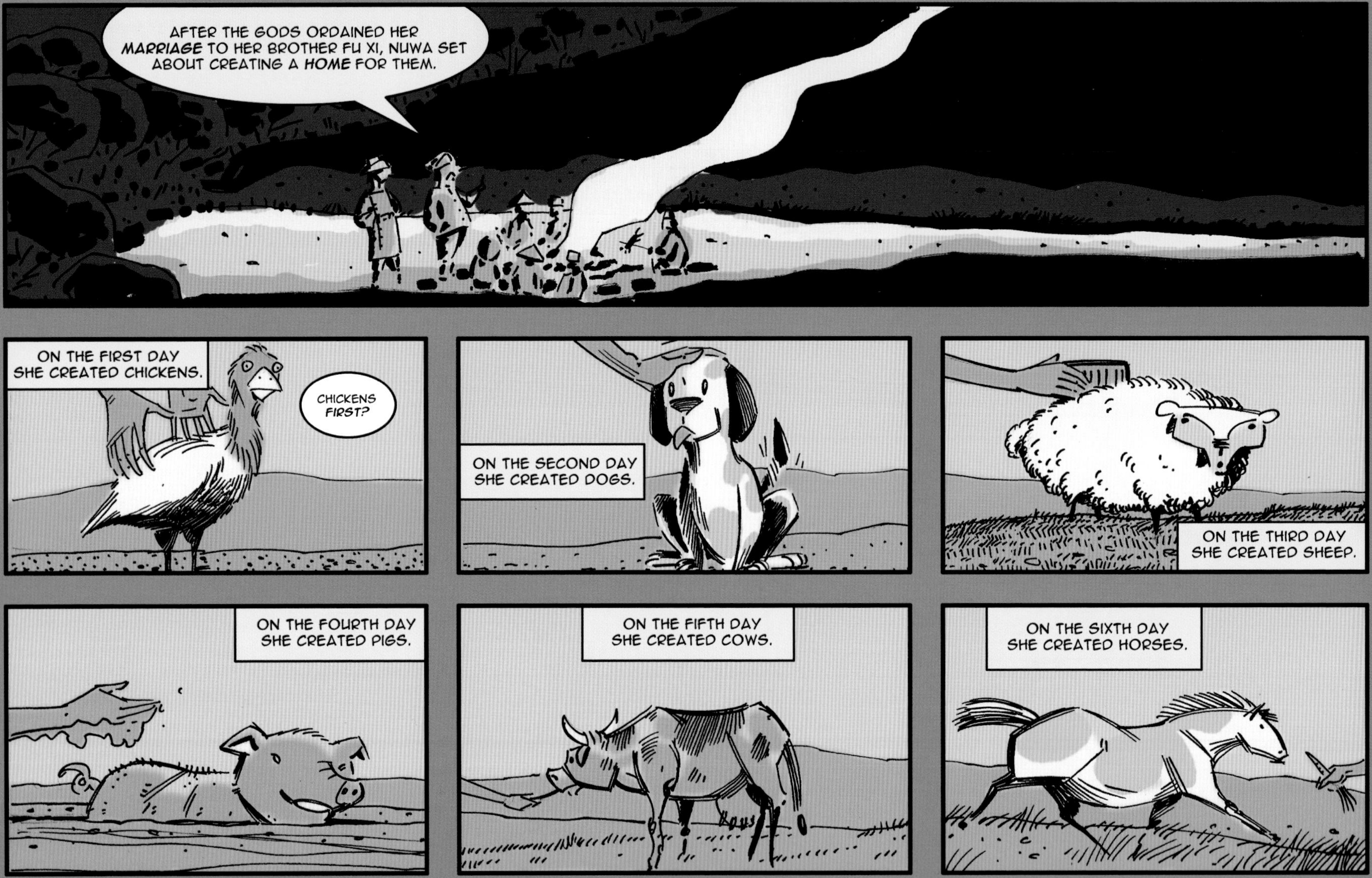
AFTER THE GODS ORDAINED HER MARRIAGE TO HER BROTHER FU XI, NUWA SET ABOUT CREATING A HOME FOR THEM.
ON THE FIRST DAY SHE CREATED CHICKENS.
CHICKENS FIRST?
ON THE SECOND DAY SHE CREATED DOGS.
ON THE THIRD DAY SHE CREATED SHEEP.
ON THE FOURTH DAY SHE CREATED PIGS.
ON THE FIFTH DAY SHE CREATED COWS.
ON THE SIXTH DAY SHE CREATED HORSES.

ON THE SEVENTH DAY SHE BEGAN SCULPTING. BEAUTIFUL MEN AND WOMEN WERE FORMED FROM YELLOW CLAY. AT NOON, SHE STOPPED TO REST AND ADMIRE HER ACHIEVEMENT.

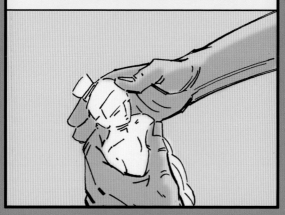

SHE HAD MADE HUNDREDS OF FIGURES THIS WAY BUT HAD GROWN TIRED OF THE LABORIOUS PROCESS.

INSTEAD, SHE DIPPED A ROPE IN CLAY AND SNAPPED IT. BLOBS OF CLAY LANDED ABOUT HER.

EACH OF THESE BLOBS BECAME A PERSON. THEY ONLY STOOD UPRIGHT BY VIRTUE OF THE ROPE INSIDE OF THEM.

IN THIS WAY OUR NOBLES WERE CREATED FROM THE HAND-CRAFTED FIGURES, AND THE BLOBS BECAME PEASANTS.

SO *THAT* EXPLAINS YOUR NOSE.

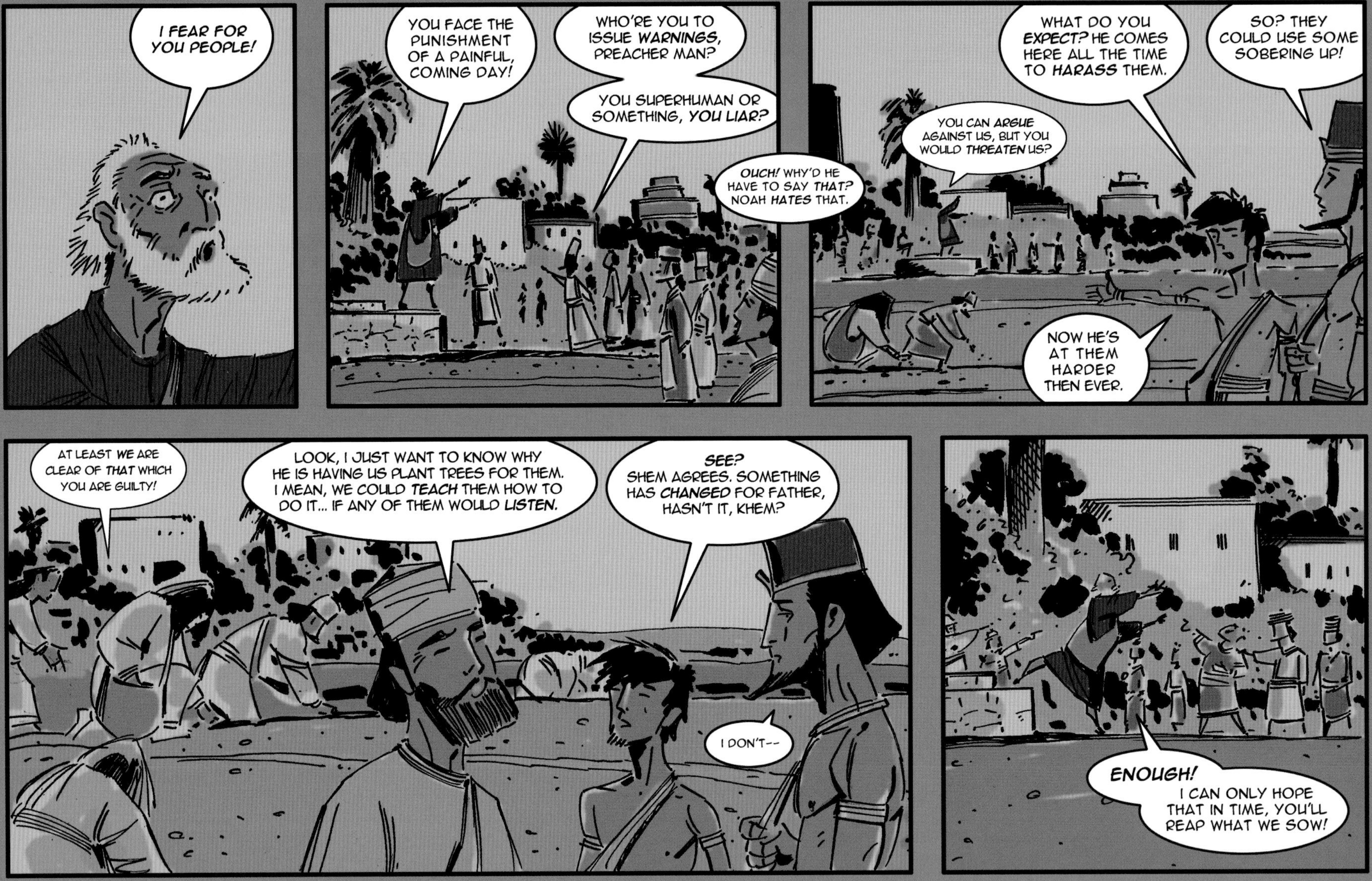
I FEAR FOR YOU PEOPLE!
YOU FACE THE PUNISHMENT OF A PAINFUL, COMING DAY!
WHO'RE YOU TO ISSUE WARNINGS, PREACHER MAN?
YOU SUPERHUMAN OR SOMETHING, YOU LIAR?
OUCH! WHY'D HE HAVE TO SAY THAT? NOAH HATES THAT.
YOU CAN ARGUE AGAINST US, BUT YOU WOULD THREATEN US?
WHAT DO YOU EXPECT? HE COMES HERE ALL THE TIME TO HARASS THEM.
SO? THEY COULD USE SOME SOBERING UP!
NOW HE'S AT THEM HARDER THEN EVER.
AT LEAST WE ARE CLEAR OF THAT WHICH YOU ARE GUILTY!
LOOK, I JUST WANT TO KNOW WHY HE IS HAVING US PLANT TREES FOR THEM. I MEAN, WE COULD TEACH THEM HOW TO DO IT... IF ANY OF THEM WOULD LISTEN.
SEE? SHEM AGREES. SOMETHING HAS CHANGED FOR FATHER, HASN'T IT, KHEM?
I DON'T--
ENOUGH! I CAN ONLY HOPE THAT IN TIME, YOU'LL REAP WHAT WE SOW!

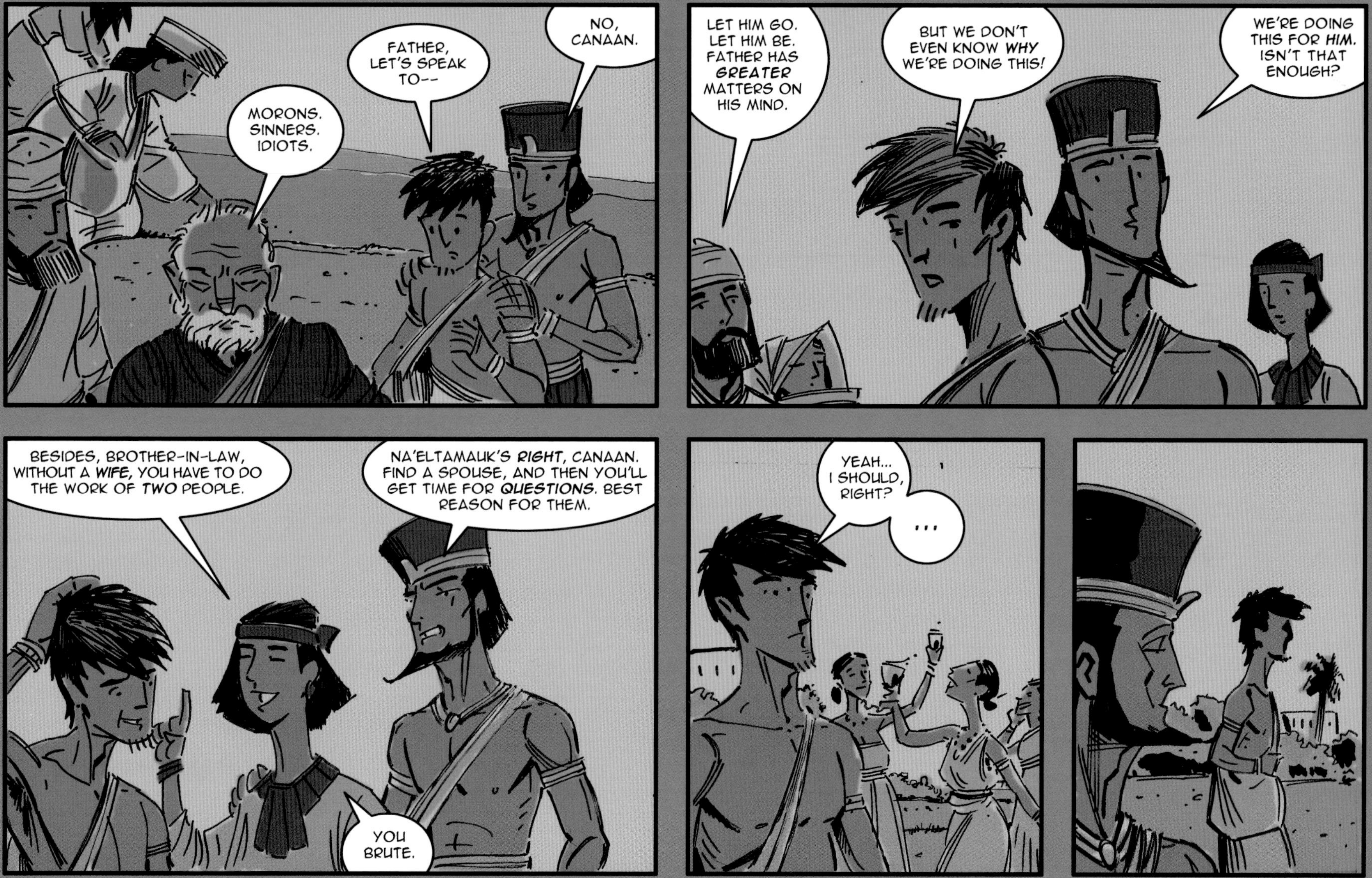
MORONS. SINNERS. IDIOTS.
FATHER, LET'S SPEAK TO--
NO, CANAAN.
LET HIM GO. LET HIM BE. FATHER HAS **GREATER** MATTERS ON HIS MIND.
BUT WE DON'T EVEN KNOW **WHY** WE'RE DOING THIS!
WE'RE DOING THIS FOR **HIM**. ISN'T THAT ENOUGH?
BESIDES, BROTHER-IN-LAW, WITHOUT A **WIFE,** YOU HAVE TO DO THE WORK OF **TWO** PEOPLE.
NA'ELTAMAUK'S **RIGHT**, CANAAN. FIND A SPOUSE, AND THEN YOU'LL GET TIME FOR **QUESTIONS**. BEST REASON FOR THEM.
YOU BRUTE.
YEAH... I SHOULD, RIGHT?
...

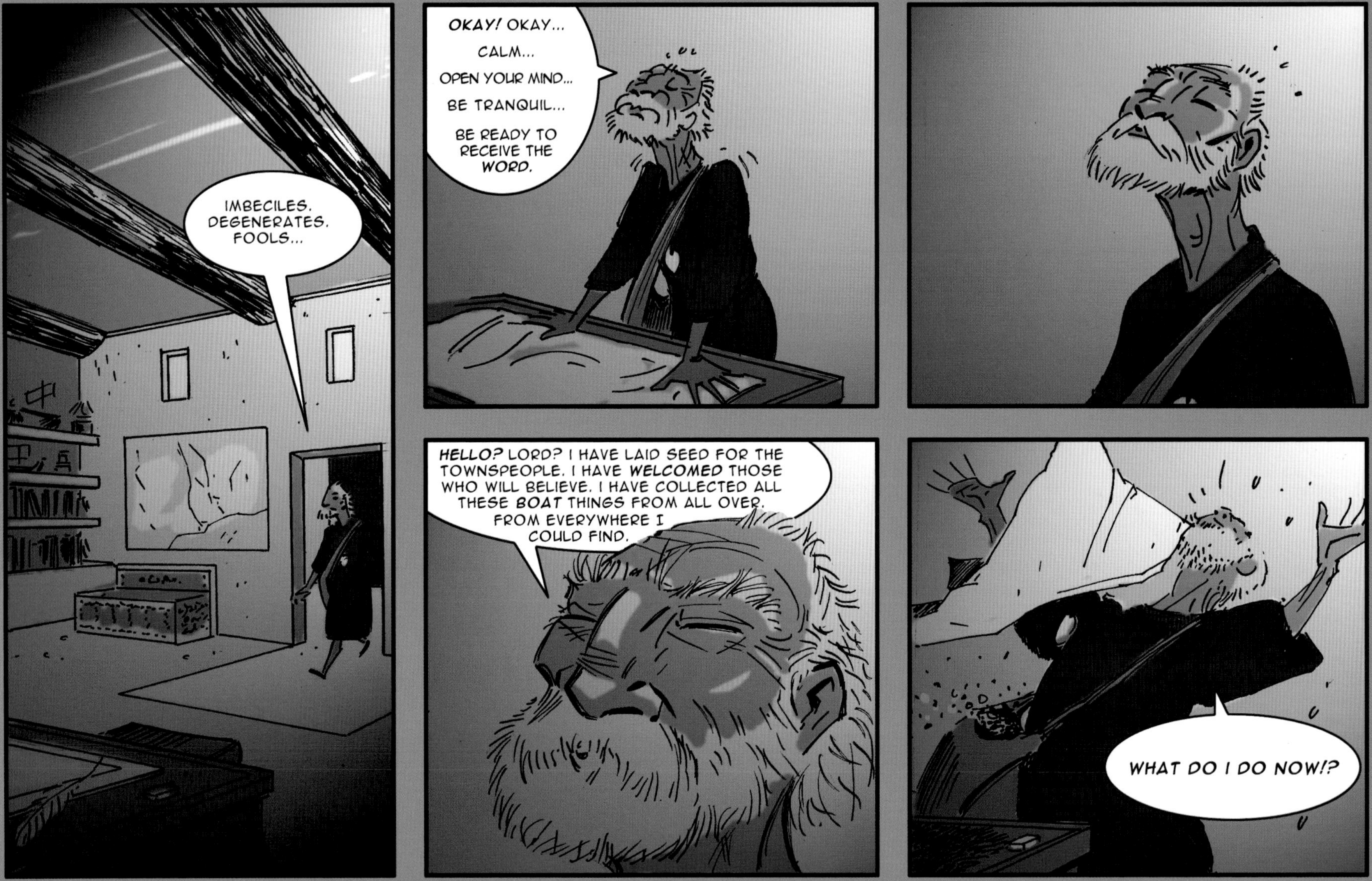
IMBECILES. DEGENERATES. FOOLS...
OKAY! OKAY...
CALM...
OPEN YOUR MIND...
BE TRANQUIL...
BE READY TO RECEIVE THE WORD.
HELLO? LORD? I HAVE LAID SEED FOR THE TOWNSPEOPLE. I HAVE WELCOMED THOSE WHO WILL BELIEVE. I HAVE COLLECTED ALL THESE BOAT THINGS FROM ALL OVER. FROM EVERYWHERE I COULD FIND.
WHAT DO I DO NOW!?

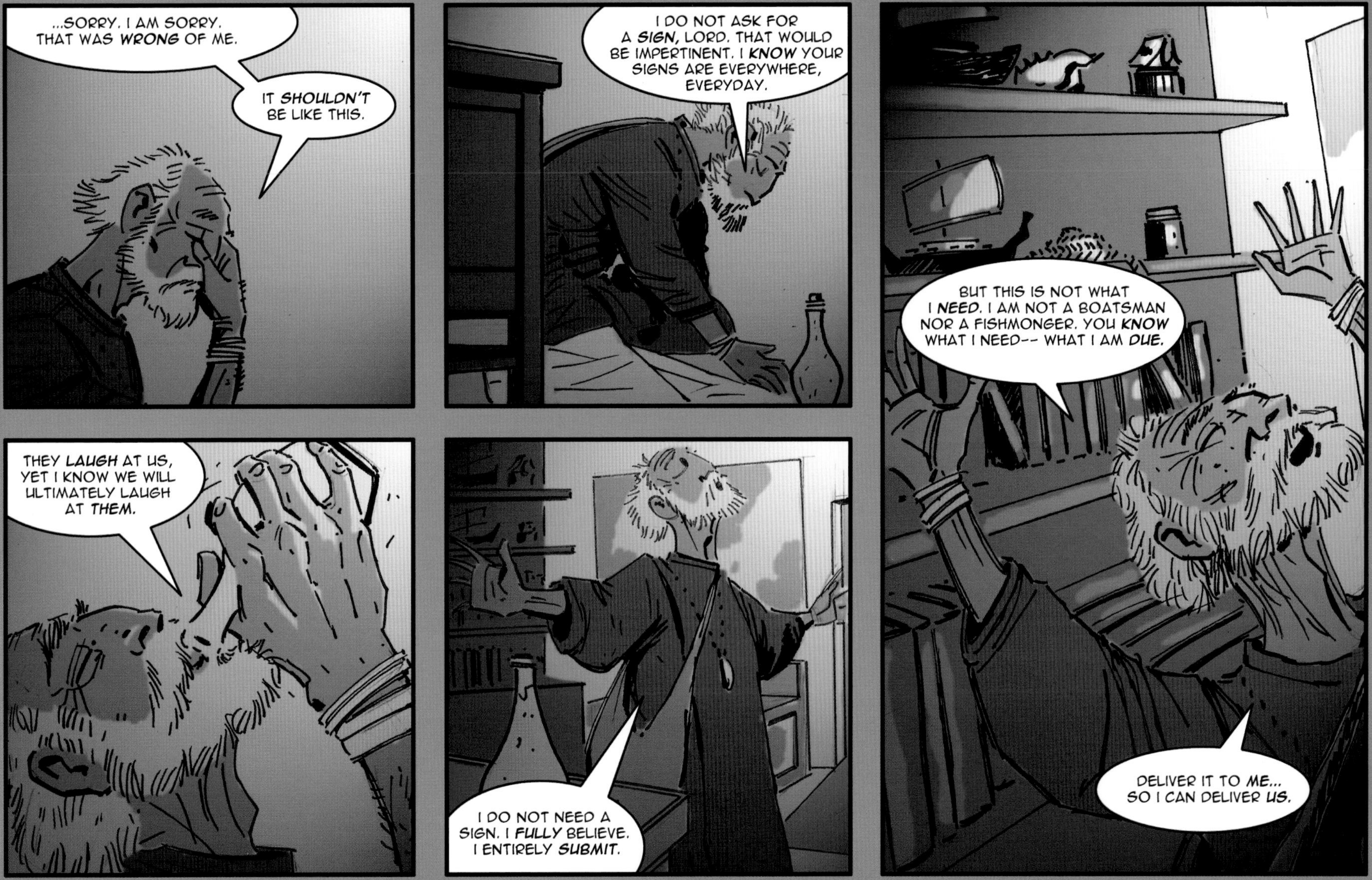
...SORRY. I AM SORRY. THAT WAS WRONG OF ME.
IT SHOULDN'T BE LIKE THIS.
I DO NOT ASK FOR A SIGN, LORD. THAT WOULD BE IMPERTINENT. I KNOW YOUR SIGNS ARE EVERYWHERE, EVERYDAY.
BUT THIS IS NOT WHAT I NEED. I AM NOT A BOATSMAN NOR A FISHMONGER. YOU KNOW WHAT I NEED-- WHAT I AM DUE.
DELIVER IT TO ME... SO I CAN DELIVER US.
THEY LAUGH AT US, YET I KNOW WE WILL ULTIMATELY LAUGH AT THEM.
I DO NOT NEED A SIGN. I FULLY BELIEVE. I ENTIRELY SUBMIT.

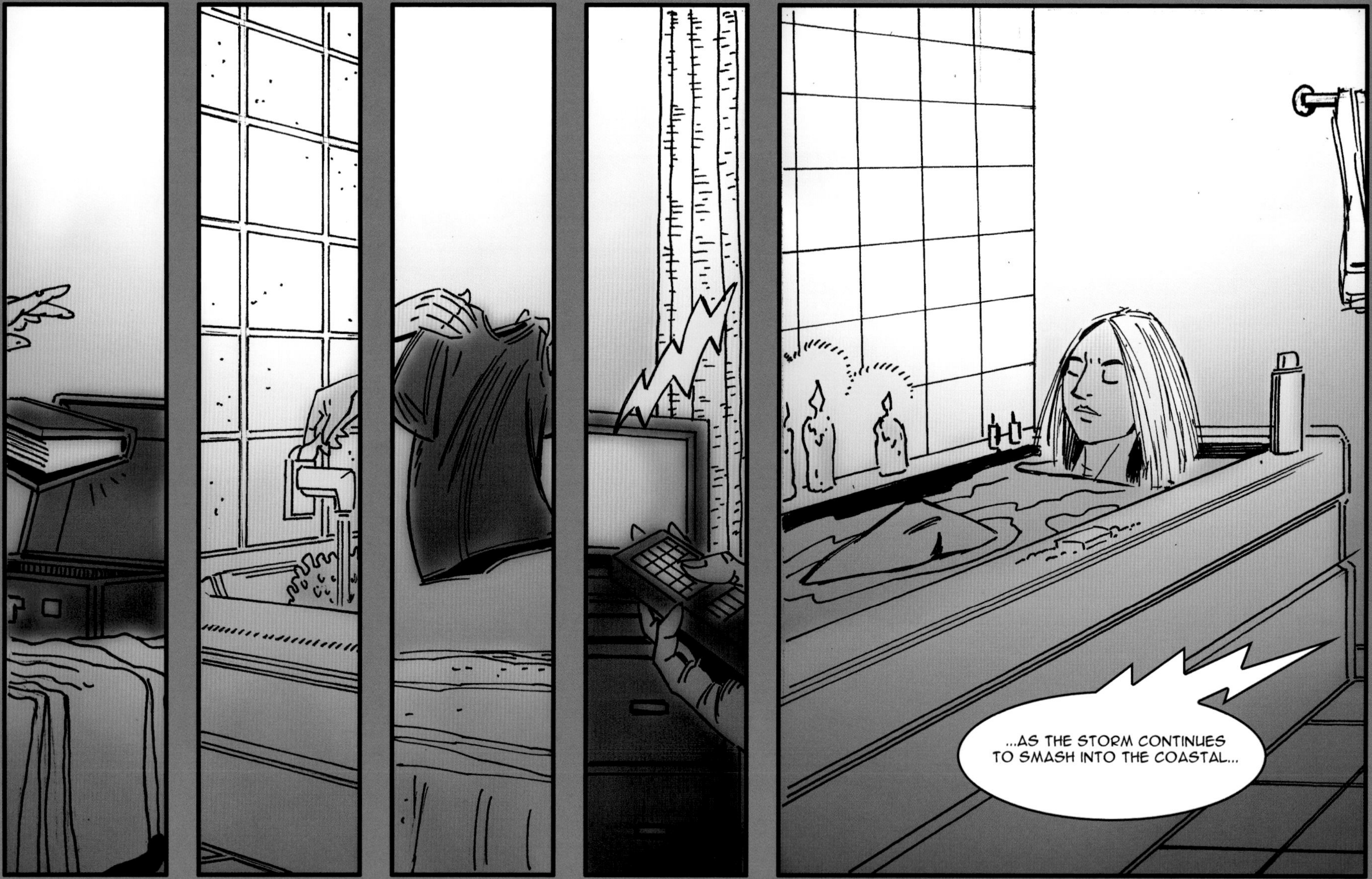
...AS THE STORM CONTINUES TO SMASH INTO THE COASTAL...

...MORE FROM THE SCENE OF DEVASTATION AS HURRICANE CARLA...

...HURRICANE CORA CONTINUES ITS PATH OF DESTRUCTION...

...YOB, YOBBLE, YOBBB...

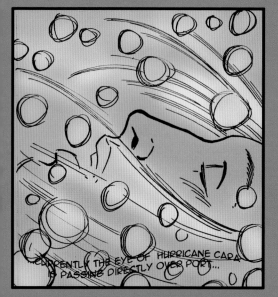

...CURRENTLY THE EYE OF HURRICANE CARA IS PASSING DIRECTLY OVER PORT...

MOMMY!

...IS LOST BEFORE THE FURY OF HURRICANE CARRIE...

...REFUGEES STILL STREAMING FROM THE PATH OF THE HURRICANE, BUT MANY, MANY ARE BELIEVED TO BE UNABLE TO GET OUT...

I MUST NOT GIVE IN TO *DESPAIR*. THROUGHOUT THE TRIP FROM SHARRUPAK TO THE COAST, I *SLEPT* LITTLE. LESS AND LESS EACH NIGHT.

BOARDING OUR SHIP AND GETTING INSTALLED CONSUMED EVERYONE'S ATTENTION FOR DAYS. NO ONE SLEPT MUCH THEN. AS THE RAINS APPROACHED, I SACRIFICED OUR SOLE REMAINING OX TO THE GODS FOR A SAFE VOYAGE.

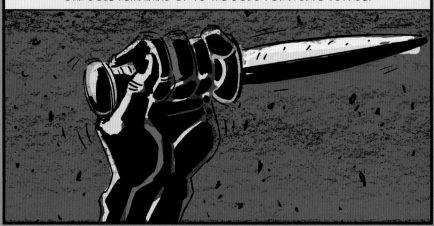

THE RAINS CAME, THE RIVER FLOODED, AND THE WATERS ROSE WITH A FURY THAT ONLY THE GODS COULD MUSTER.

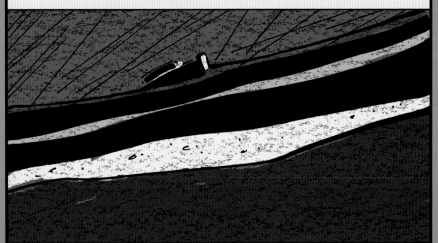

WE COULD DO NOTHING THEN BUT CLING TO EACH OTHER.

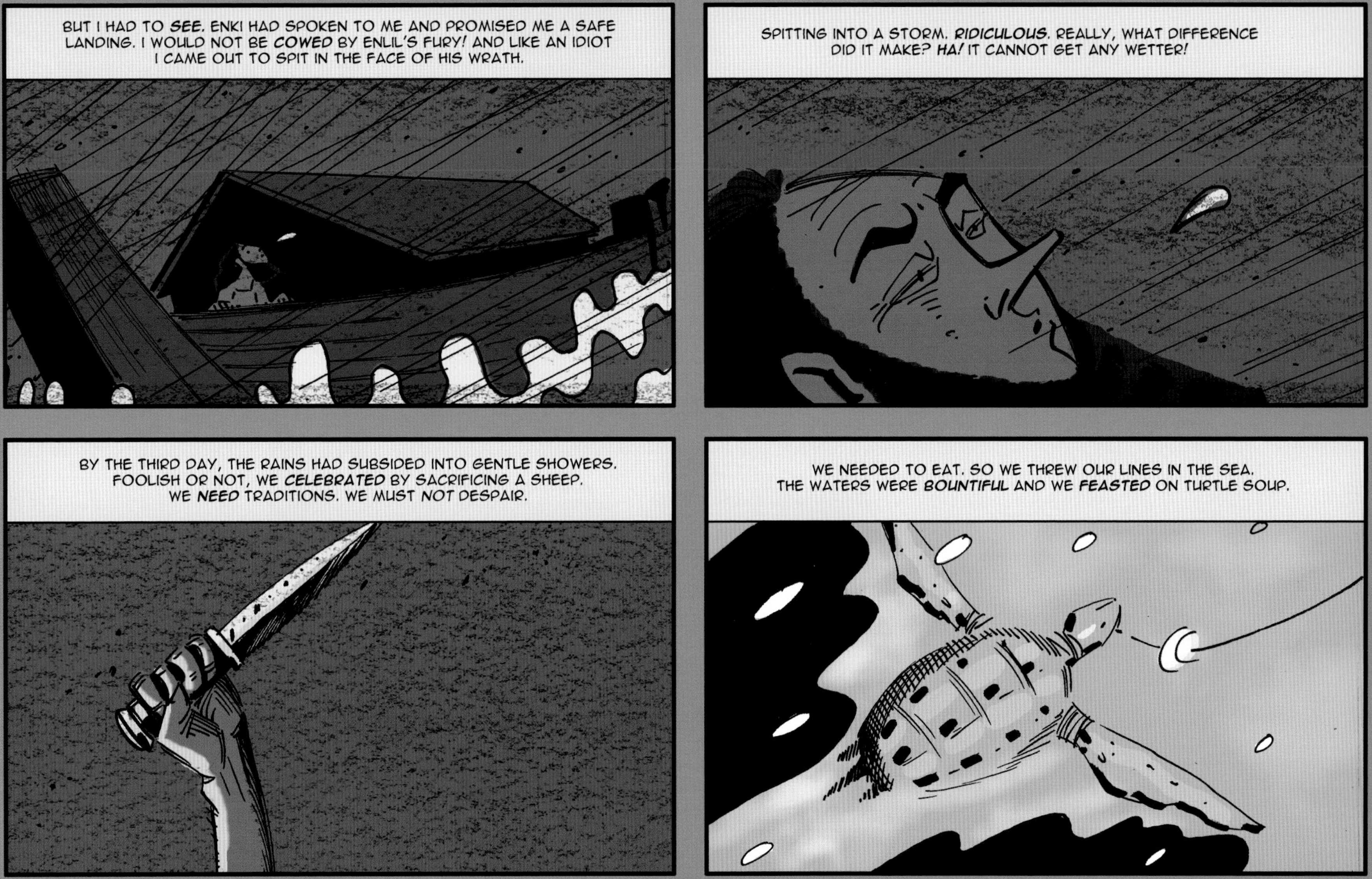
BUT I HAD TO ***SEE.*** ENKI HAD SPOKEN TO ME AND PROMISED ME A SAFE LANDING. I WOULD NOT BE ***COWED*** BY ENLIL'S *FURY!* AND LIKE AN IDIOT I CAME OUT TO SPIT IN THE FACE OF HIS WRATH.
SPITTING INTO A STORM. ***RIDICULOUS.*** REALLY, WHAT DIFFERENCE DID IT MAKE? ***HA!*** IT CANNOT GET ANY WETTER!
BY THE THIRD DAY, THE RAINS HAD SUBSIDED INTO GENTLE SHOWERS. FOOLISH OR NOT, WE ***CELEBRATED*** BY SACRIFICING A SHEEP. WE ***NEED*** TRADITIONS. WE MUST ***NOT*** DESPAIR.
WE NEEDED TO EAT. SO WE THREW OUR LINES IN THE SEA. THE WATERS WERE ***BOUNTIFUL*** AND WE ***FEASTED*** ON TURTLE SOUP.

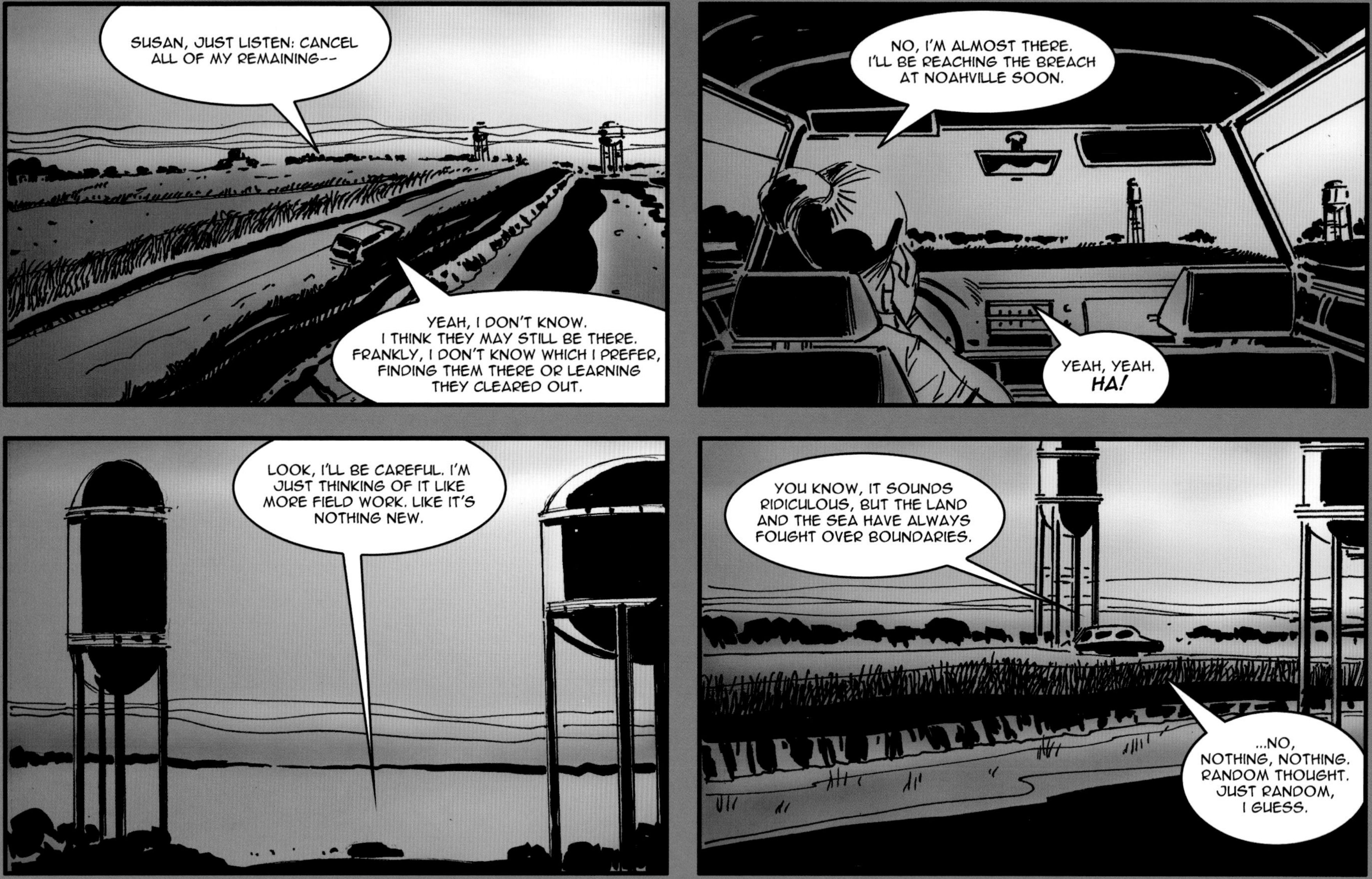
SUSAN, JUST LISTEN: CANCEL ALL OF MY REMAINING--
YEAH, I DON'T KNOW. I THINK THEY MAY STILL BE THERE. FRANKLY, I DON'T KNOW WHICH I PREFER, FINDING THEM THERE OR LEARNING THEY CLEARED OUT.
NO, I'M ALMOST THERE. I'LL BE REACHING THE BREACH AT NOAHVILLE SOON.
YEAH, YEAH. HA!
LOOK, I'LL BE CAREFUL. I'M JUST THINKING OF IT LIKE MORE FIELD WORK. LIKE IT'S NOTHING NEW.
YOU KNOW, IT SOUNDS RIDICULOUS, BUT THE LAND AND THE SEA HAVE ALWAYS FOUGHT OVER BOUNDARIES.
...NO, NOTHING, NOTHING. RANDOM THOUGHT. JUST RANDOM, I GUESS.

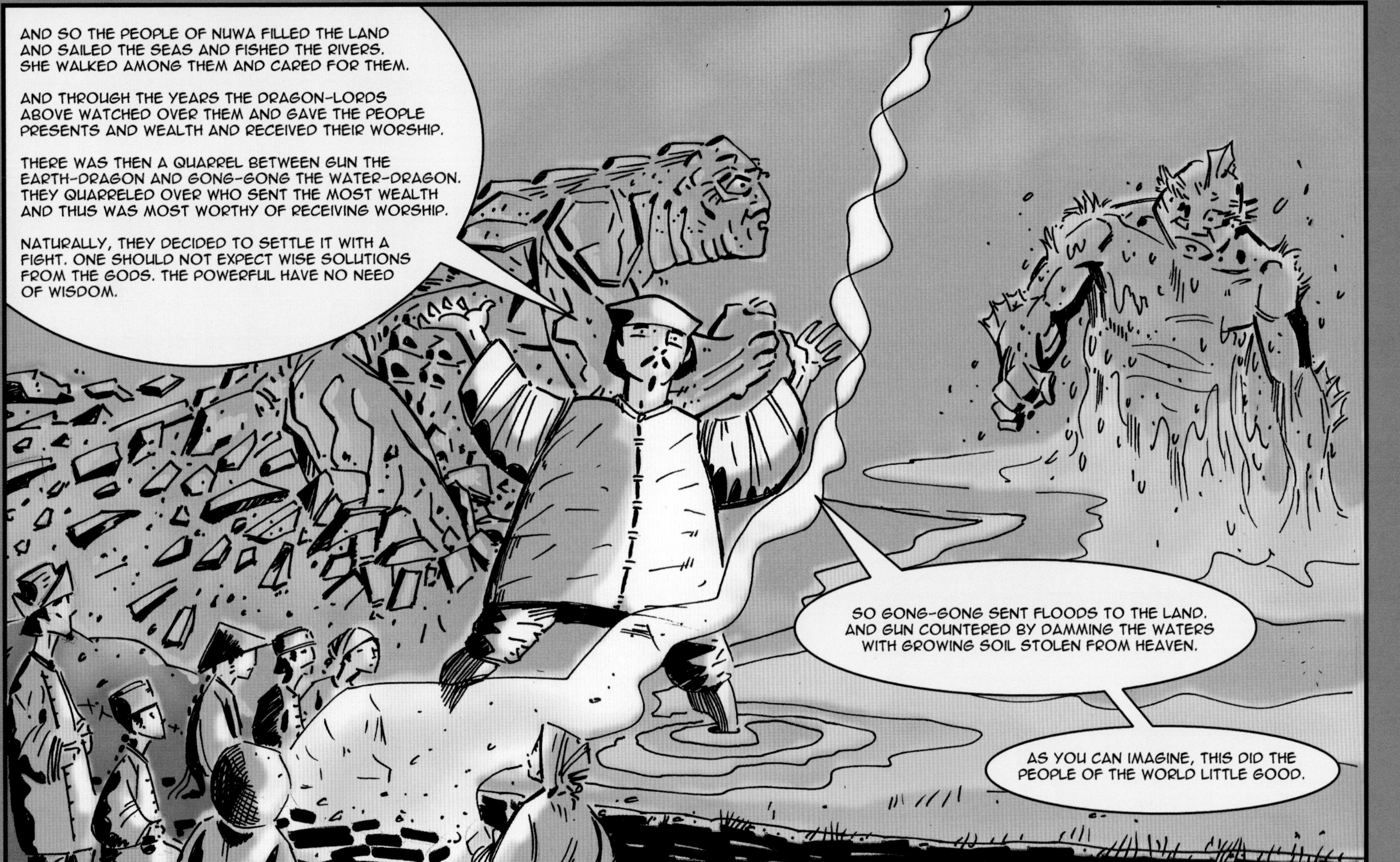
AND SO THE PEOPLE OF NUWA FILLED THE LAND AND SAILED THE SEAS AND FISHED THE RIVERS. SHE WALKED AMONG THEM AND CARED FOR THEM.
AND THROUGH THE YEARS THE DRAGON-LORDS ABOVE WATCHED OVER THEM AND GAVE THE PEOPLE PRESENTS AND WEALTH AND RECEIVED THEIR WORSHIP.
THERE WAS THEN A QUARREL BETWEEN GUN THE EARTH-DRAGON AND GONG-GONG THE WATER-DRAGON. THEY QUARRELED OVER WHO SENT THE MOST WEALTH AND THUS WAS MOST WORTHY OF RECEIVING WORSHIP.
NATURALLY, THEY DECIDED TO SETTLE IT WITH A FIGHT. ONE SHOULD NOT EXPECT WISE SOLUTIONS FROM THE GODS. THE POWERFUL HAVE NO NEED OF WISDOM.
SO GONG-GONG SENT FLOODS TO THE LAND. AND GUN COUNTERED BY DAMMING THE WATERS WITH GROWING SOIL STOLEN FROM HEAVEN.
AS YOU CAN IMAGINE, THIS DID THE PEOPLE OF THE WORLD LITTLE GOOD.

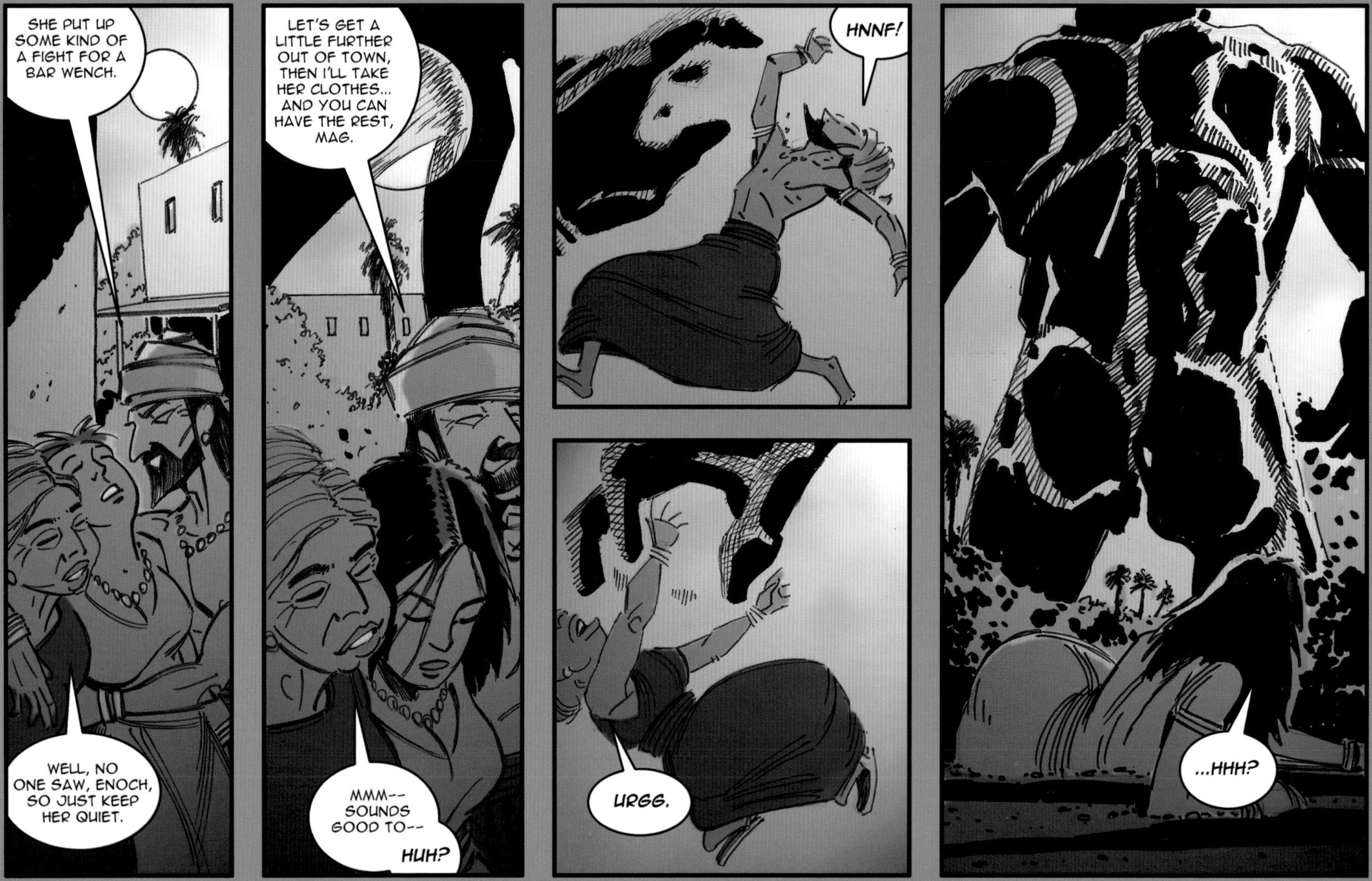
SHE PUT UP SOME KIND OF A FIGHT FOR A BAR WENCH.
WELL, NO ONE SAW, ENOCH, SO JUST KEEP HER QUIET.
LET'S GET A LITTLE FURTHER OUT OF TOWN, THEN I'LL TAKE HER CLOTHES... AND YOU CAN HAVE THE REST, MAG.
MMM-- SOUNDS GOOD TO--
HUH?
HNNF!
URGG.
...HHH?

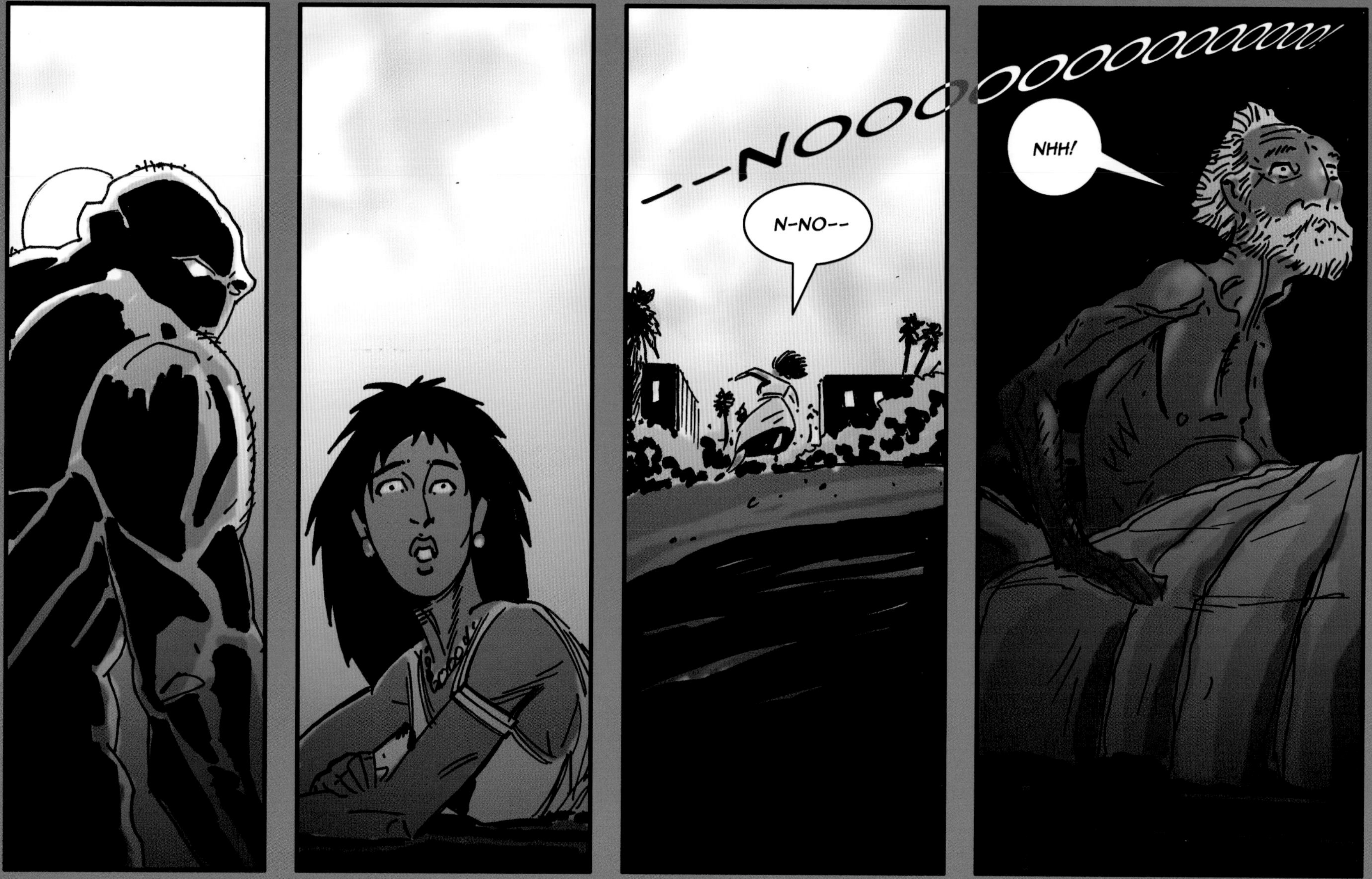
--NOOOOOOOOOOOOOOOO!
N-NO--
NHH!

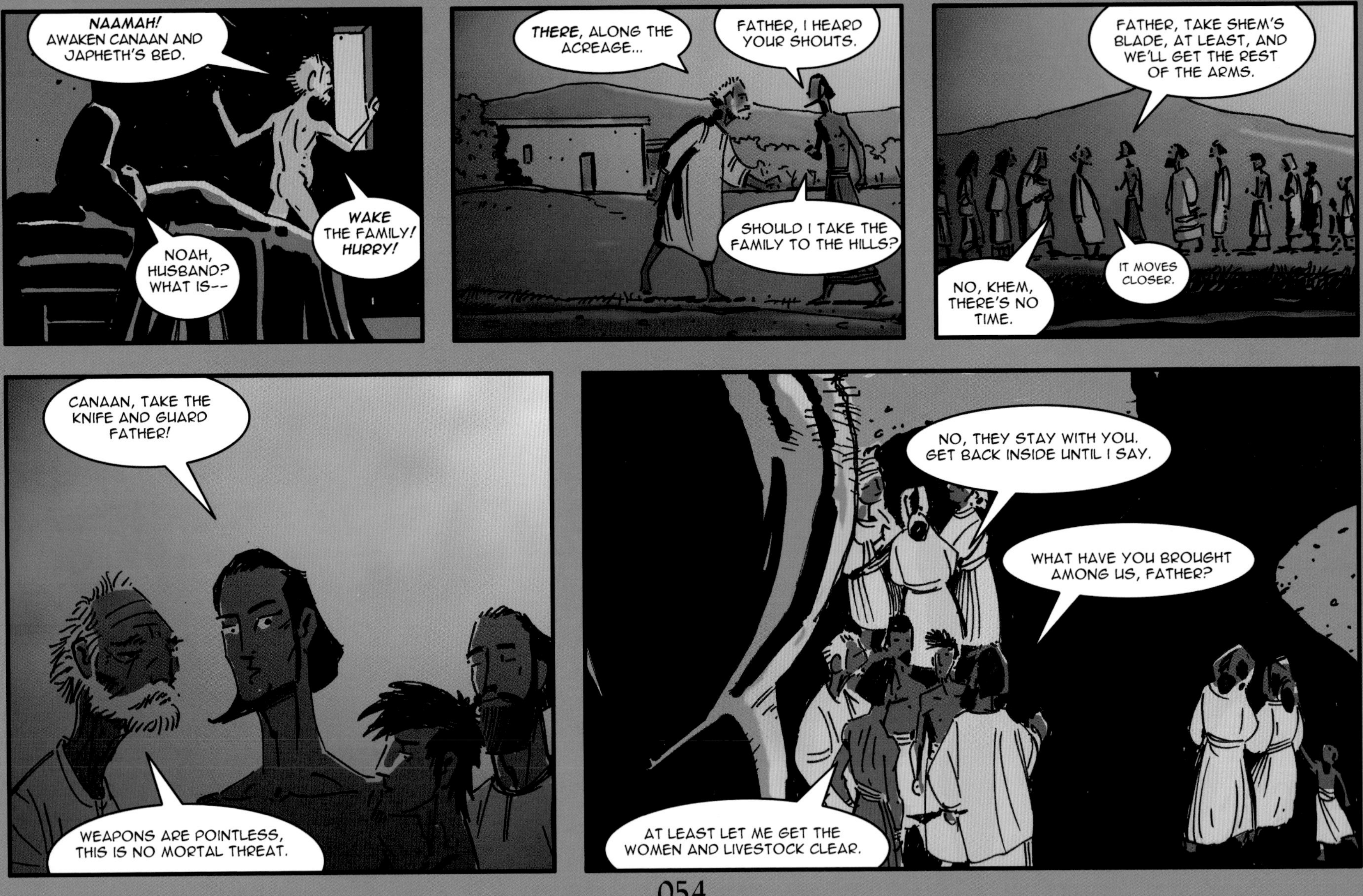
NAAMAH! AWAKEN CANAAN AND JAPHETH'S BED.
NOAH, HUSBAND? WHAT IS--
WAKE THE FAMILY! HURRY!
THERE, ALONG THE ACREAGE...
FATHER, I HEARD YOUR SHOUTS.
SHOULD I TAKE THE FAMILY TO THE HILLS?
FATHER, TAKE SHEM'S BLADE, AT LEAST, AND WE'LL GET THE REST OF THE ARMS.
NO, KHEM, THERE'S NO TIME.
IT MOVES CLOSER.
CANAAN, TAKE THE KNIFE AND GUARD FATHER!
WEAPONS ARE POINTLESS, THIS IS NO MORTAL THREAT.
NO, THEY STAY WITH YOU. GET BACK INSIDE UNTIL I SAY.
WHAT HAVE YOU BROUGHT AMONG US, FATHER?
AT LEAST LET ME GET THE WOMEN AND LIVESTOCK CLEAR.

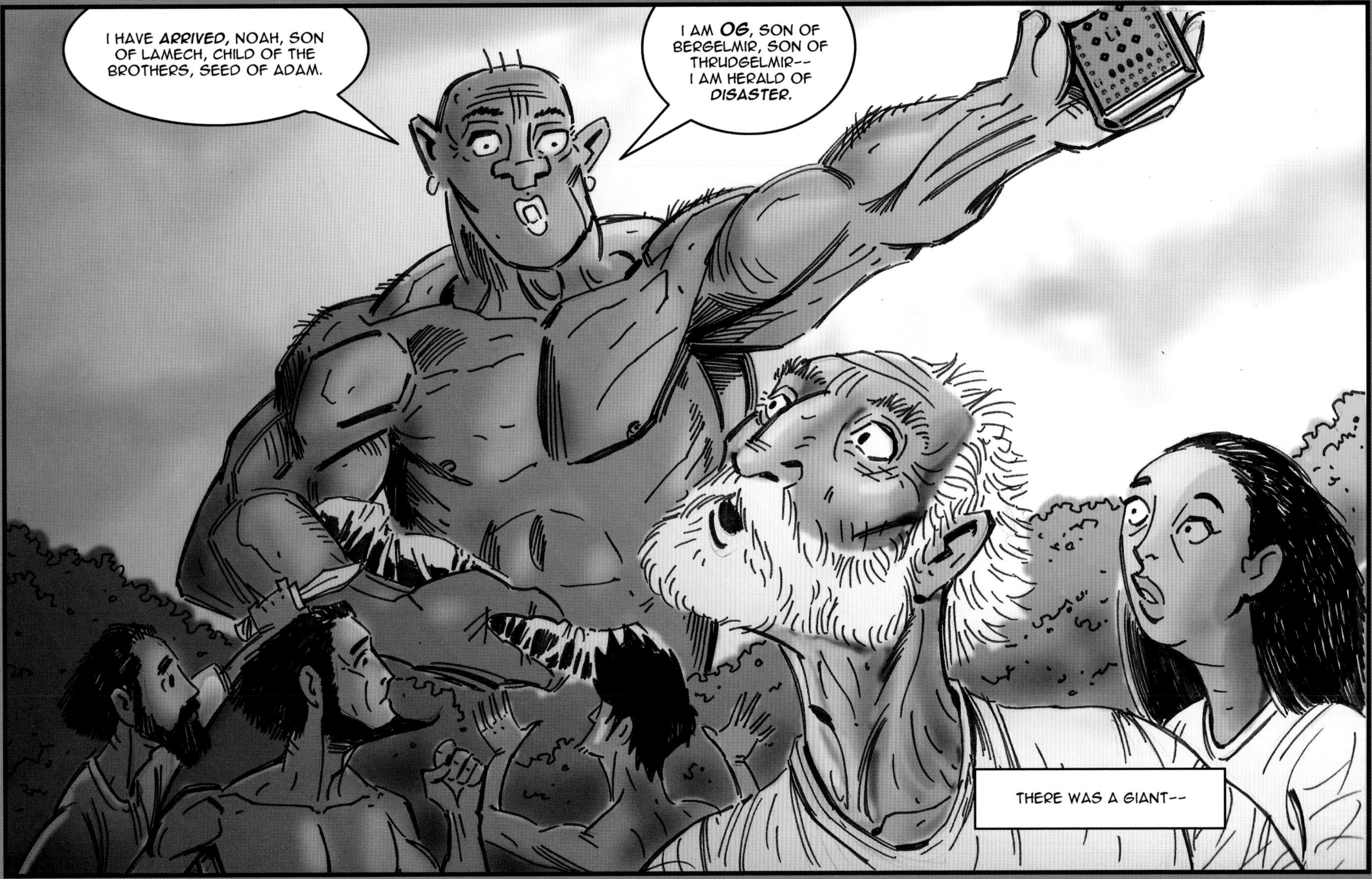
I HAVE ARRIVED, NOAH, SON OF LAMECH, CHILD OF THE BROTHERS, SEED OF ADAM.
I AM OG, SON OF BERGELMIR, SON OF THRUDGELMIR-- I AM HERALD OF DISASTER.
THERE WAS A GIANT--

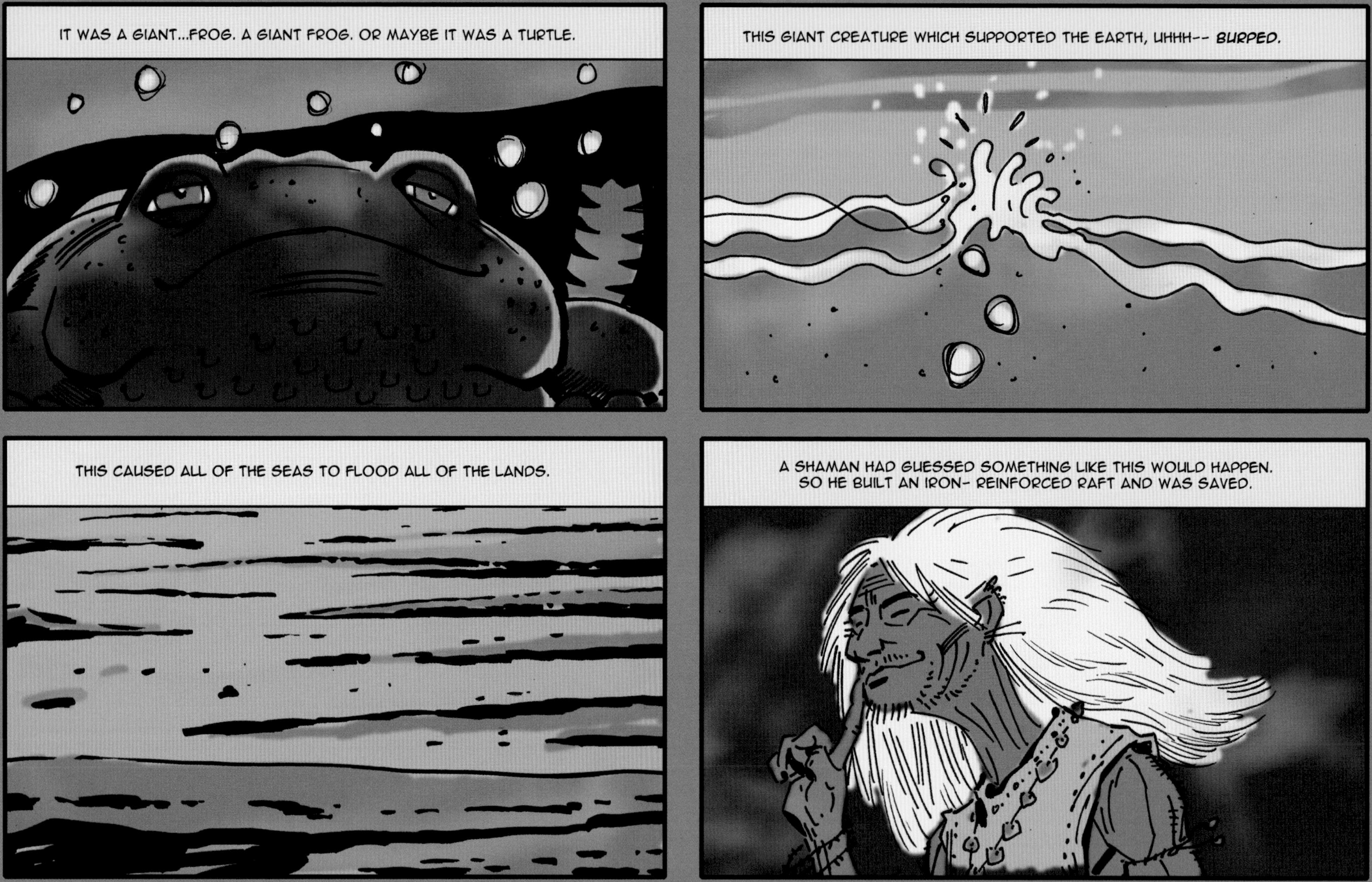
IT WAS A GIANT...FROG. A GIANT FROG. OR MAYBE IT WAS A TURTLE.
THIS GIANT CREATURE WHICH SUPPORTED THE EARTH, UHHH-- BURPED.
THIS CAUSED ALL OF THE SEAS TO FLOOD ALL OF THE LANDS.
A SHAMAN HAD GUESSED SOMETHING LIKE THIS WOULD HAPPEN. SO HE BUILT AN IRON- REINFORCED RAFT AND WAS SAVED.

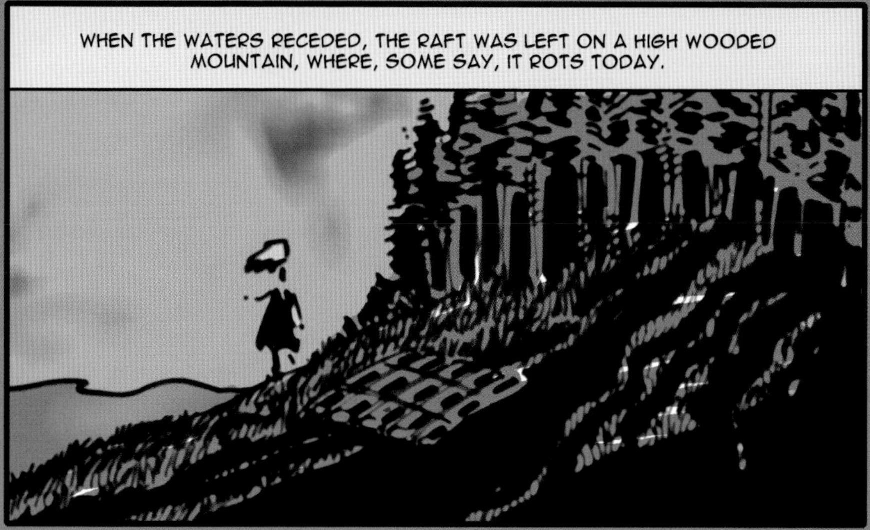
WHEN THE WATERS RECEDED, THE RAFT WAS LEFT ON A HIGH WOODED MOUNTAIN, WHERE, SOME SAY, IT ROTS TODAY.

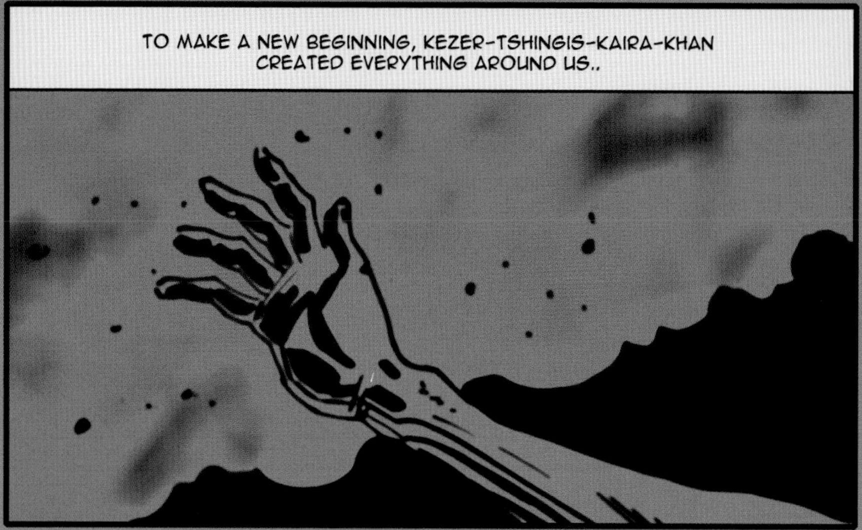
TO MAKE A NEW BEGINNING, KEZER-TSHINGIS-KAIRA-KHAN CREATED EVERYTHING AROUND US..

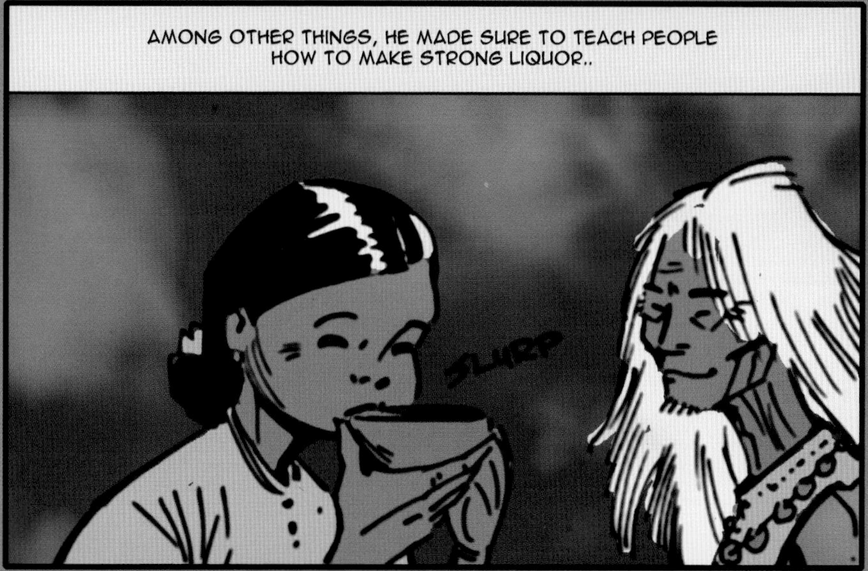
AMONG OTHER THINGS, HE MADE SURE TO TEACH PEOPLE HOW TO MAKE STRONG LIQUOR..
SLURP

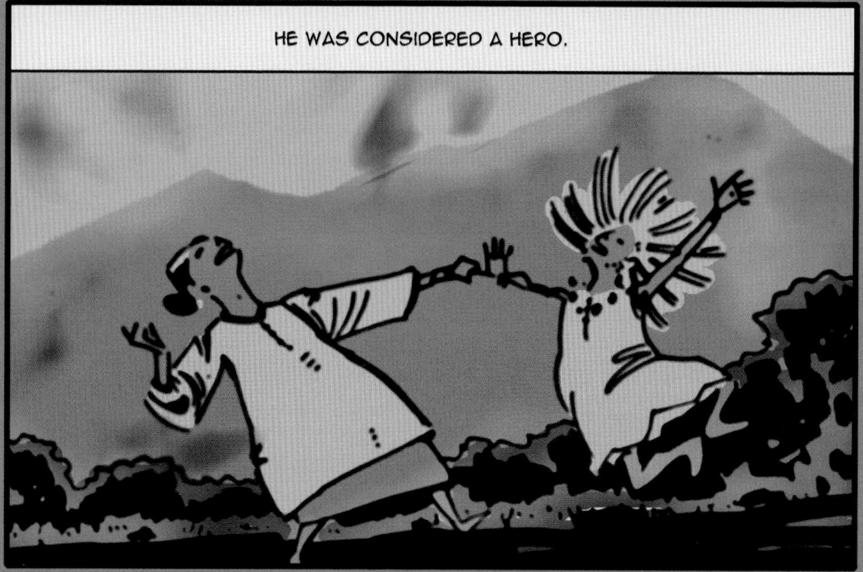
HE WAS CONSIDERED A HERO.

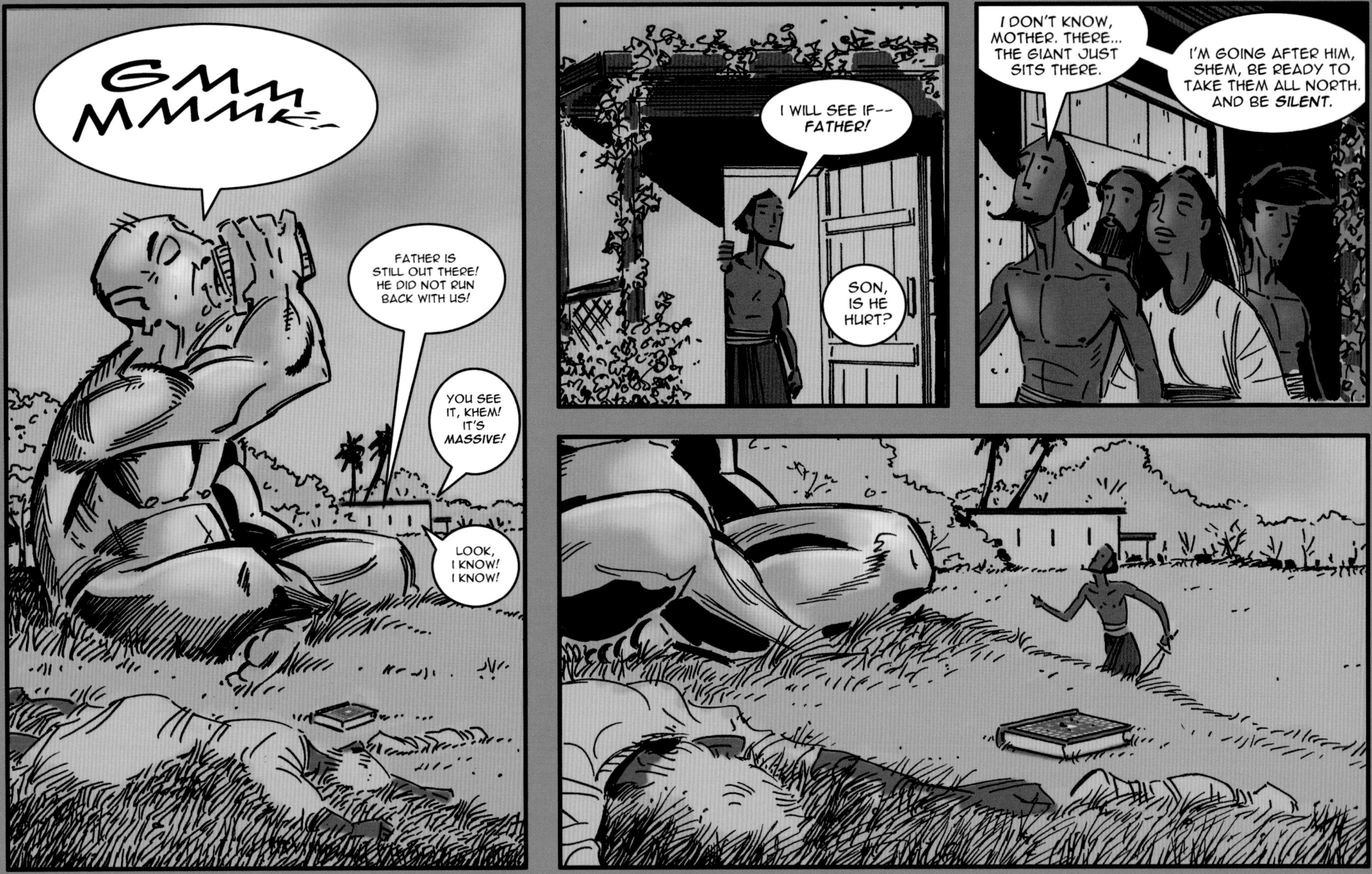

GMM MMMK-!
FATHER IS STILL OUT THERE! HE DID NOT RUN BACK WITH US!
YOU SEE IT, KHEM! IT'S MASSIVE!
LOOK, I KNOW! I KNOW!
I WILL SEE IF-- FATHER!
SON, IS HE HURT?
I DON'T KNOW, MOTHER. THERE... THE GIANT JUST SITS THERE.
I'M GOING AFTER HIM, SHEM, BE READY TO TAKE THEM ALL NORTH. AND BE SILENT.

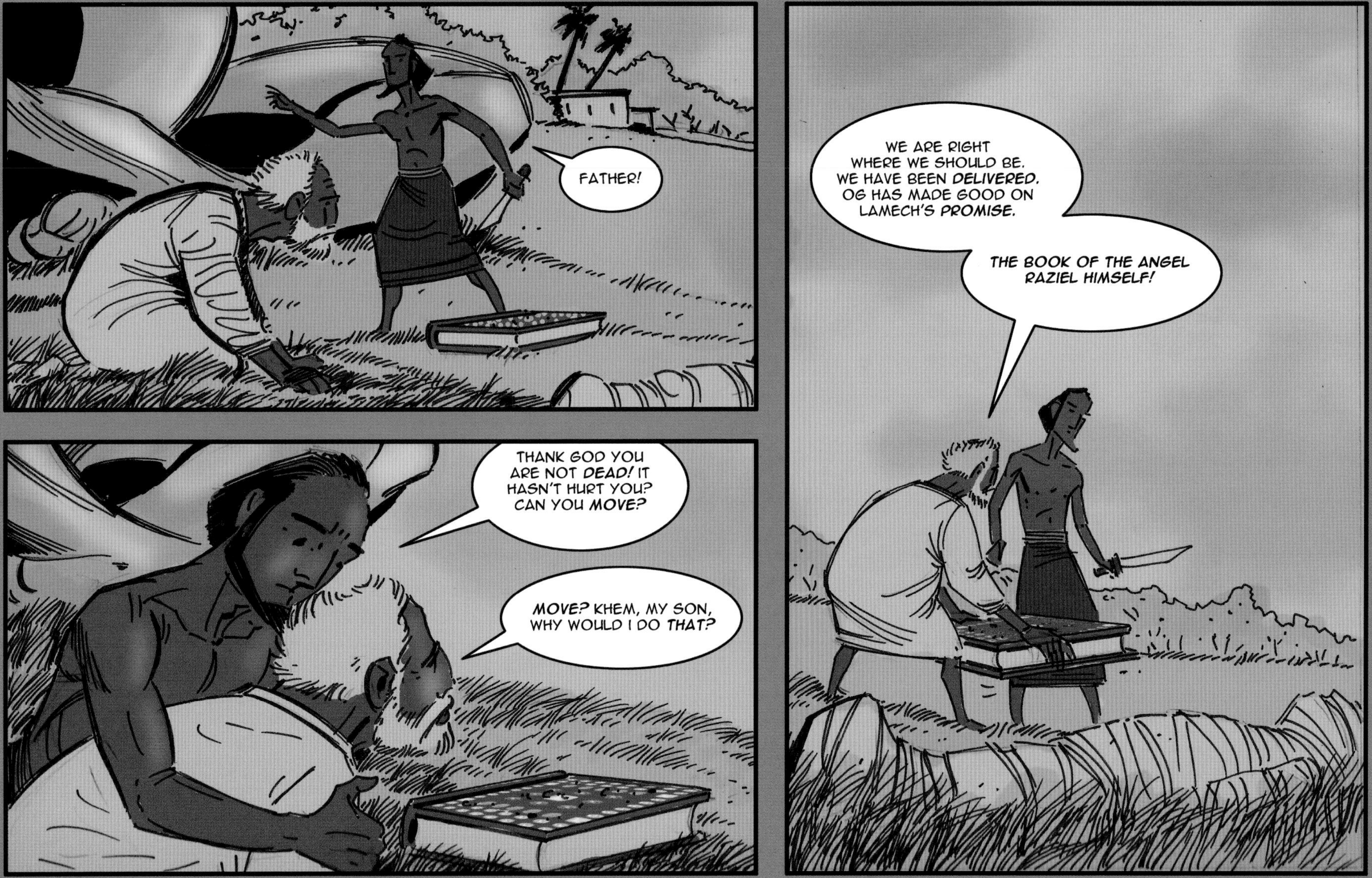
FATHER!
THANK GOD YOU ARE NOT *DEAD!* IT HASN'T HURT YOU? CAN YOU *MOVE?*
MOVE? KHEM, MY SON, WHY WOULD I DO *THAT?*
WE ARE RIGHT WHERE WE SHOULD BE. WE HAVE BEEN *DELIVERED.* OG HAS MADE GOOD ON LAMECH'S *PROMISE.*
THE BOOK OF THE ANGEL RAZIEL HIMSELF!

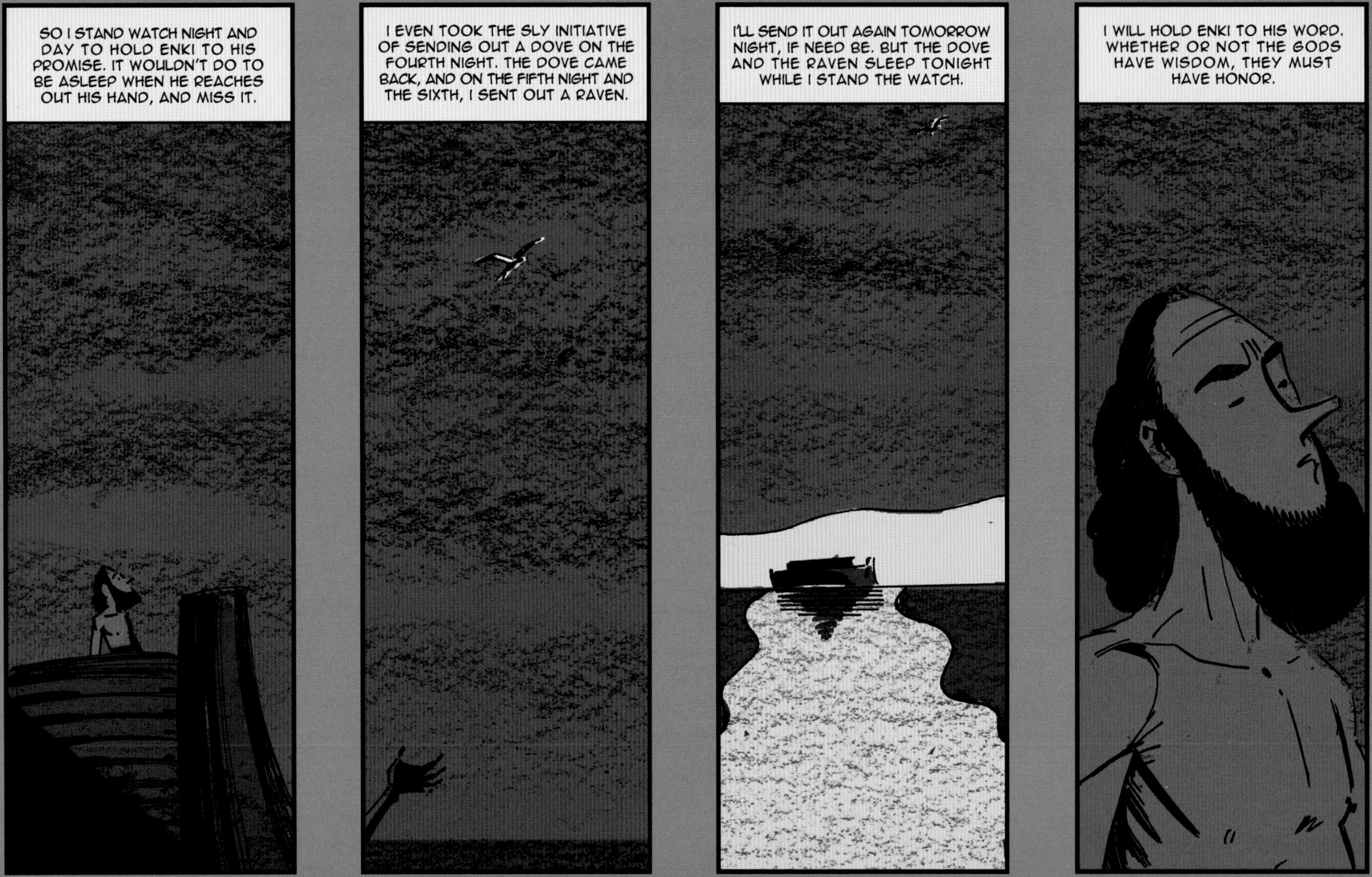
SO I STAND WATCH NIGHT AND DAY TO HOLD ENKI TO HIS PROMISE. IT WOULDN'T DO TO BE ASLEEP WHEN HE REACHES OUT HIS HAND, AND MISS IT.
I EVEN TOOK THE SLY INITIATIVE OF SENDING OUT A DOVE ON THE FOURTH NIGHT. THE DOVE CAME BACK, AND ON THE FIFTH NIGHT AND THE SIXTH, I SENT OUT A RAVEN.
I'LL SEND IT OUT AGAIN TOMORROW NIGHT, IF NEED BE. BUT THE DOVE AND THE RAVEN SLEEP TONIGHT WHILE I STAND THE WATCH.
I WILL HOLD ENKI TO HIS WORD. WHETHER OR NOT THE GODS HAVE WISDOM, THEY MUST HAVE HONOR.

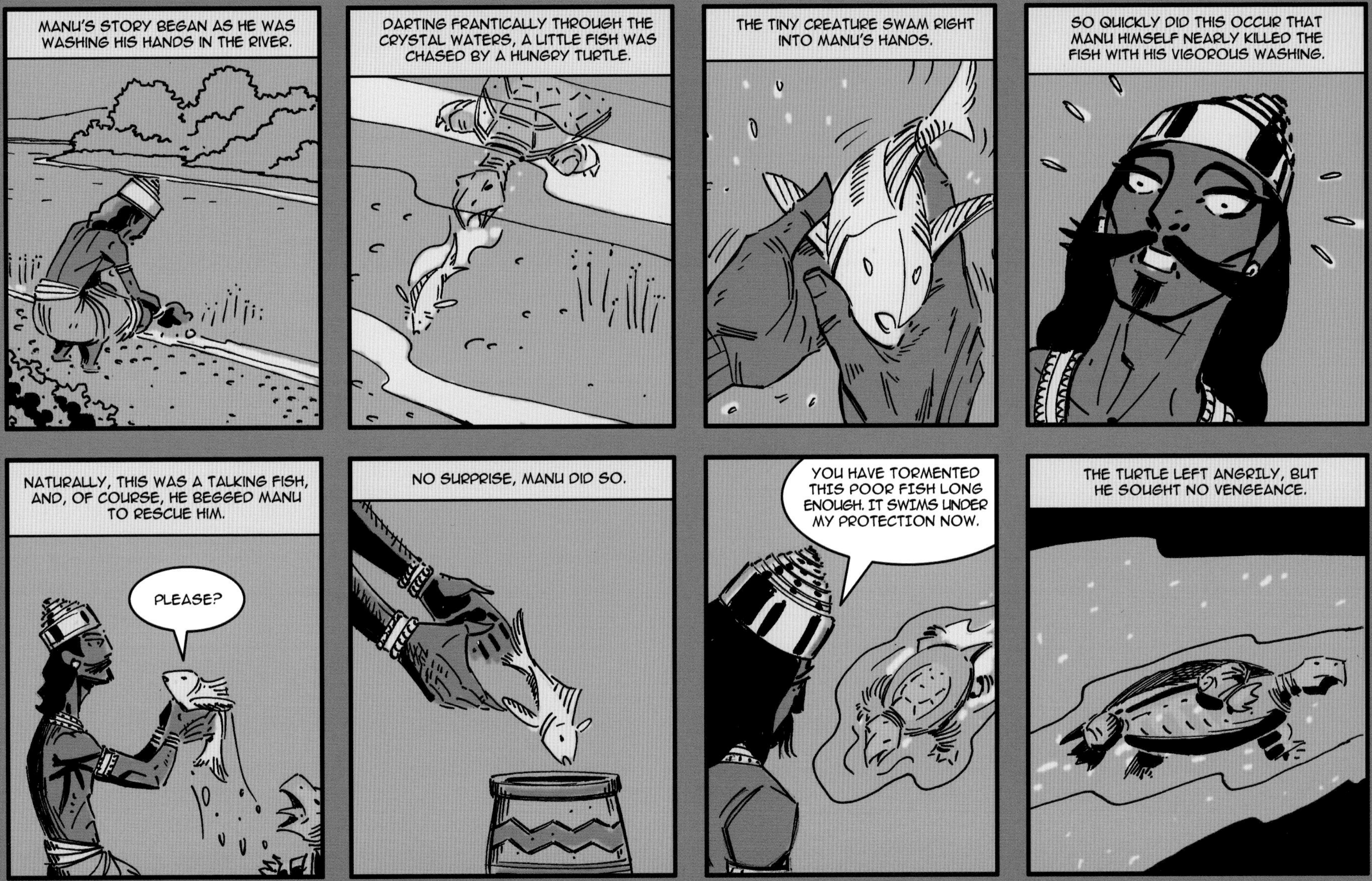
MANU'S STORY BEGAN AS HE WAS WASHING HIS HANDS IN THE RIVER.
DARTING FRANTICALLY THROUGH THE CRYSTAL WATERS, A LITTLE FISH WAS CHASED BY A HUNGRY TURTLE.
THE TINY CREATURE SWAM RIGHT INTO MANU'S HANDS.
SO QUICKLY DID THIS OCCUR THAT MANU HIMSELF NEARLY KILLED THE FISH WITH HIS VIGOROUS WASHING.
NATURALLY, THIS WAS A TALKING FISH, AND, OF COURSE, HE BEGGED MANU TO RESCUE HIM.
PLEASE?
NO SURPRISE, MANU DID SO.
YOU HAVE TORMENTED THIS POOR FISH LONG ENOUGH. IT SWIMS UNDER MY PROTECTION NOW.
THE TURTLE LEFT ANGRILY, BUT HE SOUGHT NO VENGEANCE.

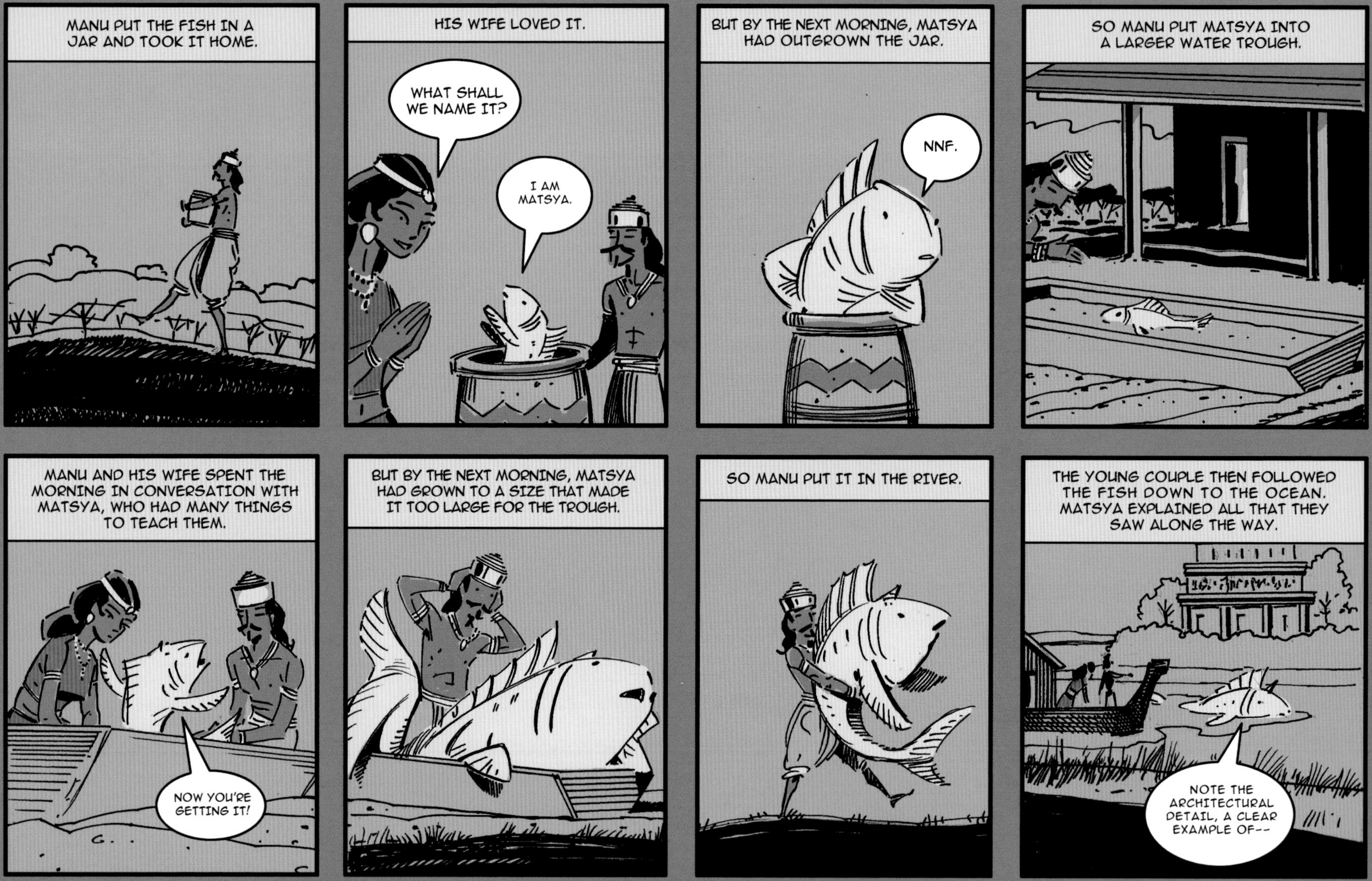
MANU PUT THE FISH IN A JAR AND TOOK IT HOME.
HIS WIFE LOVED IT.
WHAT SHALL WE NAME IT?
I AM MATSYA.
BUT BY THE NEXT MORNING, MATSYA HAD OUTGROWN THE JAR.
NNF.
SO MANU PUT MATSYA INTO A LARGER WATER TROUGH.
MANU AND HIS WIFE SPENT THE MORNING IN CONVERSATION WITH MATSYA, WHO HAD MANY THINGS TO TEACH THEM.
NOW YOU'RE GETTING IT!
BUT BY THE NEXT MORNING, MATSYA HAD GROWN TO A SIZE THAT MADE IT TOO LARGE FOR THE TROUGH.
SO MANU PUT IT IN THE RIVER.
THE YOUNG COUPLE THEN FOLLOWED THE FISH DOWN TO THE OCEAN. MATSYA EXPLAINED ALL THAT THEY SAW ALONG THE WAY.
NOTE THE ARCHITECTURAL DETAIL, A CLEAR EXAMPLE OF--

BY THE OCEAN, THEY SAW THAT IT HAD GROWN TO A VERY LARGE SIZE.

ONLY THEN DID MATSYA WARN THEM OF A GREAT FLOOD THAT WOULD COME THE NEXT WEEK TO DESTROY ALL LIFE.

OH, BY THE WAY...

THEY NEEDED TO GATHER SEEDS OF LIFE AND TAKE THEM OUT TO THE OCEAN AND WAIT.

SO, YOU REMEMBER ALL THAT STUFF I WAS TELLING YOU ABOUT?

SURE ENOUGH, THE RAINS CAME AND THE LAND DISAPPEARED.

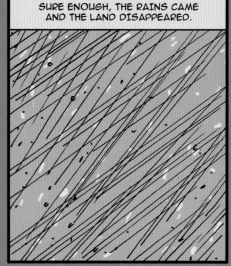

MATSYA RETURNED, BIGGER AND BETTER THAN EVER.

HEH.

MANU THREW A ROPE AROUND ITS HORN--STRANGE FISH TO HAVE A *HORN*-- AND THE FISH TOWED HIM TO SAFETY.

MANU RECEIVED THE NAME SATYAVRATA AND WAS RENOWNED FOR HIS HONESTY.

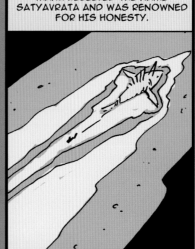

I HEAR THE FISH'S OTHER NAME, MANU. BUT ALSO SRI VISHNU, THE FIRST *AVATARA*. STRANGE WORDS. BUT MORE PROOF, WERE IT NEEDED, THAT THE GODS *WILL* SAVE US.

I KNOW THEY WILL NOT PERMIT US TO PASS TO THE NEXT WORLD. WE WILL LIVE. WE WILL CLEAVE TO THE GODS AND WHEN THE WATERS SUBSIDE WE WILL RE-ENTER THIS WORLD CROWNED WITH WISDOM. THE WORLD NEEDS US. HUMANITY HAS ITS PLACE ABOVE THE WAVES.

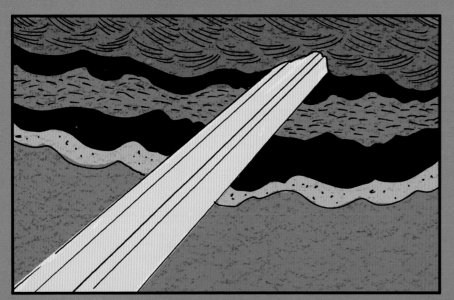

I *BELIEVE* THIS. I *MUST* BELIEVE THIS.

Deluge

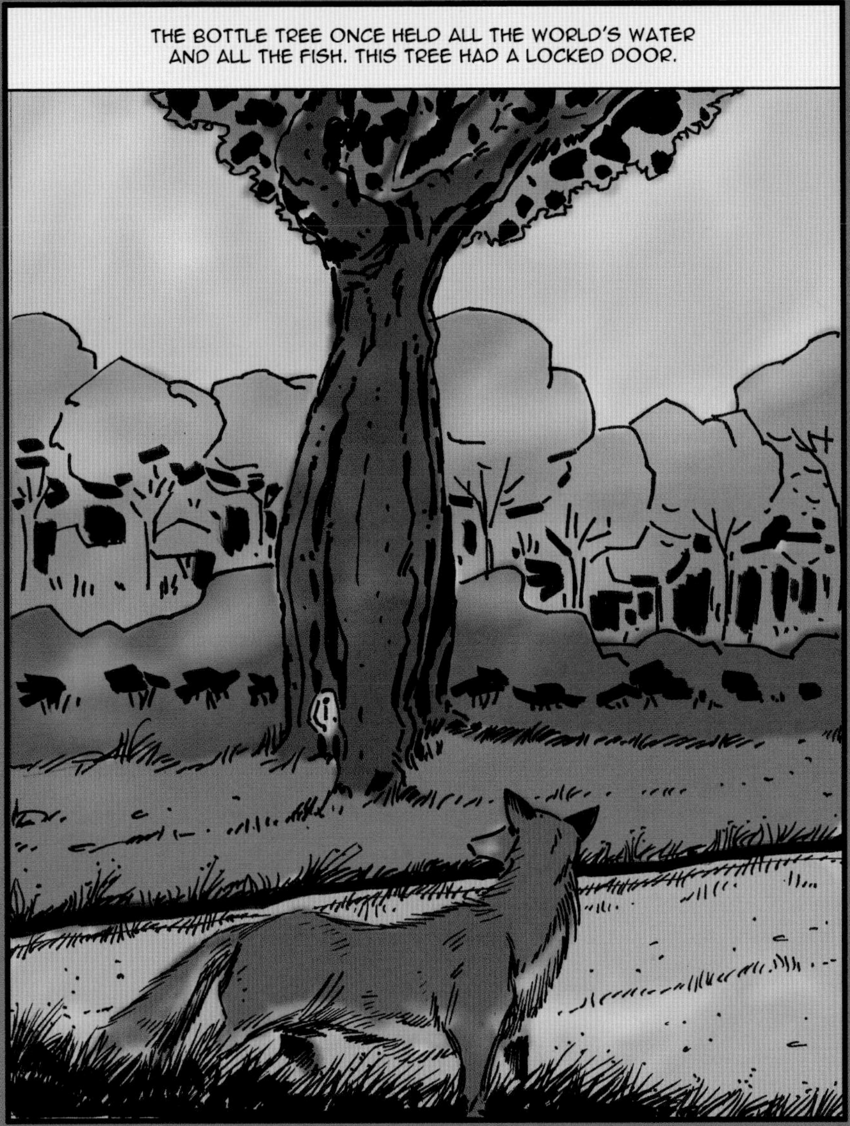
THE BOTTLE TREE ONCE HELD ALL THE WORLD'S WATER AND ALL THE FISH. THIS TREE HAD A LOCKED DOOR.

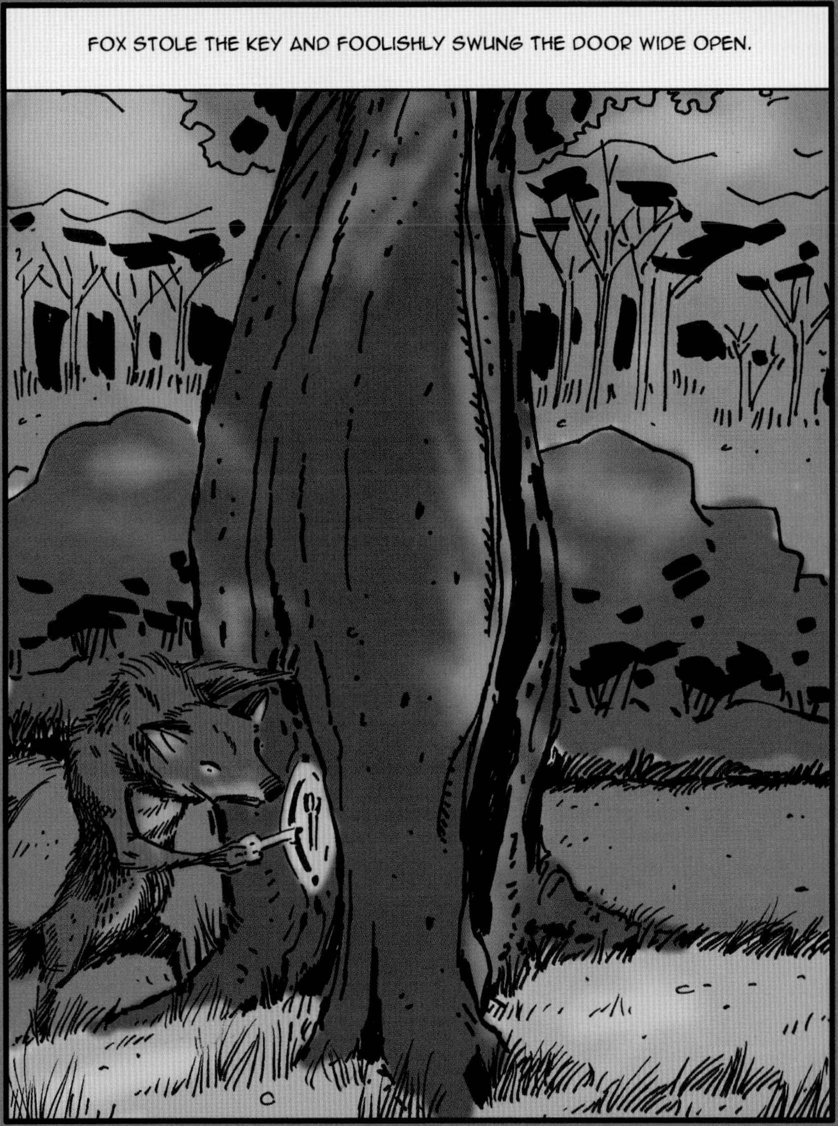
FOX STOLE THE KEY AND FOOLISHLY SWUNG THE DOOR WIDE OPEN.

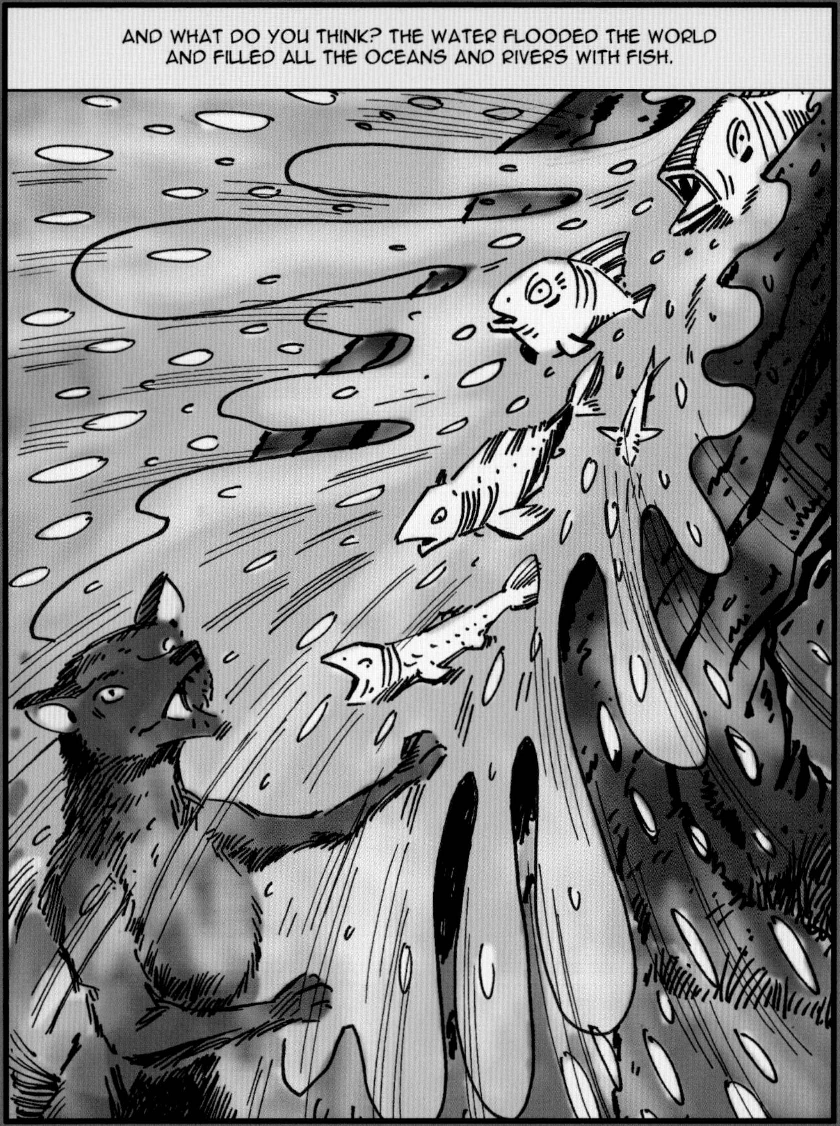
AND WHAT DO YOU THINK? THE WATER FLOODED THE WORLD
AND FILLED ALL THE OCEANS AND RIVERS WITH FISH.

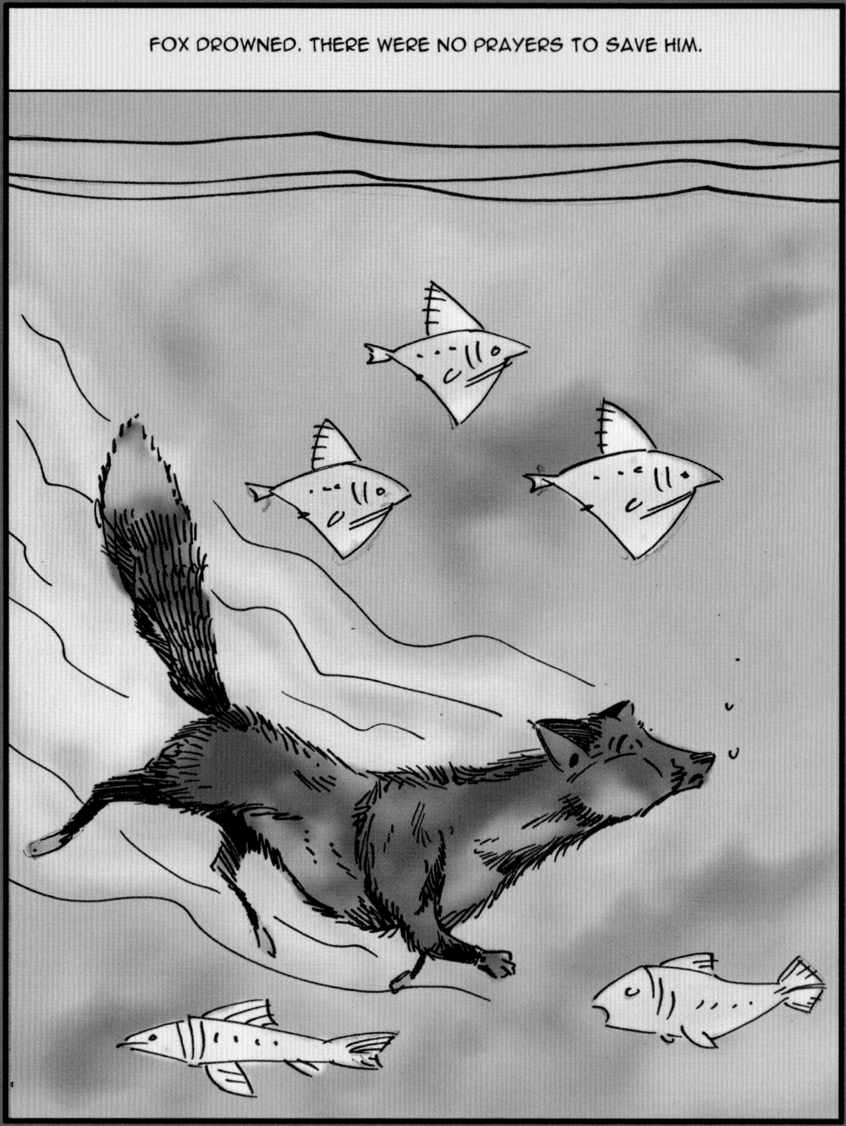
FOX DROWNED. THERE WERE NO PRAYERS TO SAVE HIM.

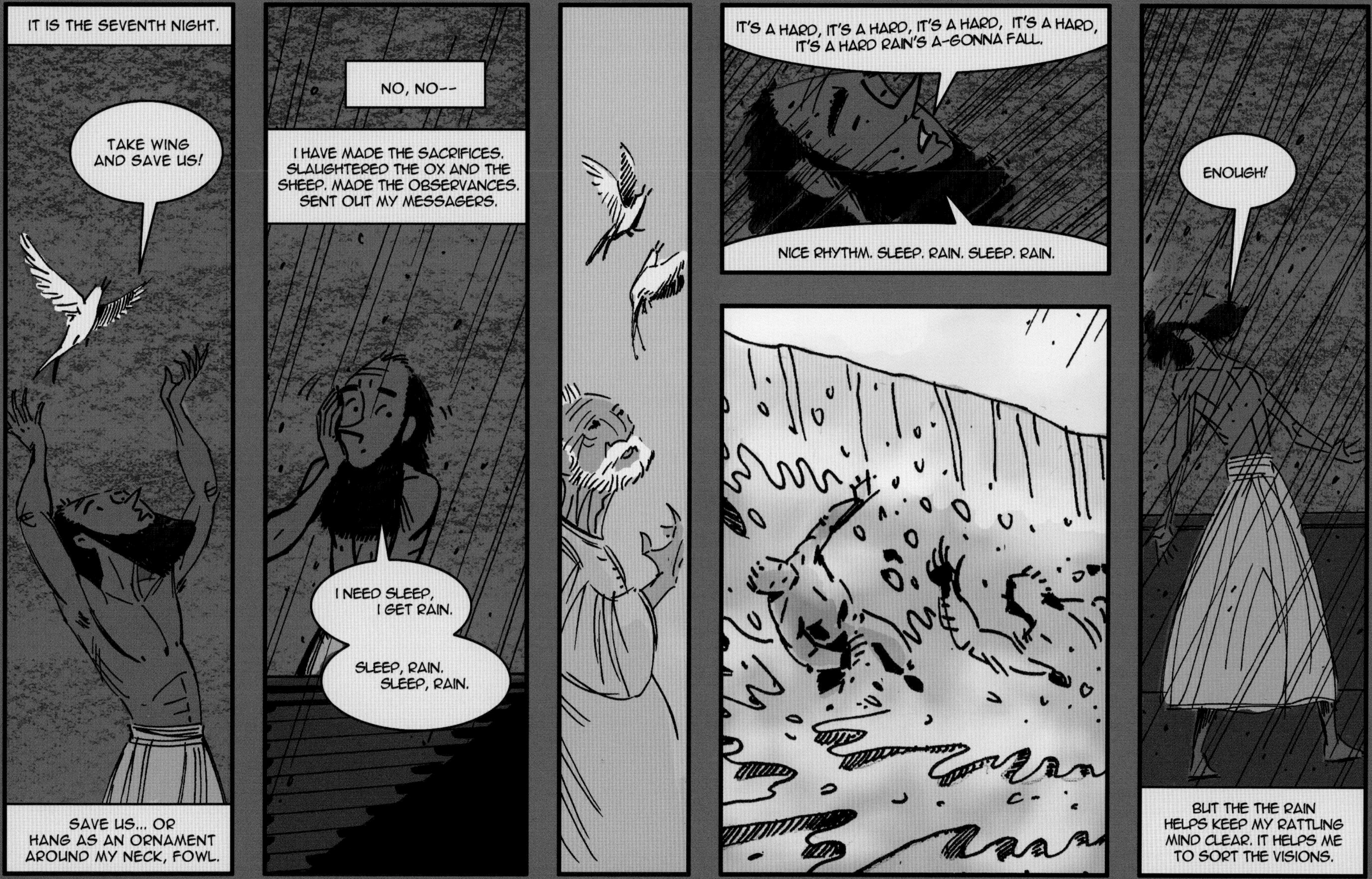
IT IS THE SEVENTH NIGHT.
TAKE WING AND SAVE US!
SAVE US... OR HANG AS AN ORNAMENT AROUND MY NECK, FOWL.
NO, NO--
I HAVE MADE THE SACRIFICES. SLAUGHTERED THE OX AND THE SHEEP. MADE THE OBSERVANCES. SENT OUT MY MESSAGERS.
I NEED SLEEP, I GET RAIN.
SLEEP, RAIN. SLEEP, RAIN.
IT'S A HARD, IT'S A HARD, IT'S A HARD, IT'S A HARD, IT'S A HARD RAIN'S A-GONNA FALL.
NICE RHYTHM. SLEEP. RAIN. SLEEP. RAIN.
ENOUGH!
BUT THE THE RAIN HELPS KEEP MY RATTLING MIND CLEAR. IT HELPS ME TO SORT THE VISIONS.

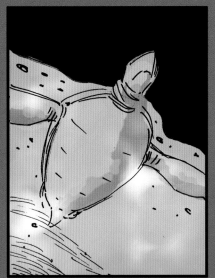

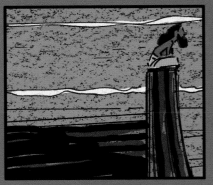

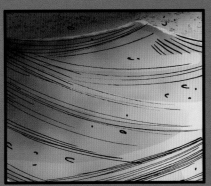

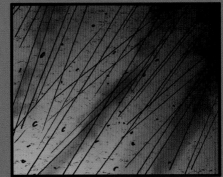

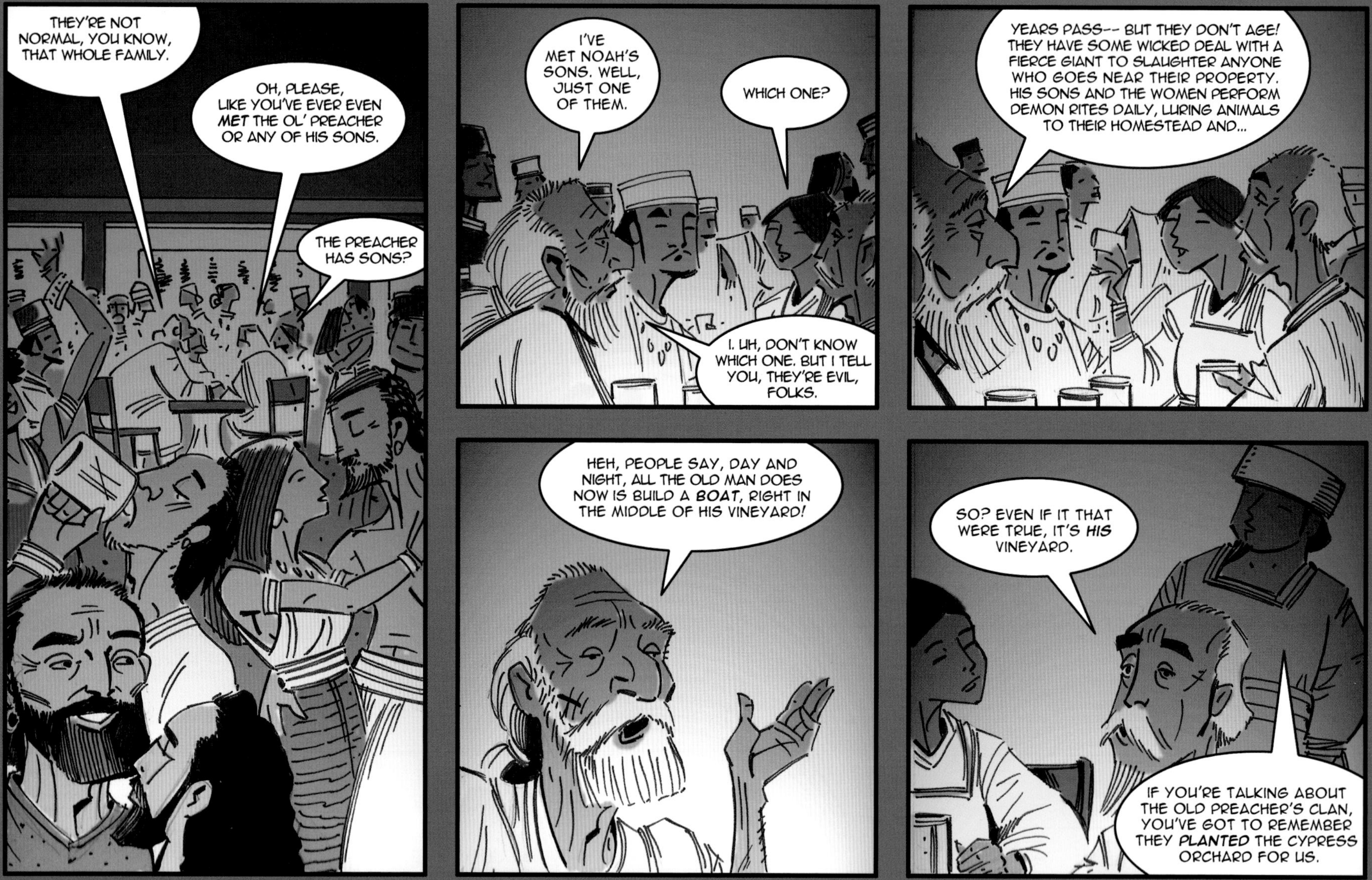

THEY'RE NOT NORMAL, YOU KNOW, THAT WHOLE FAMILY.
OH, PLEASE, LIKE YOU'VE EVER EVEN **MET** THE OL' PREACHER OR ANY OF HIS SONS.
THE PREACHER HAS SONS?
I'VE MET NOAH'S SONS. WELL, JUST ONE OF THEM.
WHICH ONE?
I. UH, DON'T KNOW WHICH ONE. BUT I TELL YOU, THEY'RE EVIL, FOLKS.
YEARS PASS-- BUT THEY DON'T AGE! THEY HAVE SOME WICKED DEAL WITH A FIERCE GIANT TO SLAUGHTER ANYONE WHO GOES NEAR THEIR PROPERTY. HIS SONS AND THE WOMEN PERFORM DEMON RITES DAILY, LURING ANIMALS TO THEIR HOMESTEAD AND...
HEH, PEOPLE SAY, DAY AND NIGHT, ALL THE OLD MAN DOES NOW IS BUILD A **BOAT**, RIGHT IN THE MIDDLE OF HIS VINEYARD!
SO? EVEN IF IT THAT WERE TRUE, IT'S **HIS** VINEYARD.
IF YOU'RE TALKING ABOUT THE OLD PREACHER'S CLAN, YOU'VE GOT TO REMEMBER THEY **PLANTED** THE CYPRESS ORCHARD FOR US.

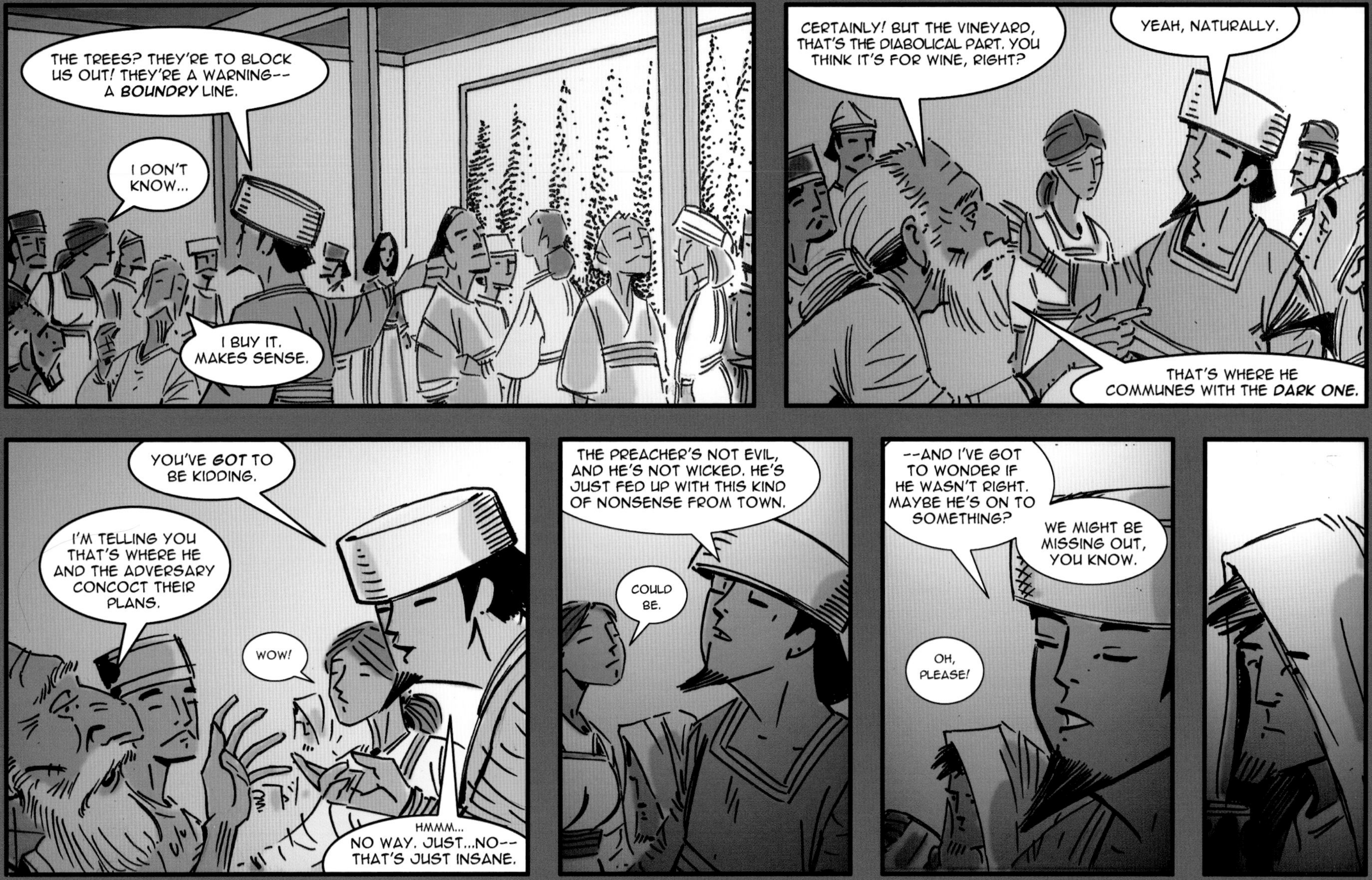
THE TREES? THEY'RE TO BLOCK US OUT! THEY'RE A WARNING-- A **BOUNDRY** LINE.
I DON'T KNOW...
I BUY IT. MAKES SENSE.
CERTAINLY! BUT THE VINEYARD, THAT'S THE DIABOLICAL PART. YOU THINK IT'S FOR WINE, RIGHT?
YEAH, NATURALLY.
THAT'S WHERE HE COMMUNES WITH THE ***DARK ONE.***
YOU'VE **GOT** TO BE KIDDING.
I'M TELLING YOU THAT'S WHERE HE AND THE ADVERSARY CONCOCT THEIR PLANS.
WOW!
HMMM... NO WAY. JUST...NO-- THAT'S JUST INSANE.
THE PREACHER'S NOT EVIL, AND HE'S NOT WICKED. HE'S JUST FED UP WITH THIS KIND OF NONSENSE FROM TOWN.
COULD BE.
--AND I'VE GOT TO WONDER IF HE WASN'T RIGHT. MAYBE HE'S ON TO SOMETHING?
WE MIGHT BE MISSING OUT, YOU KNOW.
OH, PLEASE!

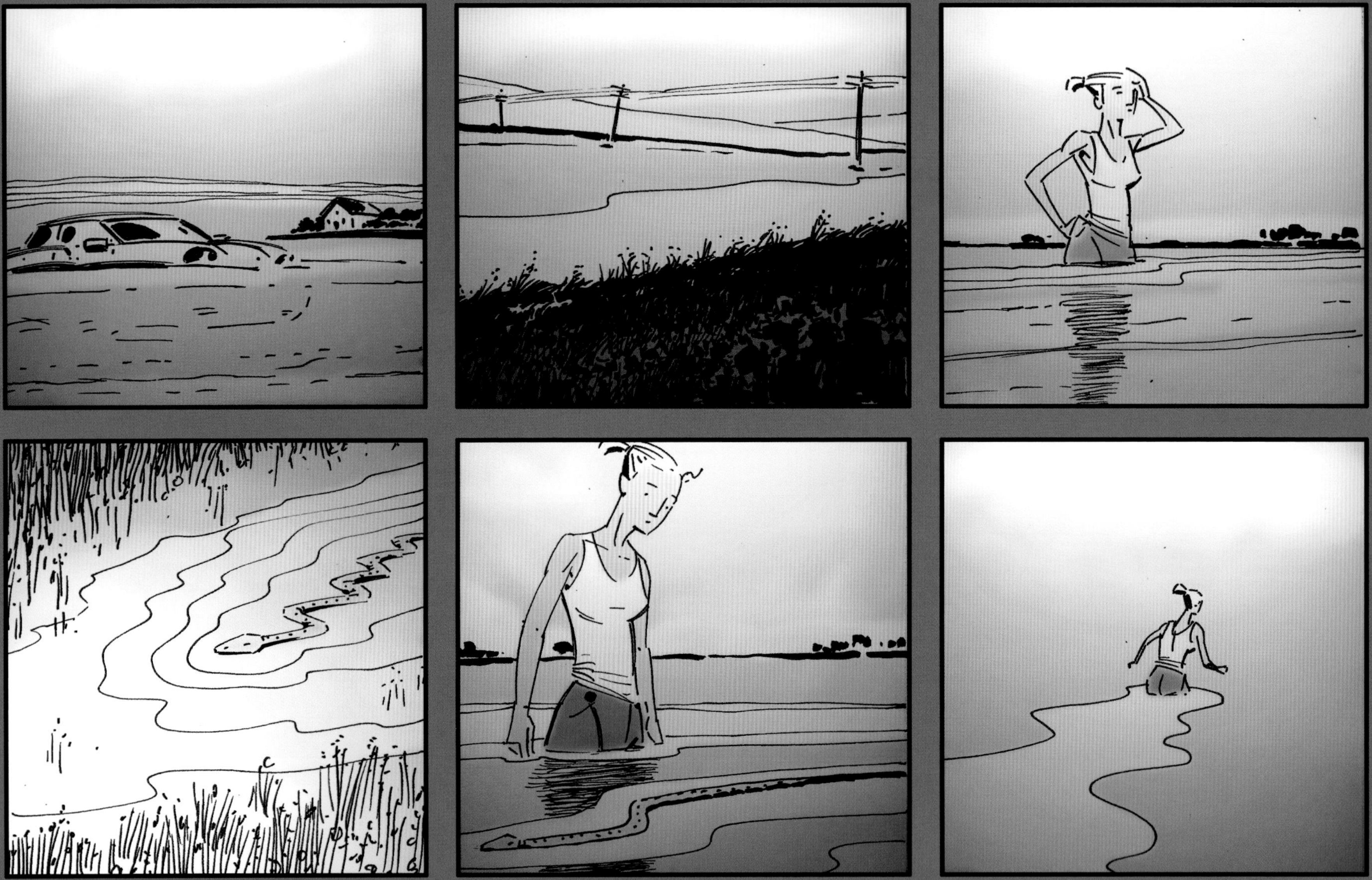

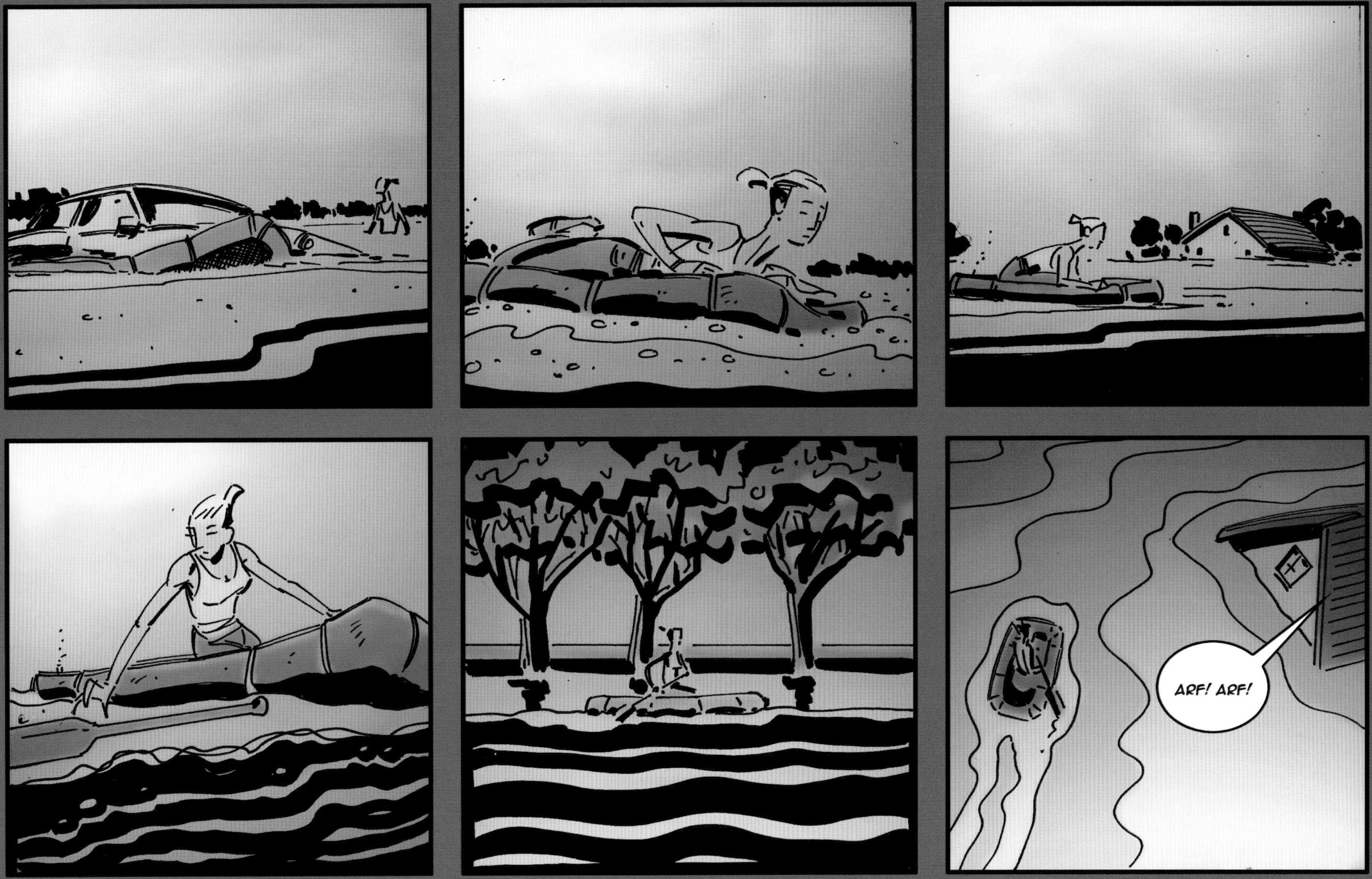
ARF! ARF!

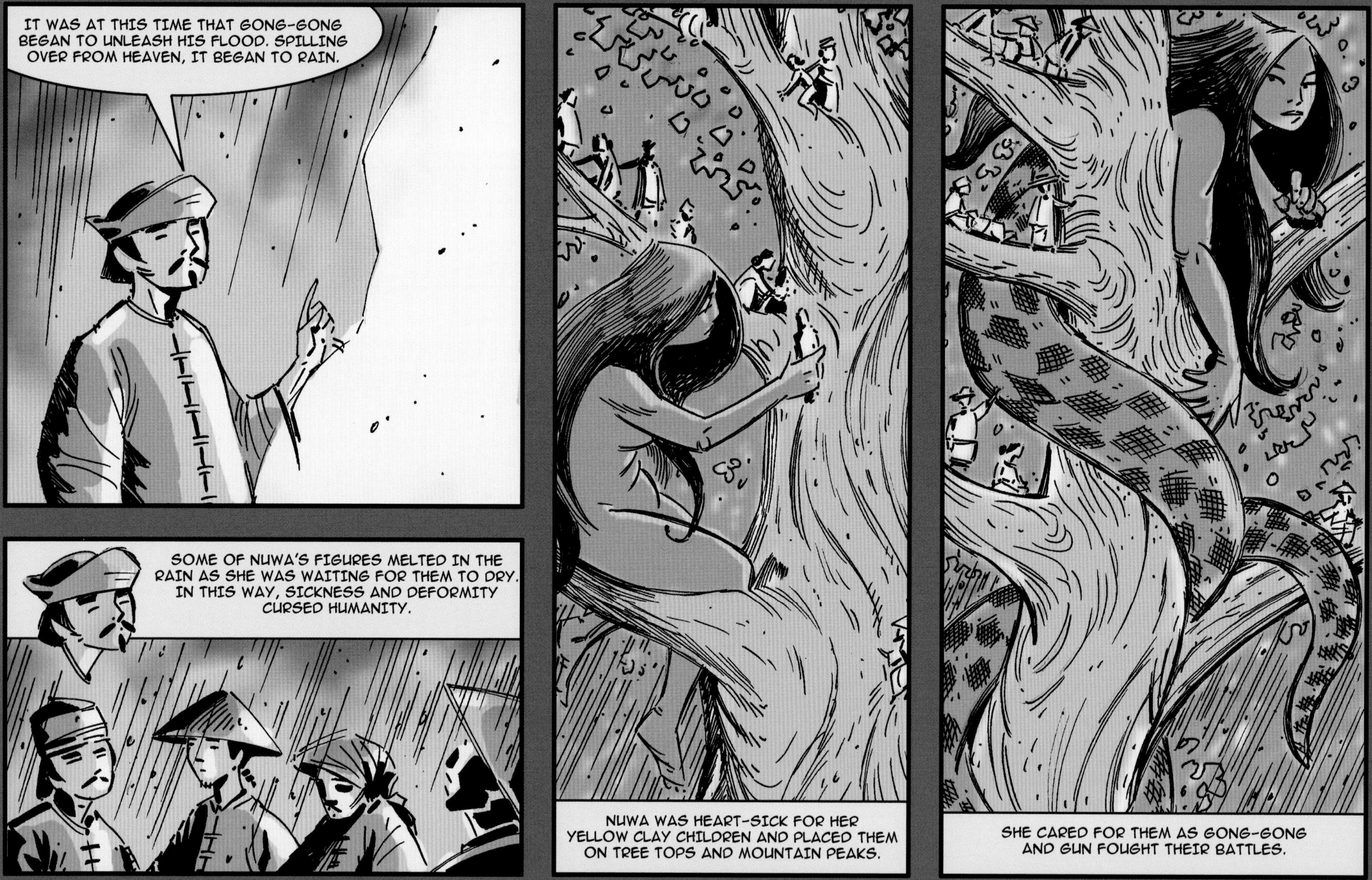
IT WAS AT THIS TIME THAT GONG-GONG BEGAN TO UNLEASH HIS FLOOD. SPILLING OVER FROM HEAVEN, IT BEGAN TO RAIN.
SOME OF NUWA'S FIGURES MELTED IN THE RAIN AS SHE WAS WAITING FOR THEM TO DRY. IN THIS WAY, SICKNESS AND DEFORMITY CURSED HUMANITY.
NUWA WAS HEART-SICK FOR HER YELLOW CLAY CHILDREN AND PLACED THEM ON TREE TOPS AND MOUNTAIN PEAKS.
SHE CARED FOR THEM AS GONG-GONG AND GUN FOUGHT THEIR BATTLES.

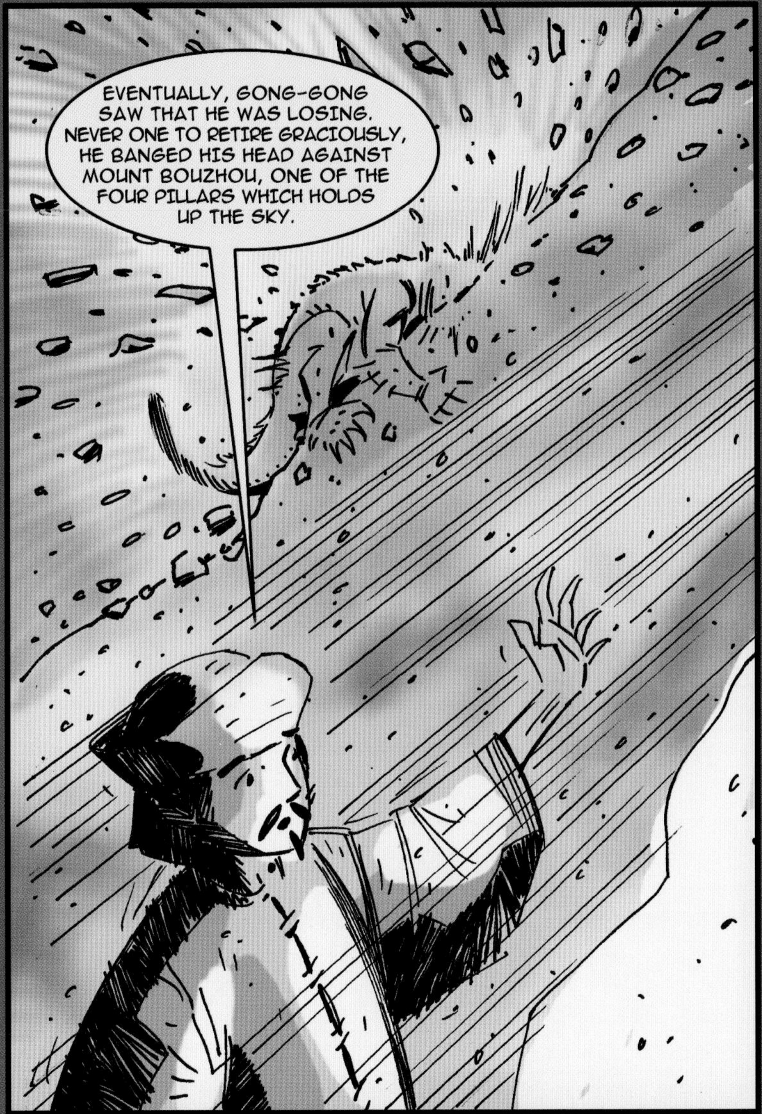
EVENTUALLY, GONG-GONG SAW THAT HE WAS LOSING. NEVER ONE TO RETIRE GRACIOUSLY, HE BANGED HIS HEAD AGAINST MOUNT BOUZHOU, ONE OF THE FOUR PILLARS WHICH HOLDS UP THE SKY.

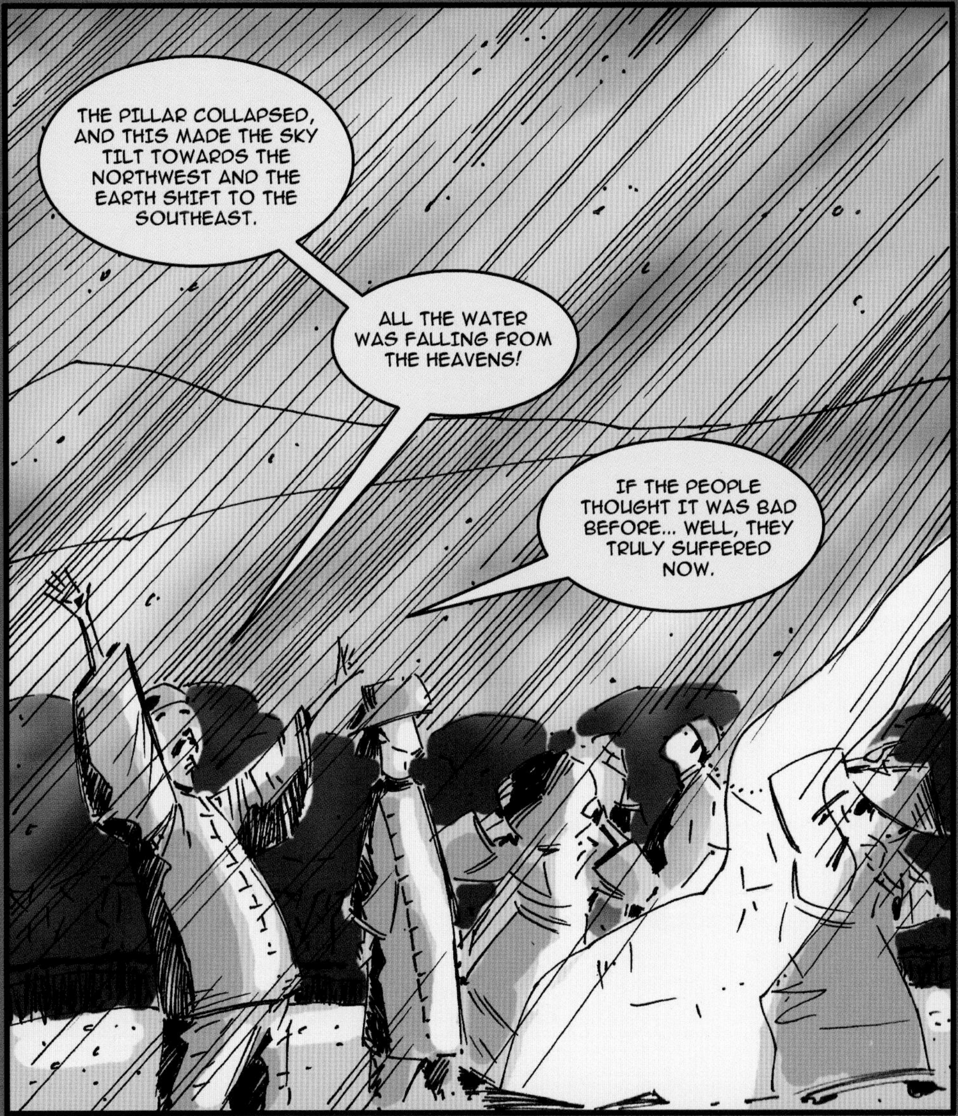
THE PILLAR COLLAPSED, AND THIS MADE THE SKY TILT TOWARDS THE NORTHWEST AND THE EARTH SHIFT TO THE SOUTHEAST.
ALL THE WATER WAS FALLING FROM THE HEAVENS!
IF THE PEOPLE THOUGHT IT WAS BAD BEFORE... WELL, THEY TRULY SUFFERED NOW.

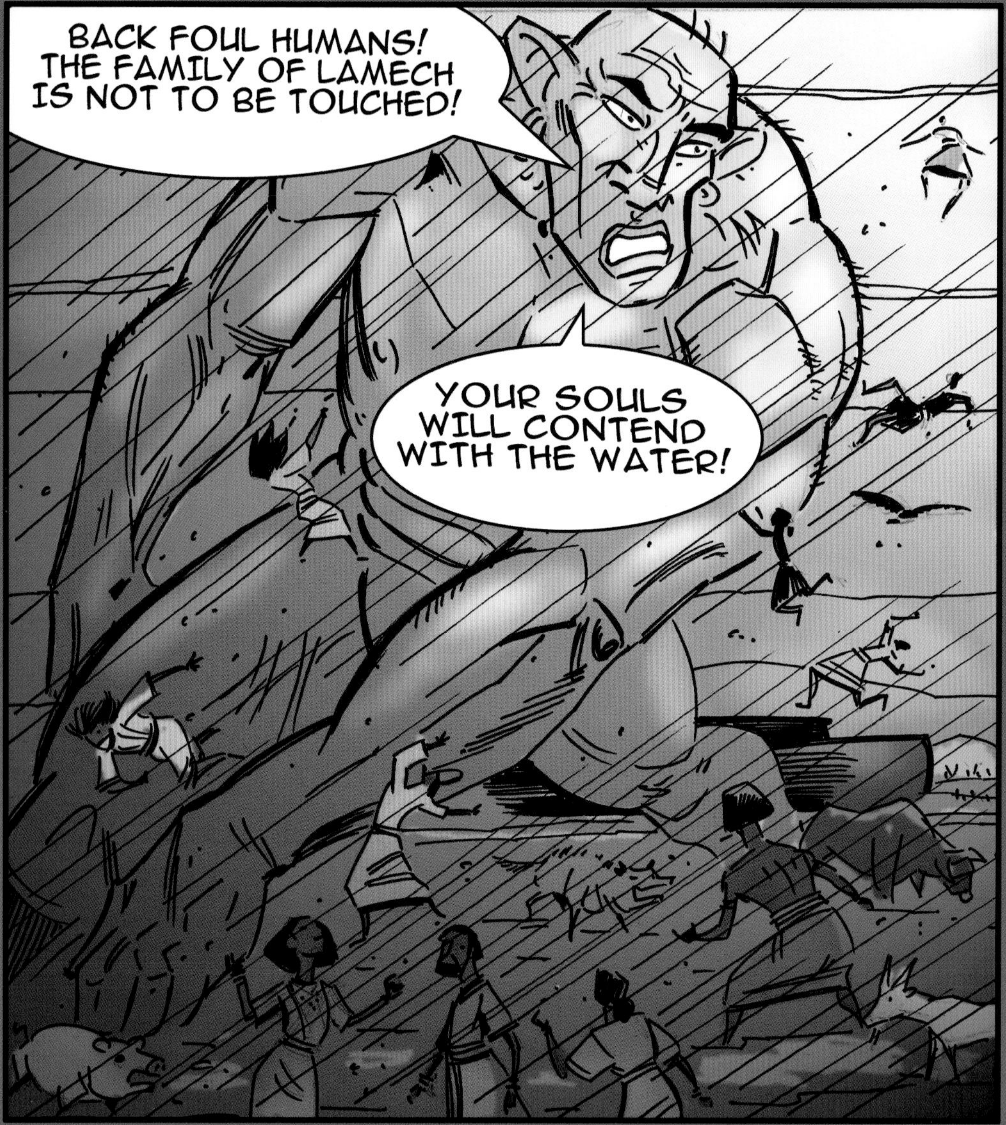
BACK FOUL HUMANS! THE FAMILY OF LAMECH IS NOT TO BE TOUCHED!
YOUR SOULS WILL CONTEND WITH THE WATER!

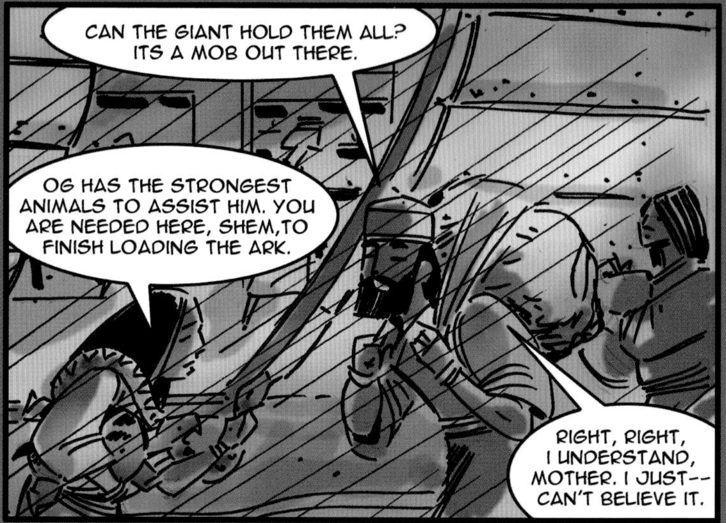
CAN THE GIANT HOLD THEM ALL? ITS A MOB OUT THERE.
OG HAS THE STRONGEST ANIMALS TO ASSIST HIM. YOU ARE NEEDED HERE, SHEM,TO FINISH LOADING THE ARK.
RIGHT, RIGHT, I UNDERSTAND, MOTHER. I JUST--CAN'T BELIEVE IT.

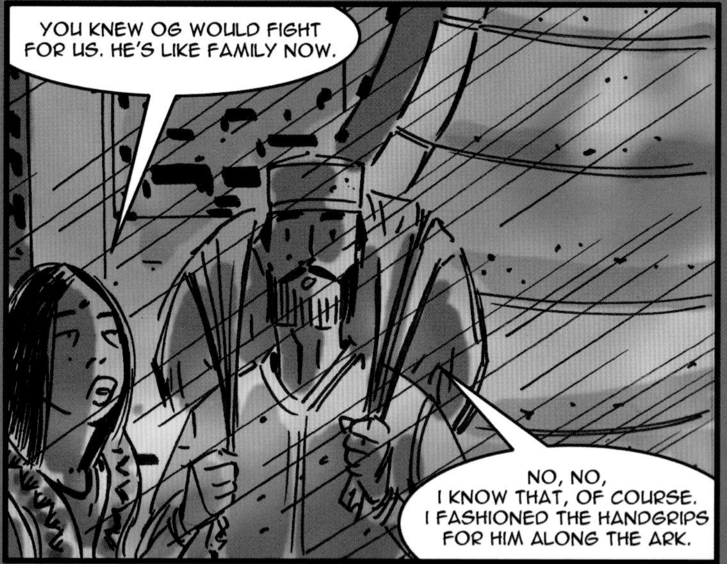
YOU KNEW OG WOULD FIGHT FOR US. HE'S LIKE FAMILY NOW.
NO, NO, I KNOW THAT, OF COURSE. I FASHIONED THE HANDGRIPS FOR HIM ALONG THE ARK.

IT'S ALL OF IT. OG, THE ARK, THE RAIN. AND NOW THE DESPARATE TOWNSPEOPLE. IT'S ALL AS FATHER PREDICTED.

DESPITE YOUR MOTHER'S MISGIVINGS, YOU SHOULD KNOW BETTER THAN TO DOUBT YOUR FATHER, SHEM.

I NEVER DOUBTED YOU, SIR. RATHER, I NEVER TRULY KNEW WHAT THIS DAY WOULD ACTUALLY BRING.

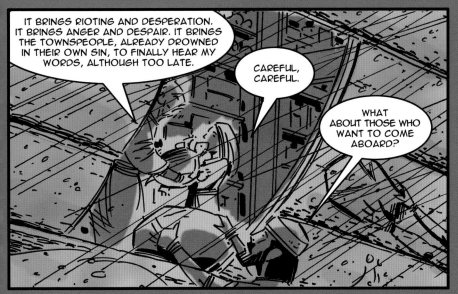

IT BRINGS RIOTING AND DESPERATION. IT BRINGS ANGER AND DESPAIR. IT BRINGS THE TOWNSPEOPLE, ALREADY DROWNED IN THEIR OWN SIN, TO FINALLY HEAR MY WORDS, ALTHOUGH TOO LATE.

CAREFUL, CAREFUL.

WHAT ABOUT THOSE WHO WANT TO COME ABOARD?

ALL THEY WANT IS TO SACK OUR SUPPLIES AND TAKE OUT THEIR RAGE ON US. ANY WHO WOULD EMPLOY VIOLENCE TO JOIN US PROVES MY POINT FOR ME. IF THEY WERE TRULY FAITHFUL, THEY WOULD HAVE SOUGHT US OUT LONG AGO, AS THE ANIMALS DID. ON THIS, MY CONSCIENCE IS CLEAR.

NOW, HURRY. LOAD THE REST, AND FIND YOUR BROTHERS. THIS SEASON'S AIR WILL SOON MAKE IT TOO COLD FOR THE WOMEN TO BE WADING WITH YOU.

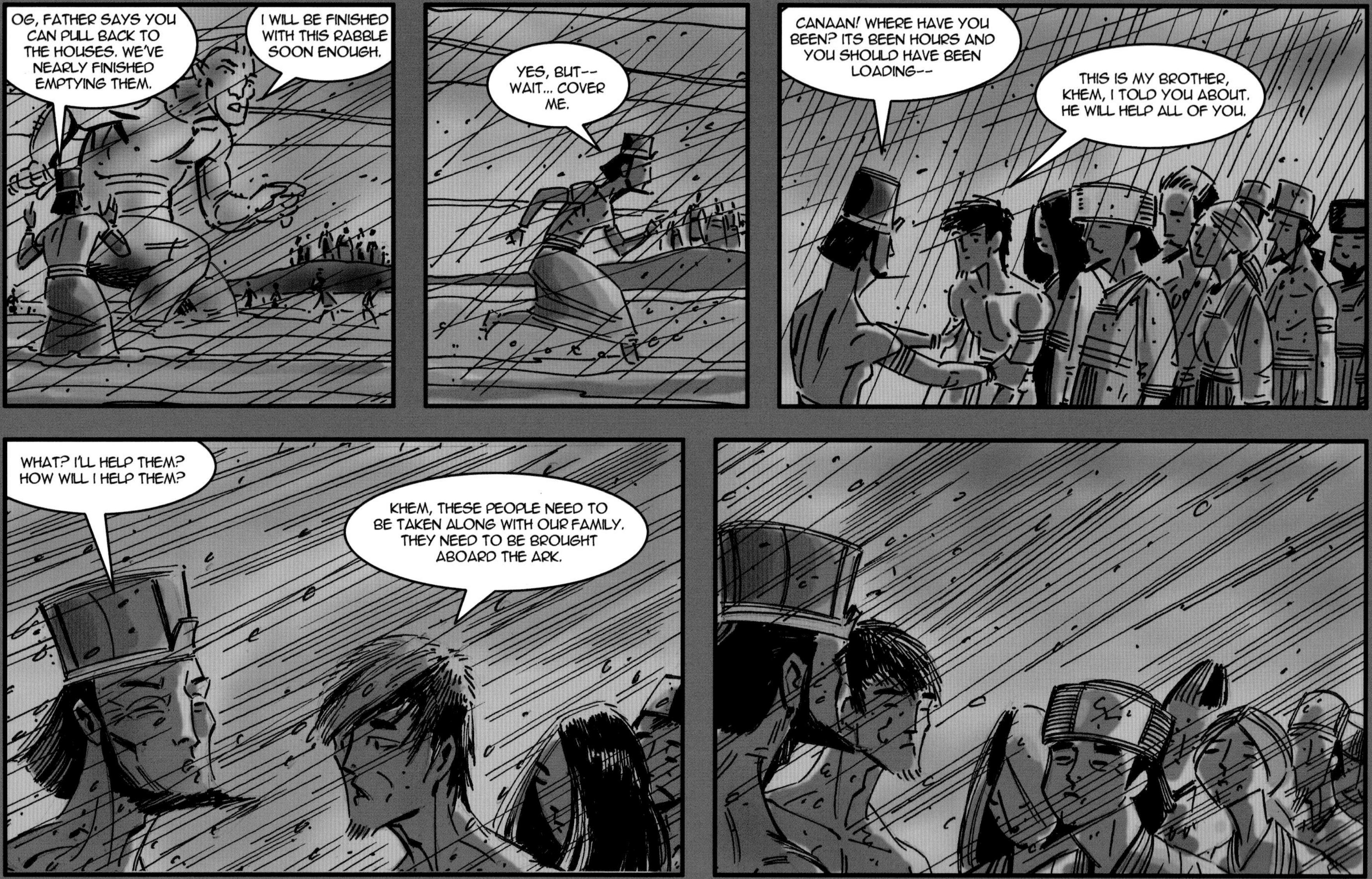
OG, FATHER SAYS YOU CAN PULL BACK TO THE HOUSES. WE'VE NEARLY FINISHED EMPTYING THEM.
I WILL BE FINISHED WITH THIS RABBLE SOON ENOUGH.
YES, BUT-- WAIT... COVER ME.
CANAAN! WHERE HAVE YOU BEEN? ITS BEEN HOURS AND YOU SHOULD HAVE BEEN LOADING--
THIS IS MY BROTHER, KHEM, I TOLD YOU ABOUT. HE WILL HELP ALL OF YOU.
WHAT? I'LL HELP THEM? HOW WILL I HELP THEM?
KHEM, THESE PEOPLE NEED TO BE TAKEN ALONG WITH OUR FAMILY. THEY NEED TO BE BROUGHT ABOARD THE ARK.

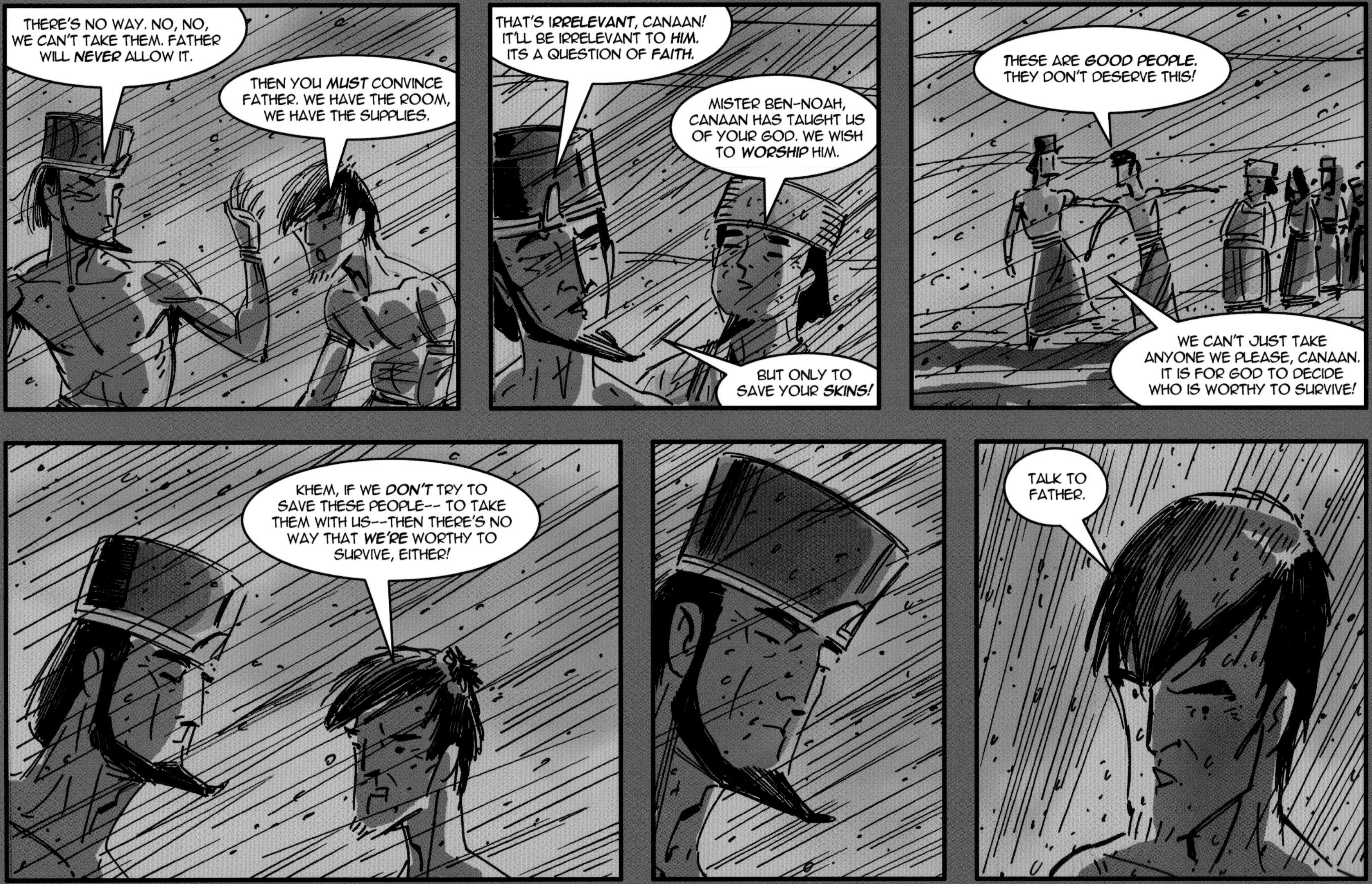
THERE'S NO WAY. NO, NO, WE CAN'T TAKE THEM. FATHER WILL NEVER ALLOW IT.
THEN YOU MUST CONVINCE FATHER. WE HAVE THE ROOM, WE HAVE THE SUPPLIES.
THAT'S IRRELEVANT, CANAAN! IT'LL BE IRRELEVANT TO HIM. ITS A QUESTION OF FAITH.
MISTER BEN-NOAH, CANAAN HAS TAUGHT US OF YOUR GOD. WE WISH TO WORSHIP HIM.
BUT ONLY TO SAVE YOUR SKINS!
THESE ARE GOOD PEOPLE. THEY DON'T DESERVE THIS!
WE CAN'T JUST TAKE ANYONE WE PLEASE, CANAAN. IT IS FOR GOD TO DECIDE WHO IS WORTHY TO SURVIVE!
KHEM, IF WE DON'T TRY TO SAVE THESE PEOPLE-- TO TAKE THEM WITH US--THEN THERE'S NO WAY THAT WE'RE WORTHY TO SURVIVE, EITHER!
TALK TO FATHER.

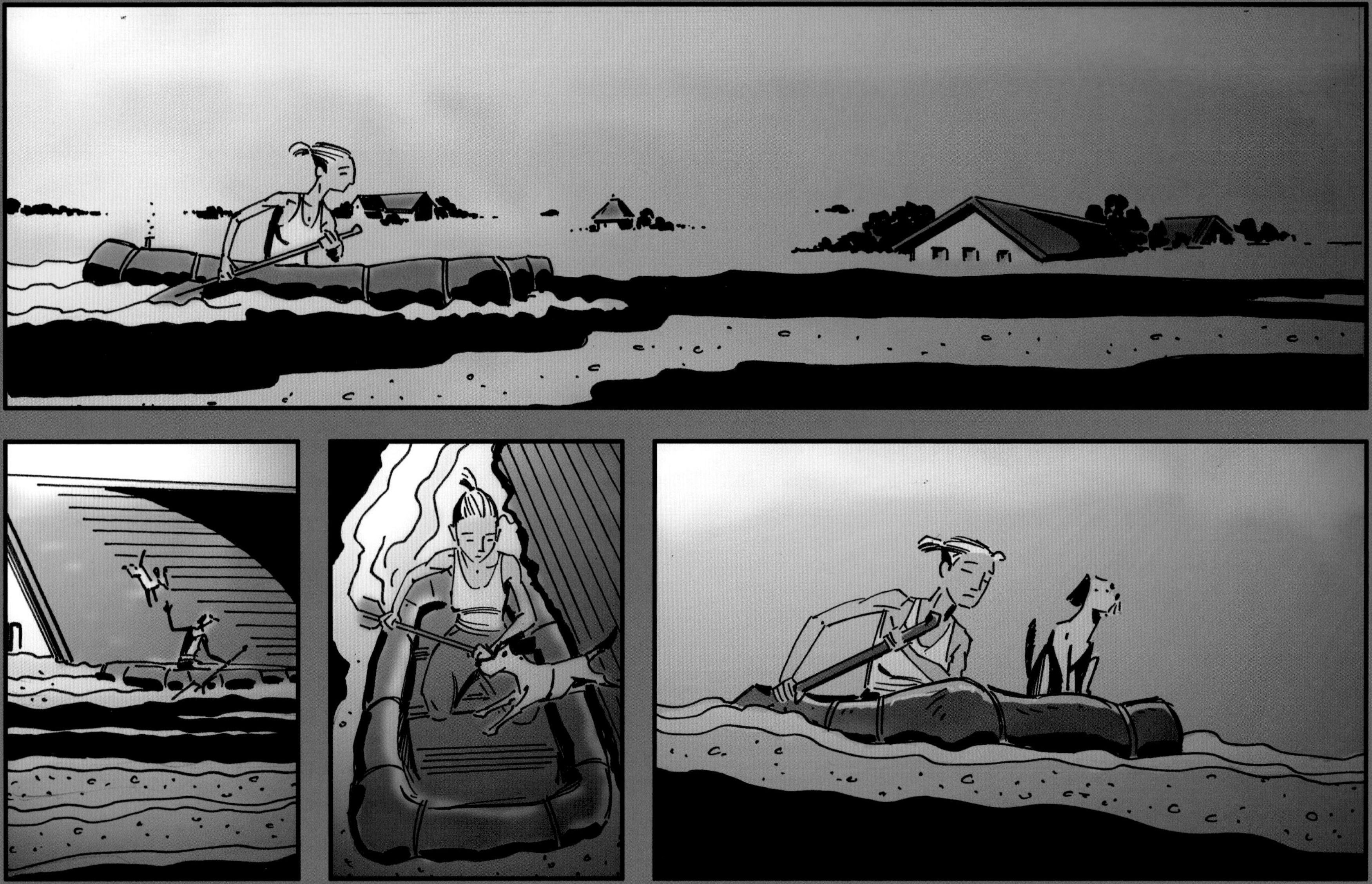

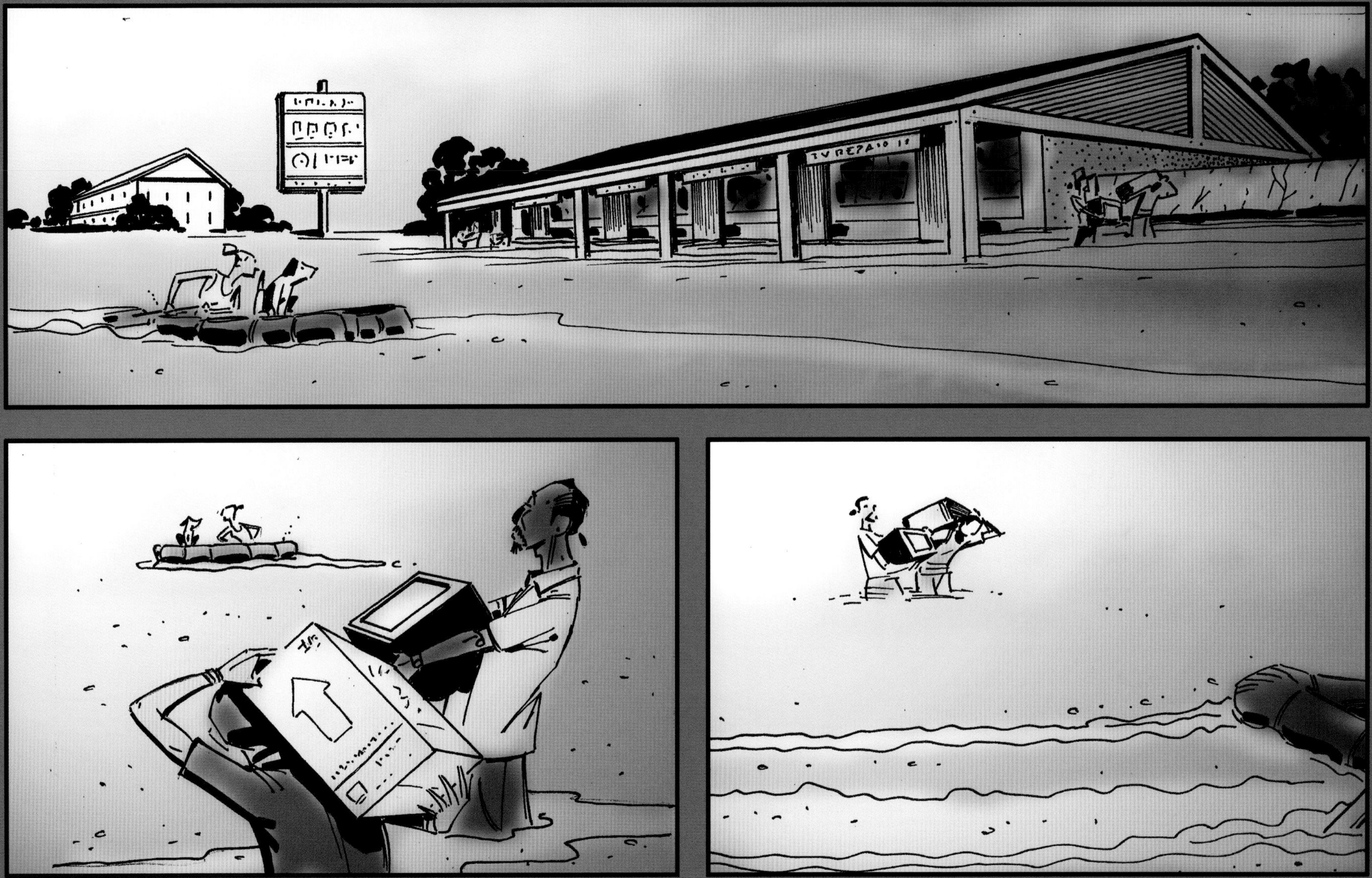

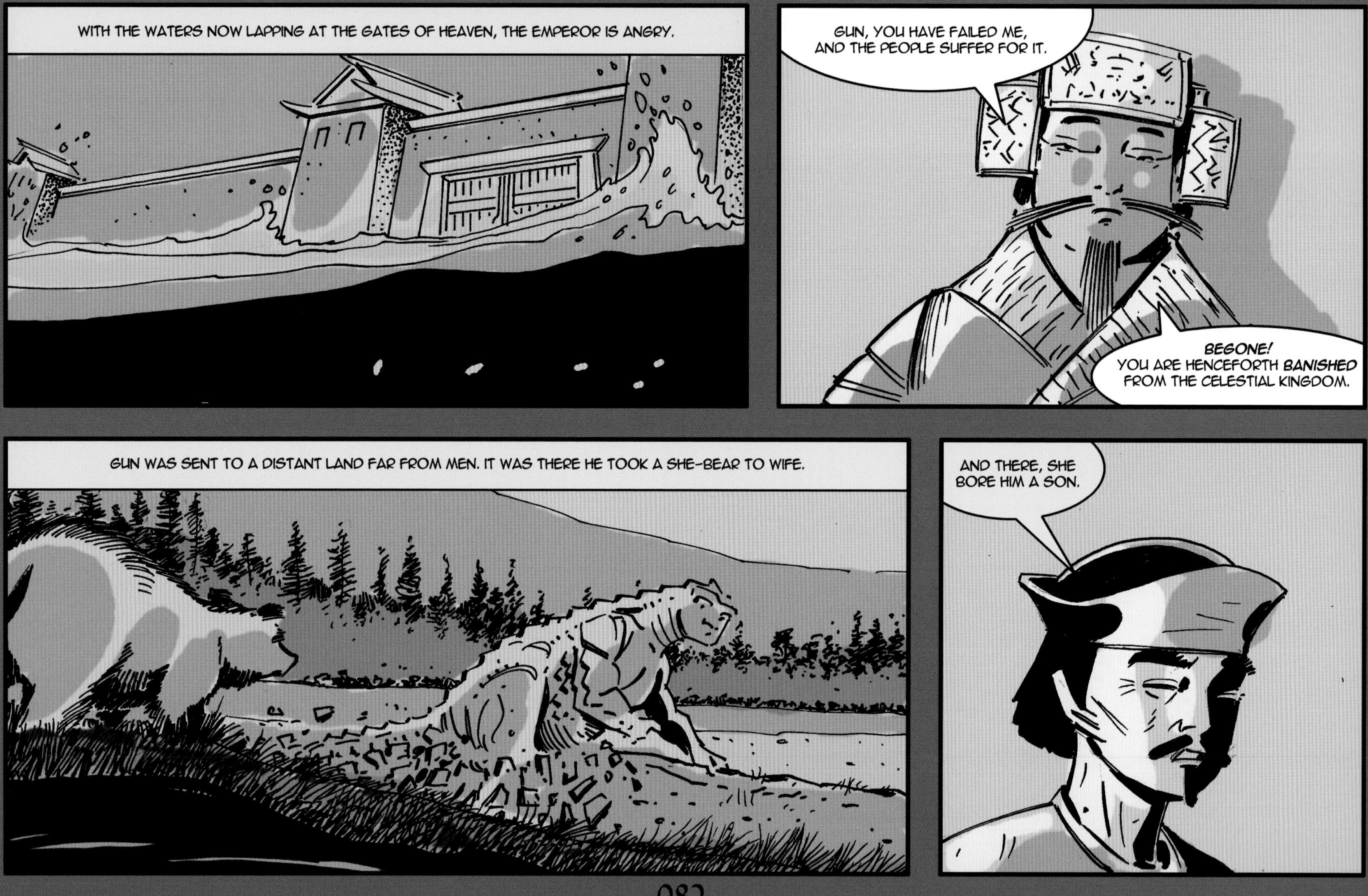
WITH THE WATERS NOW LAPPING AT THE GATES OF HEAVEN, THE EMPEROR IS ANGRY.
GUN, YOU HAVE FAILED ME, AND THE PEOPLE SUFFER FOR IT.
BEGONE! YOU ARE HENCEFORTH BANISHED FROM THE CELESTIAL KINGDOM.
GUN WAS SENT TO A DISTANT LAND FAR FROM MEN. IT WAS THERE HE TOOK A SHE-BEAR TO WIFE.
AND THERE, SHE BORE HIM A SON.

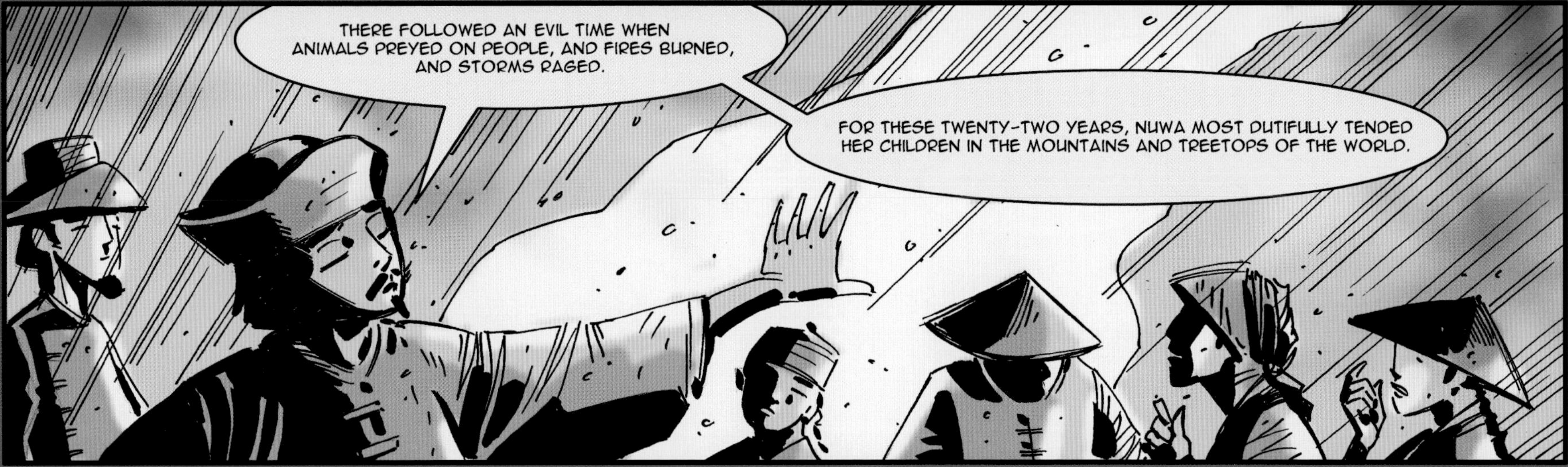
THERE FOLLOWED AN EVIL TIME WHEN ANIMALS PREYED ON PEOPLE, AND FIRES BURNED, AND STORMS RAGED.
FOR THESE TWENTY-TWO YEARS, NUWA MOST DUTIFULLY TENDED HER CHILDREN IN THE MOUNTAINS AND TREETOPS OF THE WORLD.

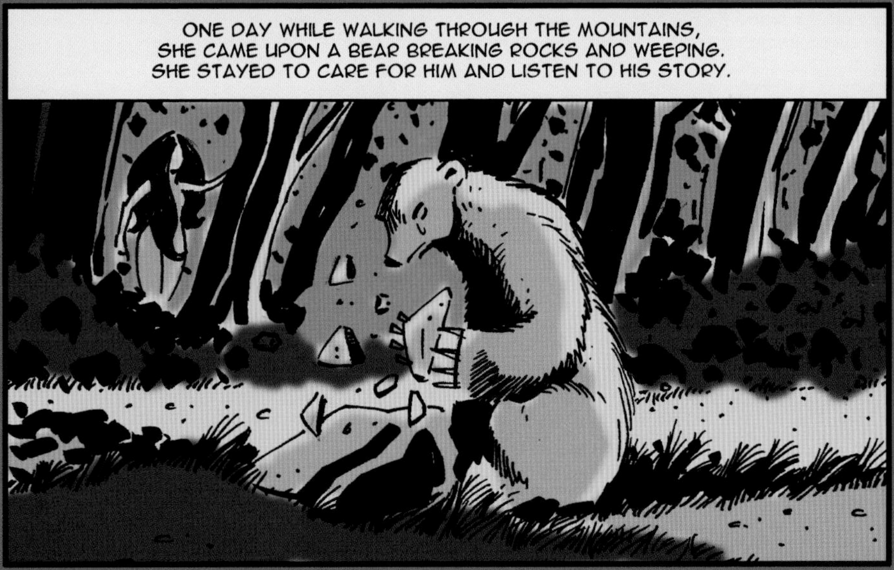
ONE DAY WHILE WALKING THROUGH THE MOUNTAINS, SHE CAME UPON A BEAR BREAKING ROCKS AND WEEPING. SHE STAYED TO CARE FOR HIM AND LISTEN TO HIS STORY.

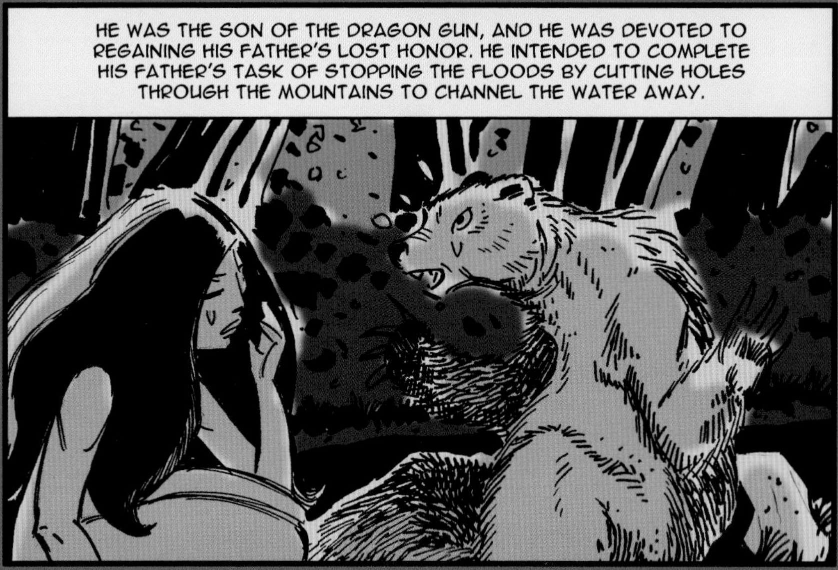
HE WAS THE SON OF THE DRAGON GUN, AND HE WAS DEVOTED TO REGAINING HIS FATHER'S LOST HONOR. HE INTENDED TO COMPLETE HIS FATHER'S TASK OF STOPPING THE FLOODS BY CUTTING HOLES THROUGH THE MOUNTAINS TO CHANNEL THE WATER AWAY.

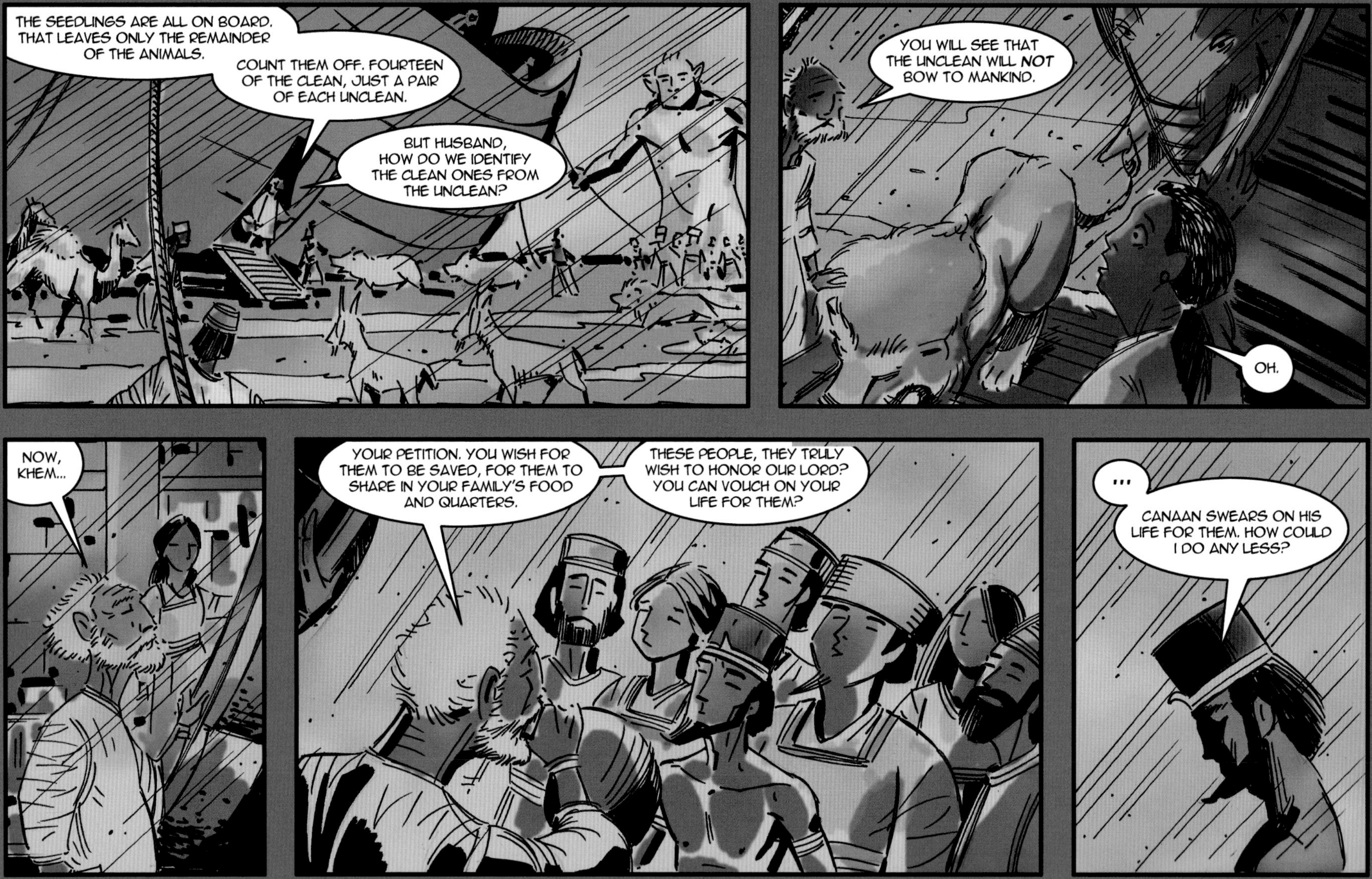
THE SEEDLINGS ARE ALL ON BOARD. THAT LEAVES ONLY THE REMAINDER OF THE ANIMALS.
COUNT THEM OFF. FOURTEEN OF THE CLEAN, JUST A PAIR OF EACH UNCLEAN.
BUT HUSBAND, HOW DO WE IDENTIFY THE CLEAN ONES FROM THE UNCLEAN?
YOU WILL SEE THAT THE UNCLEAN WILL **NOT** BOW TO MANKIND.
OH.
NOW, KHEM...
YOUR PETITION. YOU WISH FOR THEM TO BE SAVED, FOR THEM TO SHARE IN YOUR FAMILY'S FOOD AND QUARTERS.
THESE PEOPLE, THEY TRULY WISH TO HONOR OUR LORD? YOU CAN VOUCH ON YOUR LIFE FOR THEM?
...
CANAAN SWEARS ON HIS LIFE FOR THEM. HOW COULD I DO ANY LESS?

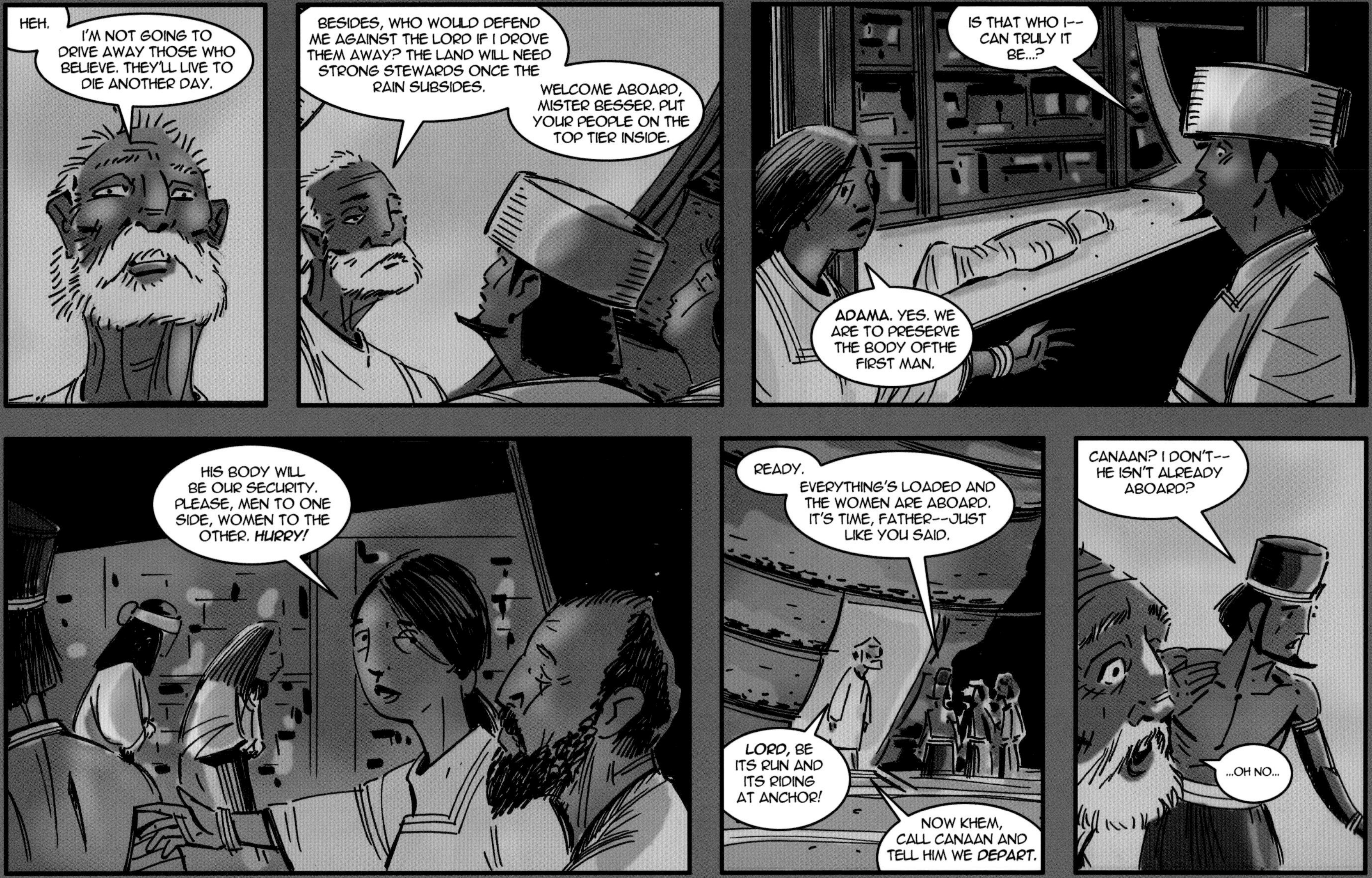
HEH.
I'M NOT GOING TO DRIVE AWAY THOSE WHO BELIEVE. THEY'LL LIVE TO DIE ANOTHER DAY.
BESIDES, WHO WOULD DEFEND ME AGAINST THE LORD IF I DROVE THEM AWAY? THE LAND WILL NEED STRONG STEWARDS ONCE THE RAIN SUBSIDES.
WELCOME ABOARD, MISTER BESSER. PUT YOUR PEOPLE ON THE TOP TIER INSIDE.
IS THAT WHO I-- CAN TRULY IT BE...?
ADAMA. YES. WE ARE TO PRESERVE THE BODY OFTHE FIRST MAN.
HIS BODY WILL BE OUR SECURITY. PLEASE, MEN TO ONE SIDE, WOMEN TO THE OTHER. *HURRY!*
READY.
EVERYTHING'S LOADED AND THE WOMEN ARE ABOARD. IT'S TIME, FATHER--JUST LIKE YOU SAID.
LORD, BE ITS RUN AND ITS RIDING AT ANCHOR!
NOW KHEM, CALL CANAAN AND TELL HIM WE *DEPART*.
CANAAN? I DON'T-- HE ISN'T ALREADY ABOARD?
...OH NO...

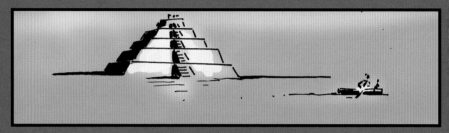

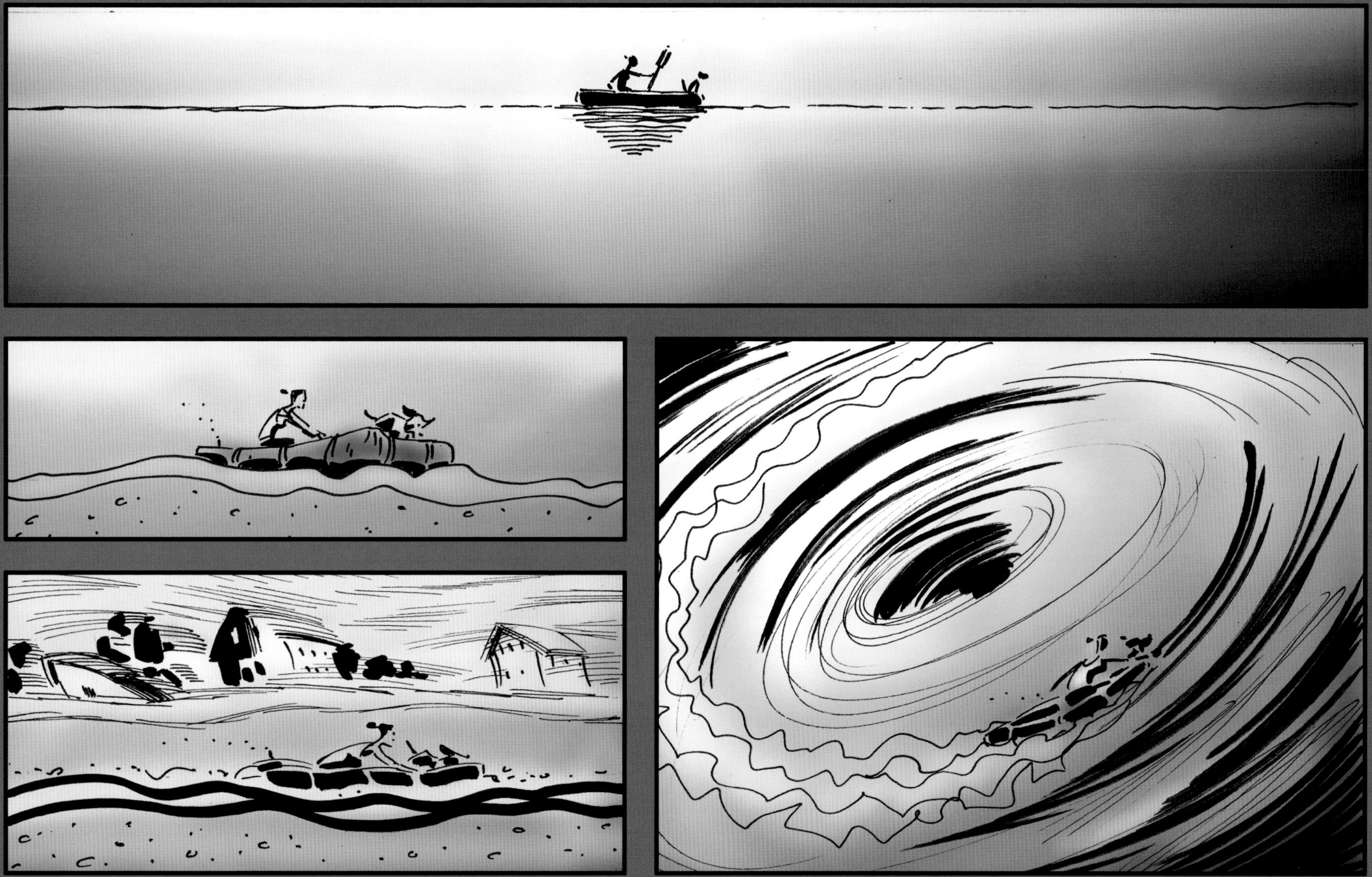

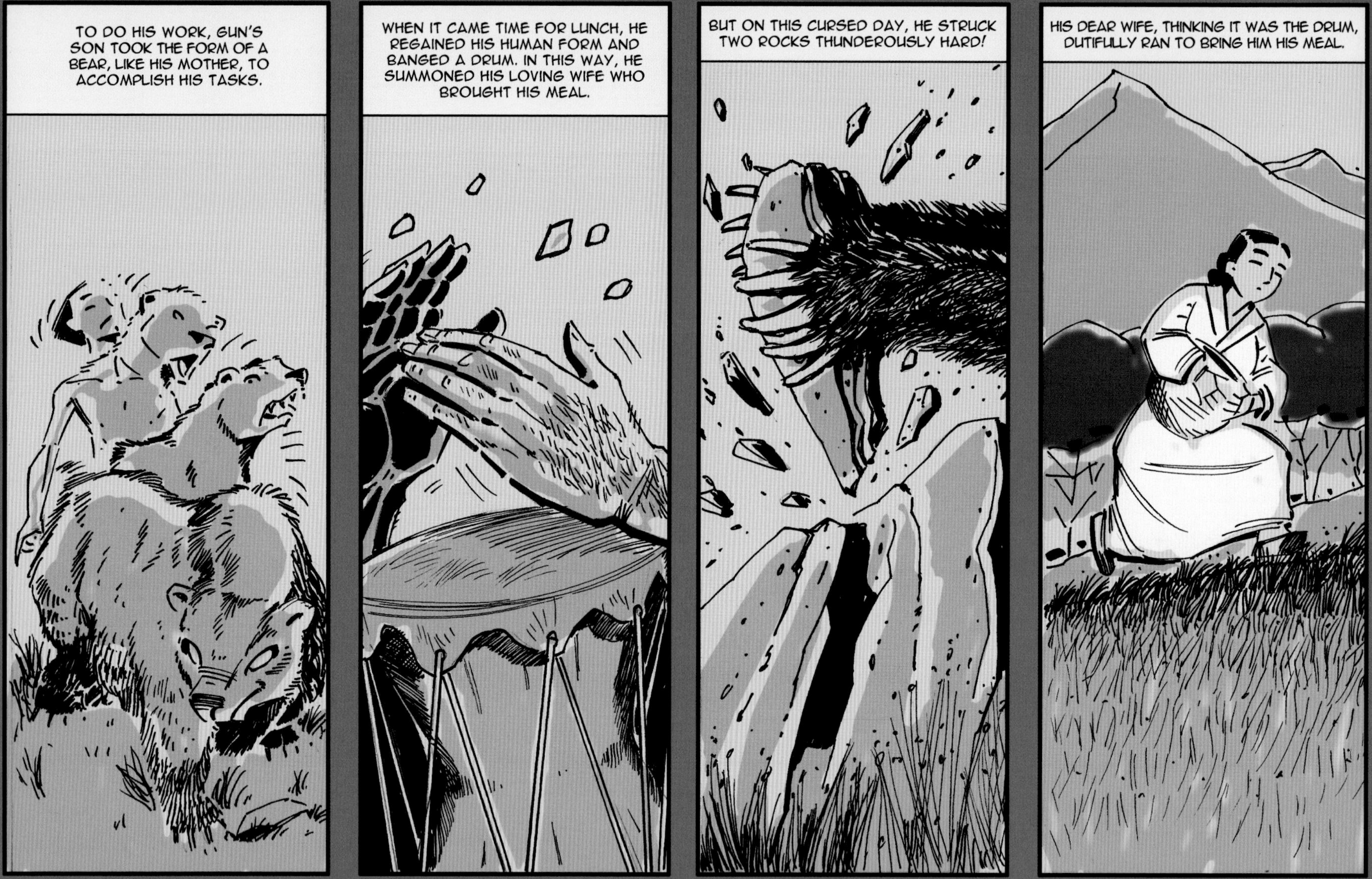
TO DO HIS WORK, GUN'S SON TOOK THE FORM OF A BEAR, LIKE HIS MOTHER, TO ACCOMPLISH HIS TASKS.
WHEN IT CAME TIME FOR LUNCH, HE REGAINED HIS HUMAN FORM AND BANGED A DRUM. IN THIS WAY, HE SUMMONED HIS LOVING WIFE WHO BROUGHT HIS MEAL.
BUT ON THIS CURSED DAY, HE STRUCK TWO ROCKS THUNDEROUSLY HARD!
HIS DEAR WIFE, THINKING IT WAS THE DRUM, DUTIFULLY RAN TO BRING HIM HIS MEAL.

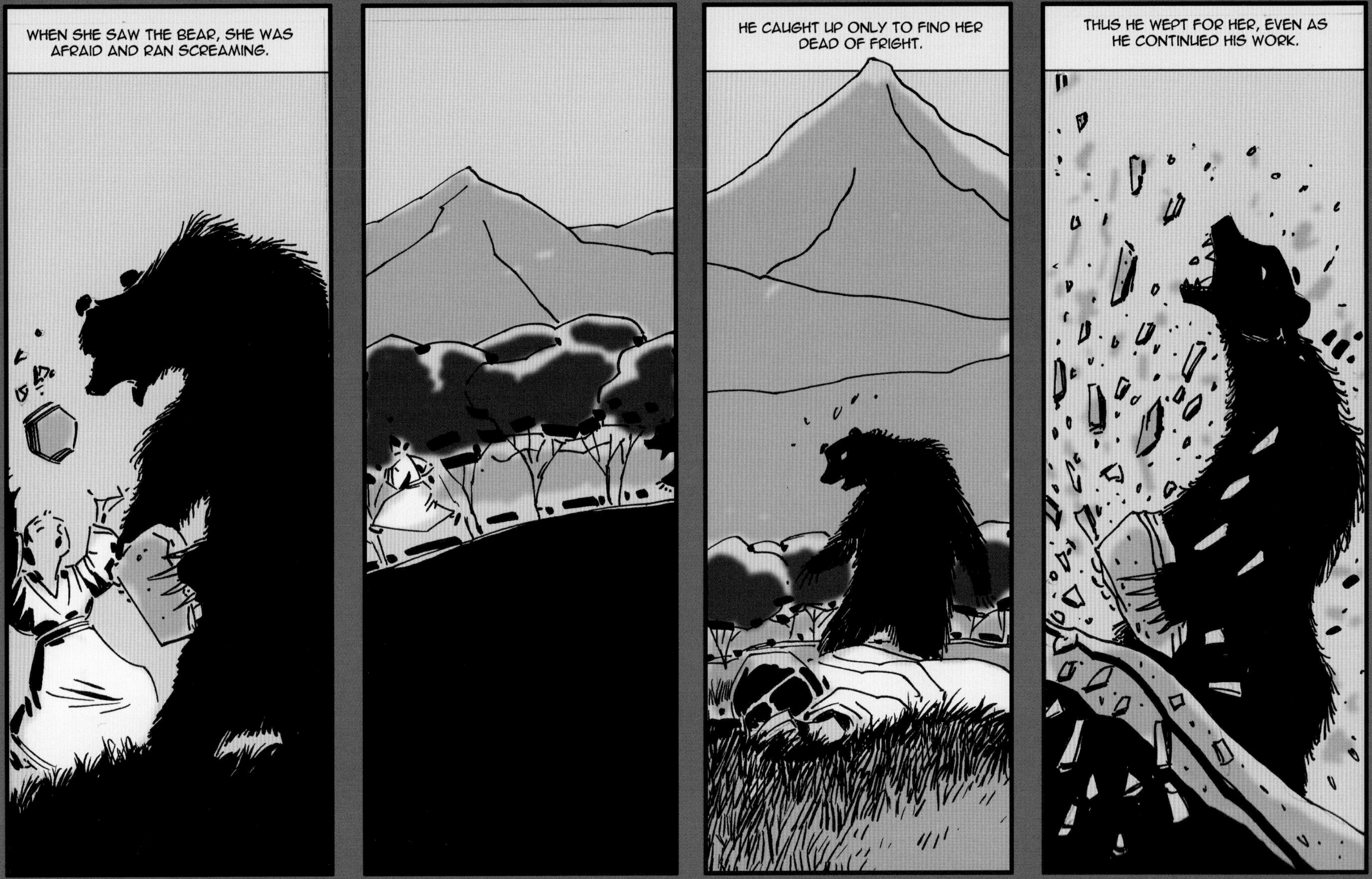
WHEN SHE SAW THE BEAR, SHE WAS AFRAID AND RAN SCREAMING.
HE CAUGHT UP ONLY TO FIND HER DEAD OF FRIGHT.
THUS HE WEPT FOR HER, EVEN AS HE CONTINUED HIS WORK.

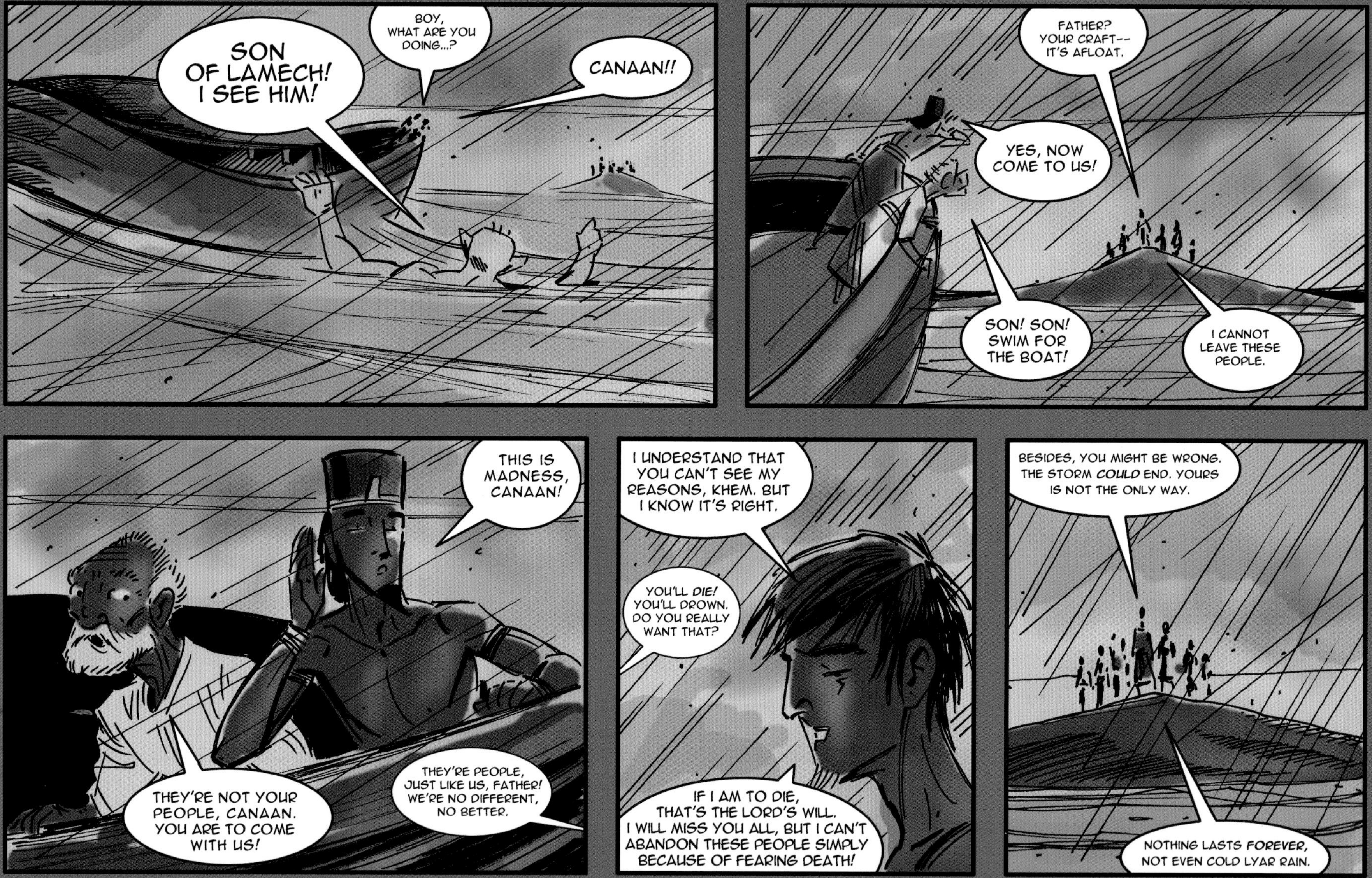

SON OF LAMECH! I SEE HIM!
BOY, WHAT ARE YOU DOING...?
CANAAN!!
FATHER? YOUR CRAFT-- IT'S AFLOAT.
YES, NOW COME TO US!
SON! SON! SWIM FOR THE BOAT!
I CANNOT LEAVE THESE PEOPLE.
THIS IS MADNESS, CANAAN!
THEY'RE NOT YOUR PEOPLE, CANAAN. YOU ARE TO COME WITH US!
THEY'RE PEOPLE, JUST LIKE US, FATHER! WE'RE NO DIFFERENT, NO BETTER.
I UNDERSTAND THAT YOU CAN'T SEE MY REASONS, KHEM. BUT I KNOW IT'S RIGHT.
YOU'LL *DIE!* YOU'LL DROWN. DO YOU REALLY WANT THAT?
IF I AM TO DIE, THAT'S THE LORD'S WILL. I WILL MISS YOU ALL, BUT I CAN'T ABANDON THESE PEOPLE SIMPLY BECAUSE OF FEARING DEATH!
BESIDES, YOU MIGHT BE WRONG. THE STORM *COULD* END. YOURS IS NOT THE ONLY WAY.
NOTHING LASTS *FOREVER,* NOT EVEN COLD LYAR RAIN.

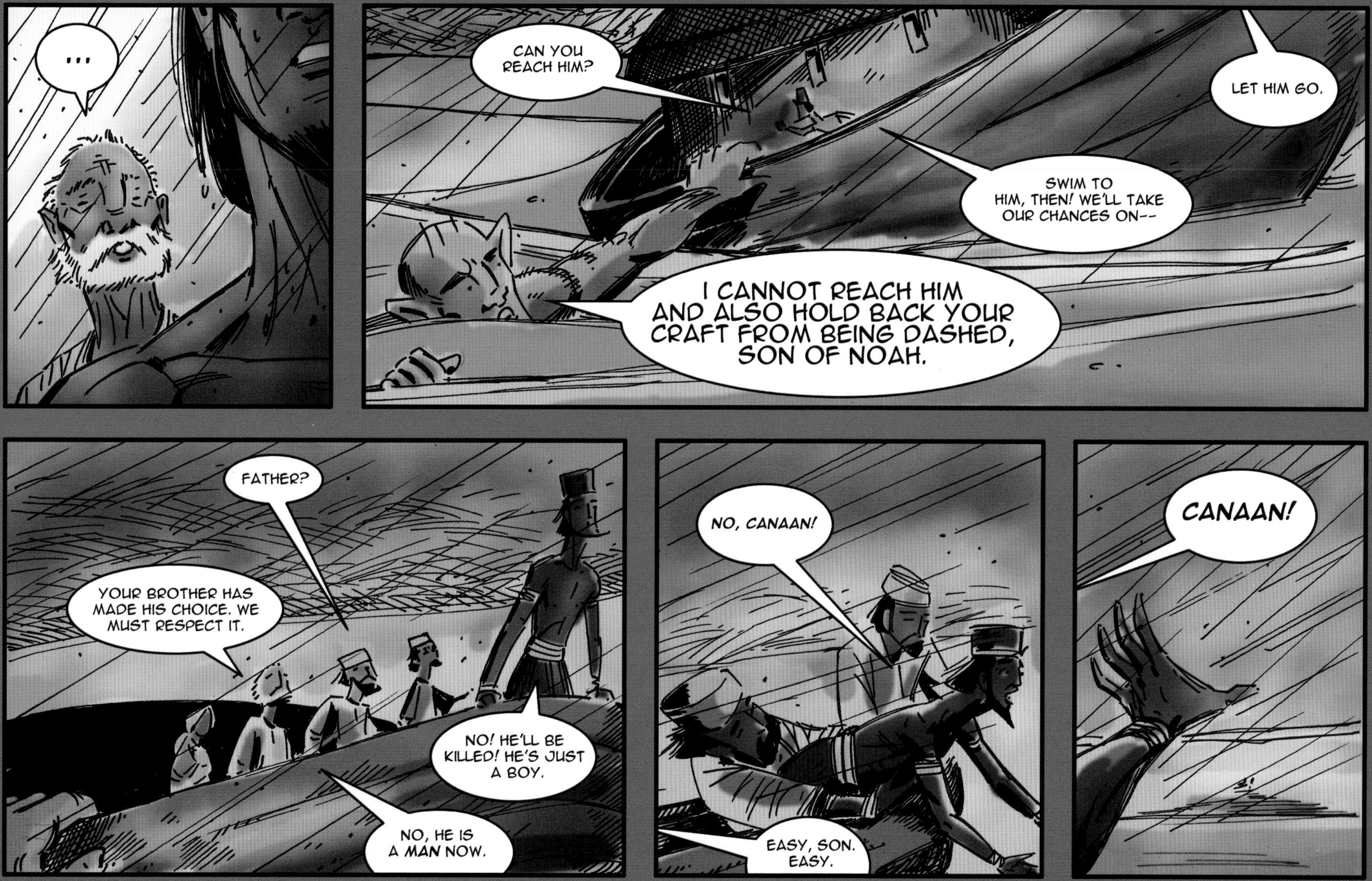
...
CAN YOU REACH HIM?
LET HIM GO.
SWIM TO HIM, THEN! WE'LL TAKE OUR CHANCES ON--
I CANNOT REACH HIM AND ALSO HOLD BACK YOUR CRAFT FROM BEING DASHED, SON OF NOAH.
FATHER?
YOUR BROTHER HAS MADE HIS CHOICE. WE MUST RESPECT IT.
NO! HE'LL BE KILLED! HE'S JUST A BOY.
NO, HE IS A MAN NOW.
NO, CANAAN!
EASY, SON. EASY.
CANAAN!

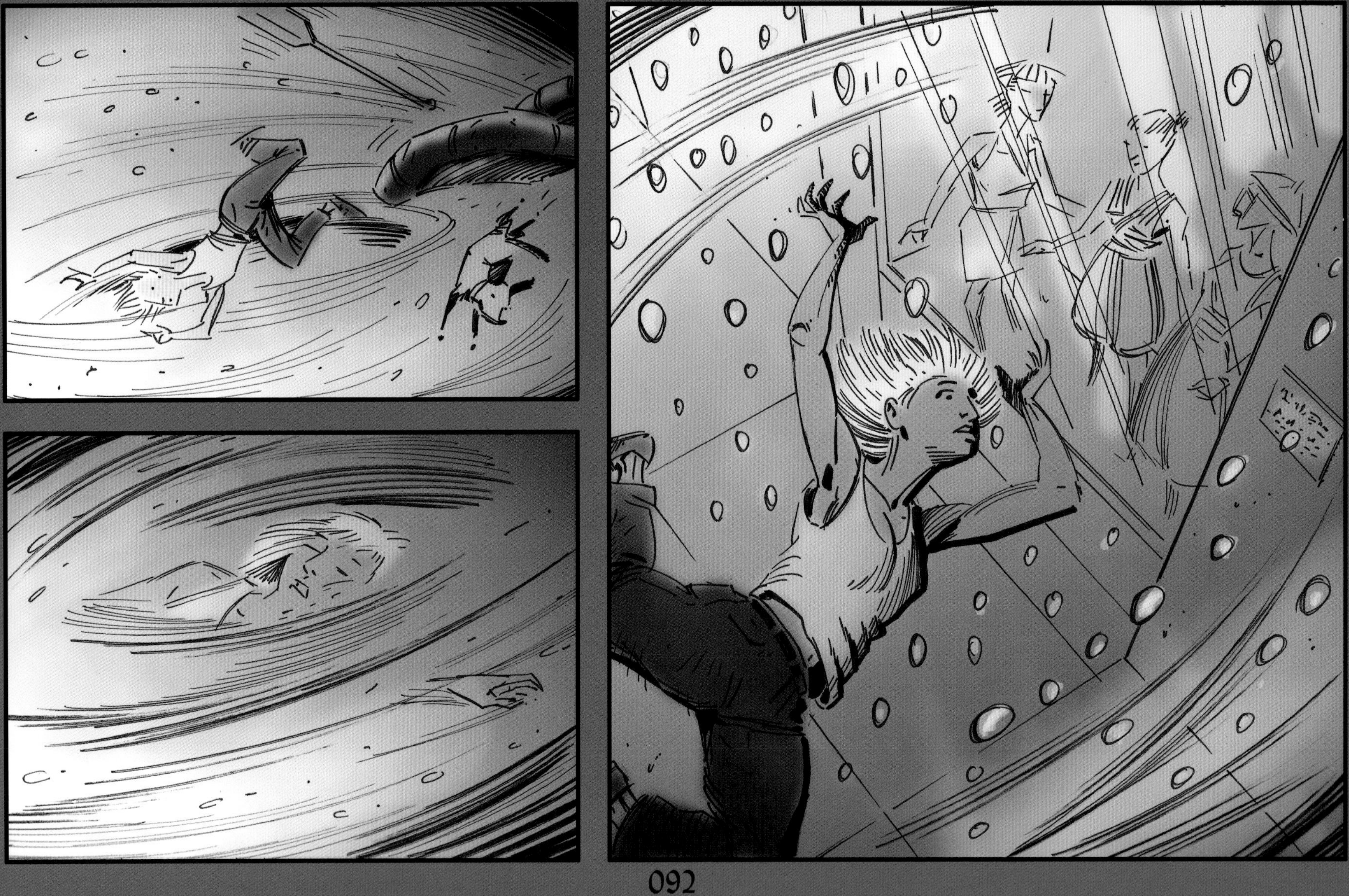

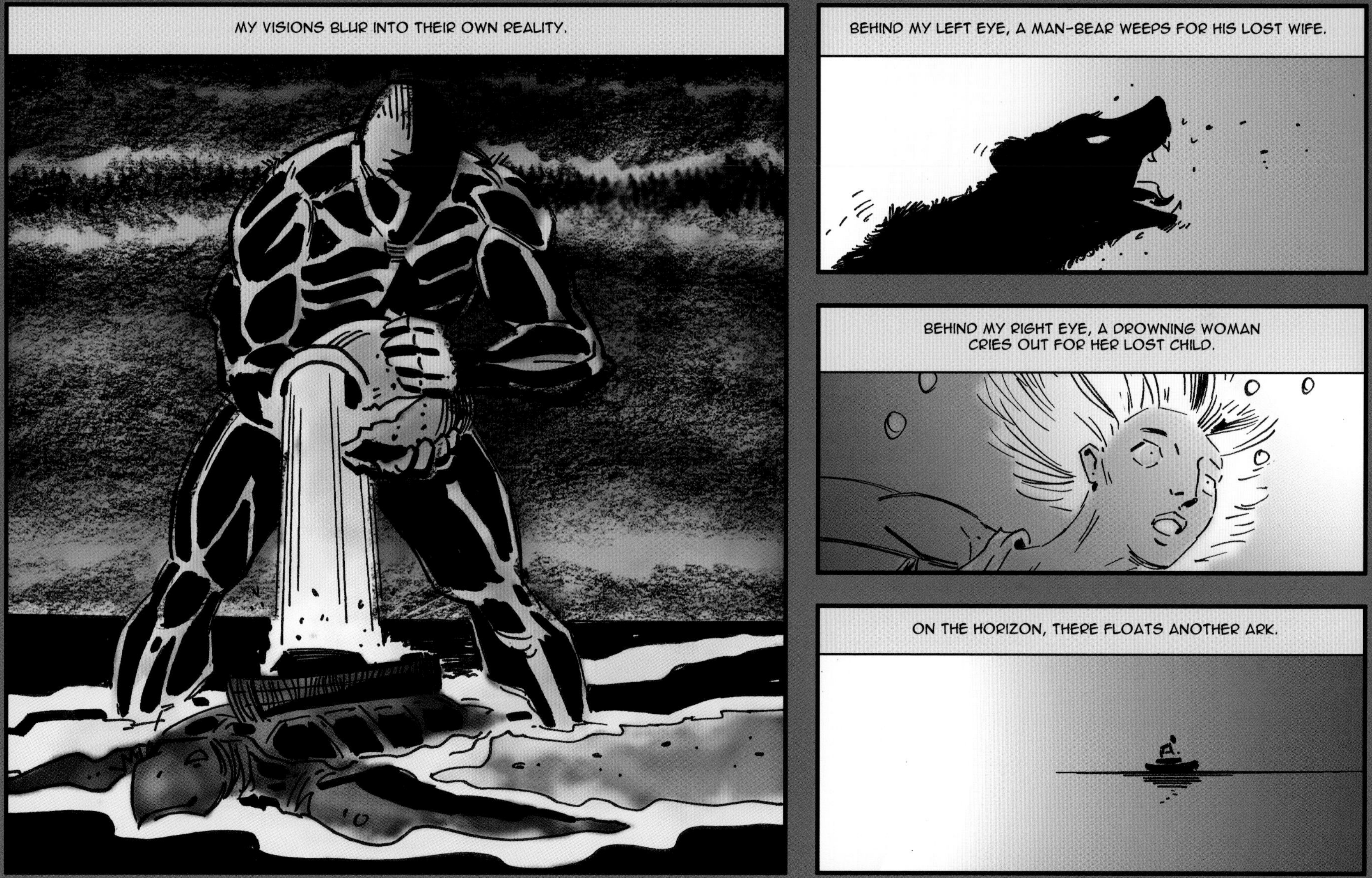
MY VISIONS BLUR INTO THEIR OWN REALITY.
BEHIND MY LEFT EYE, A MAN-BEAR WEEPS FOR HIS LOST WIFE.
BEHIND MY RIGHT EYE, A DROWNING WOMAN CRIES OUT FOR HER LOST CHILD.
ON THE HORIZON, THERE FLOATS ANOTHER ARK.

BELOW ME SWIMS THE TURTLE.

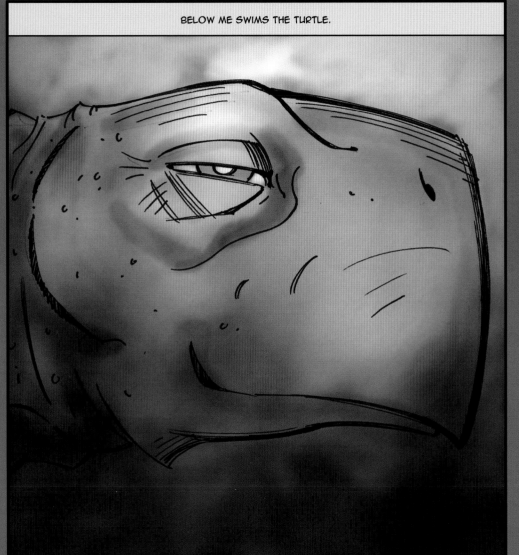

ABOVE, I SEE THE HEAVENS.

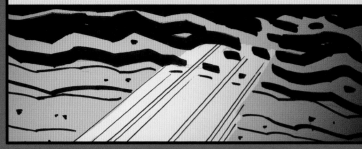

BEFORE MY EYES, NO BIRDS TO BE SEEN.

THE FUTURE, THE PAST, THE ETERNAL NOW,
ALL CONFLATE IN THE EYE OF A GOD.

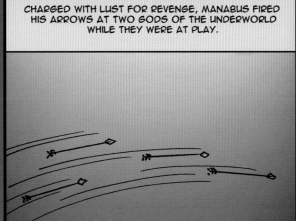

CHARGED WITH LUST FOR REVENGE, MANABUS FIRED HIS ARROWS AT TWO GODS OF THE UNDERWORLD WHILE THEY WERE AT PLAY.

WHEN THE GODS FELL INTO THE WATER, A HUGE FLOOD AROSE.

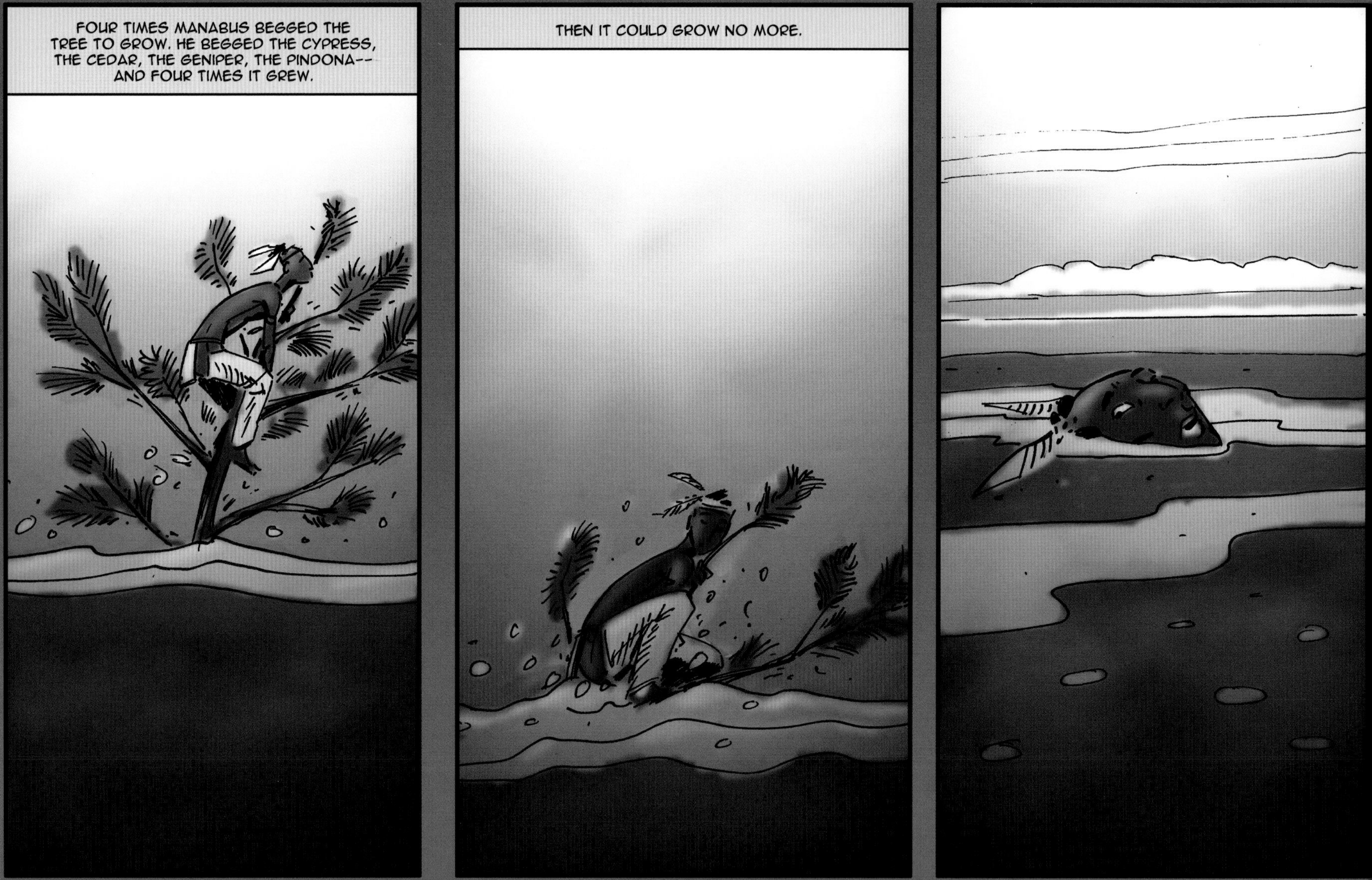
FOUR TIMES MANABUS BEGGED THE TREE TO GROW. HE BEGGED THE CYPRESS, THE CEDAR, THE GENIPER, THE PINDONA-- AND FOUR TIMES IT GREW.
THEN IT COULD GROW NO MORE.

Aftermath

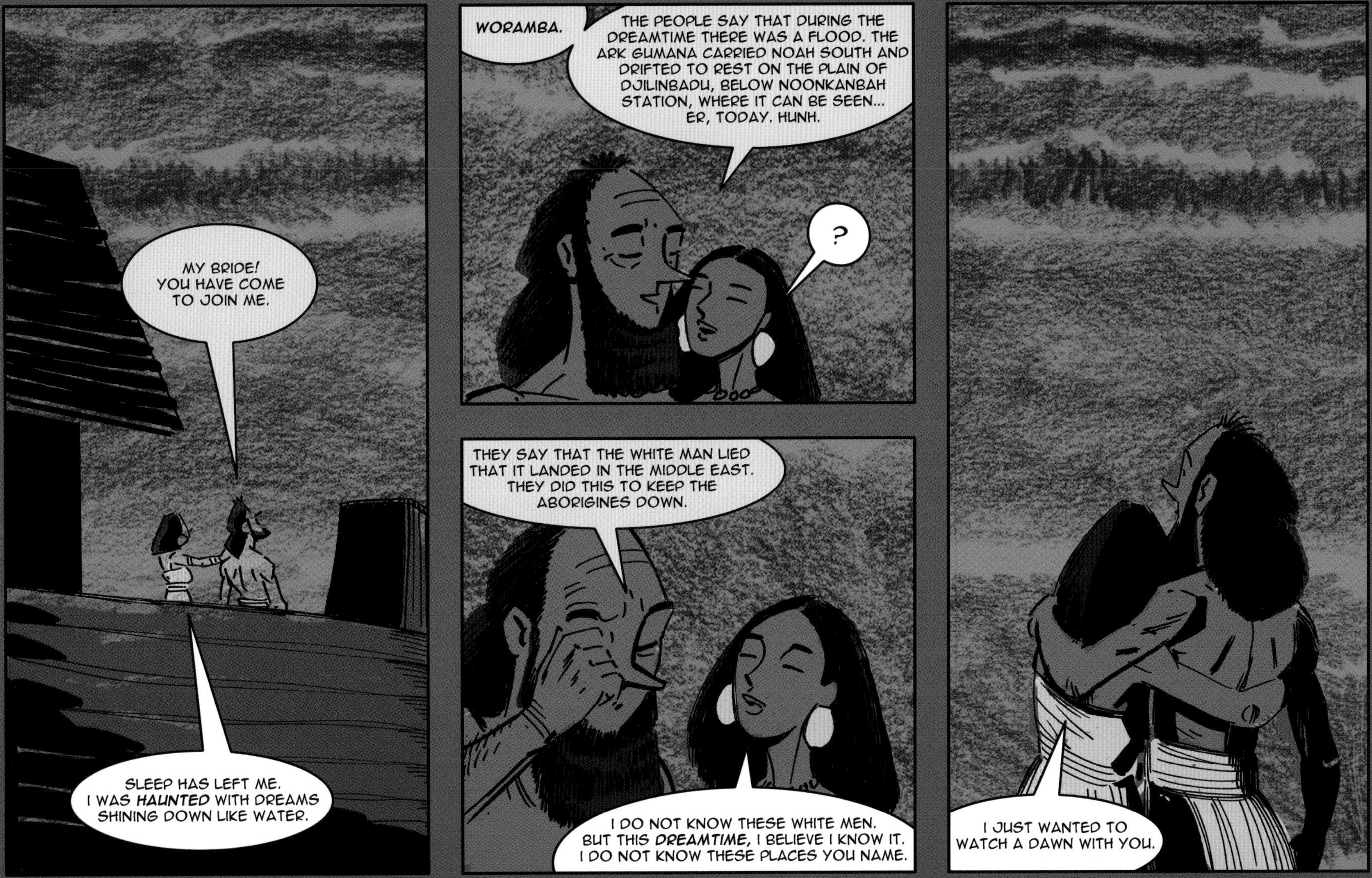
MY BRIDE! YOU HAVE COME TO JOIN ME.
SLEEP HAS LEFT ME. I WAS **HAUNTED** WITH DREAMS SHINING DOWN LIKE WATER.
WORAMBA.
THE PEOPLE SAY THAT DURING THE DREAMTIME THERE WAS A FLOOD. THE ARK GUMANA CARRIED NOAH SOUTH AND DRIFTED TO REST ON THE PLAIN OF DJILINBADU, BELOW NOONKANBAH STATION, WHERE IT CAN BE SEEN... ER, TODAY. HUNH.
?
THEY SAY THAT THE WHITE MAN LIED THAT IT LANDED IN THE MIDDLE EAST. THEY DID THIS TO KEEP THE ABORIGINES DOWN.
I DO NOT KNOW THESE WHITE MEN. BUT THIS ***DREAMTIME,*** I BELIEVE I KNOW IT. I DO NOT KNOW THESE PLACES YOU NAME.
I JUST WANTED TO WATCH A DAWN WITH YOU.

IN MAKIRITARE, THERE WERE STAR PEOPLE WHO LIVED GOOD LIVES; UNTIL THE DAY THEY LISTENED TO JAGUAR, WHO ADVISED THEM TO KILL AND EAT A WOMAN.

THIS THEY DID, AND THEREBY ENRAGED KUAMACHI. TO PUNISH THEM, HE INVITED THEM TO HELP HIM HARVEST THE DEWAKI FRUIT.

AFTER THE HARVEST, WHILE THEY WERE FEASTING ON THE FRUIT, KUAMACHI DROPPED ONE.

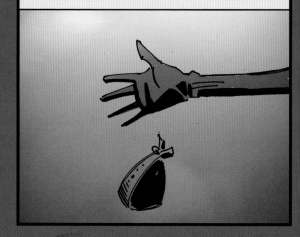

WATER GUSHED OUT OF IT AND CAUSED THE RIVER TO FLOOD. KUAMACHI AND HIS GRANDFATHER FOUND SAFETY IN A CANOE.

WITH BOWS AND ARROWS, THEY SHOT THESE PEOPLE WHO HAD SURVIVED BY CLIMBING TREES.

THE PEOPLE FELL DOWN INTO THE RIVER, WHERE THEY WERE ATTACKED BY DANGEROUS ANIMALS LIKE SNAKES AND CARNIVOROUS FISH AND GRUMPY TURTLES.

THE CARNAGE WAS MASSIVE.

AND YET IT WAS SOON OVER.

SOMEHOW, WLAHA, THE LEADER OF THE STAR PEOPLE, ESCAPED DESTRUCTION.

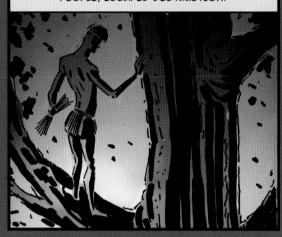

HE AVOIDED KUAMACHI'S VIOLENCE BY AVOIDING VIOLENCE ITSELF. HE HAD CAUGHT SEVEN ARROWS.

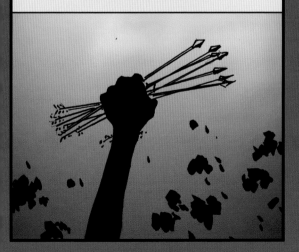

INSTEAD OF RETALIATION, HE FIRED THEM AT THE HEAVENS TO CREATE A LADDER WHICH HE HAD A FEW OF THE SURVIVING STAR PEOPLE THEN CLIMBED.

KUAMACHI PURSUED THEM, BUT THEY TURNED INTO STARS TO EVADE CAPTURE.

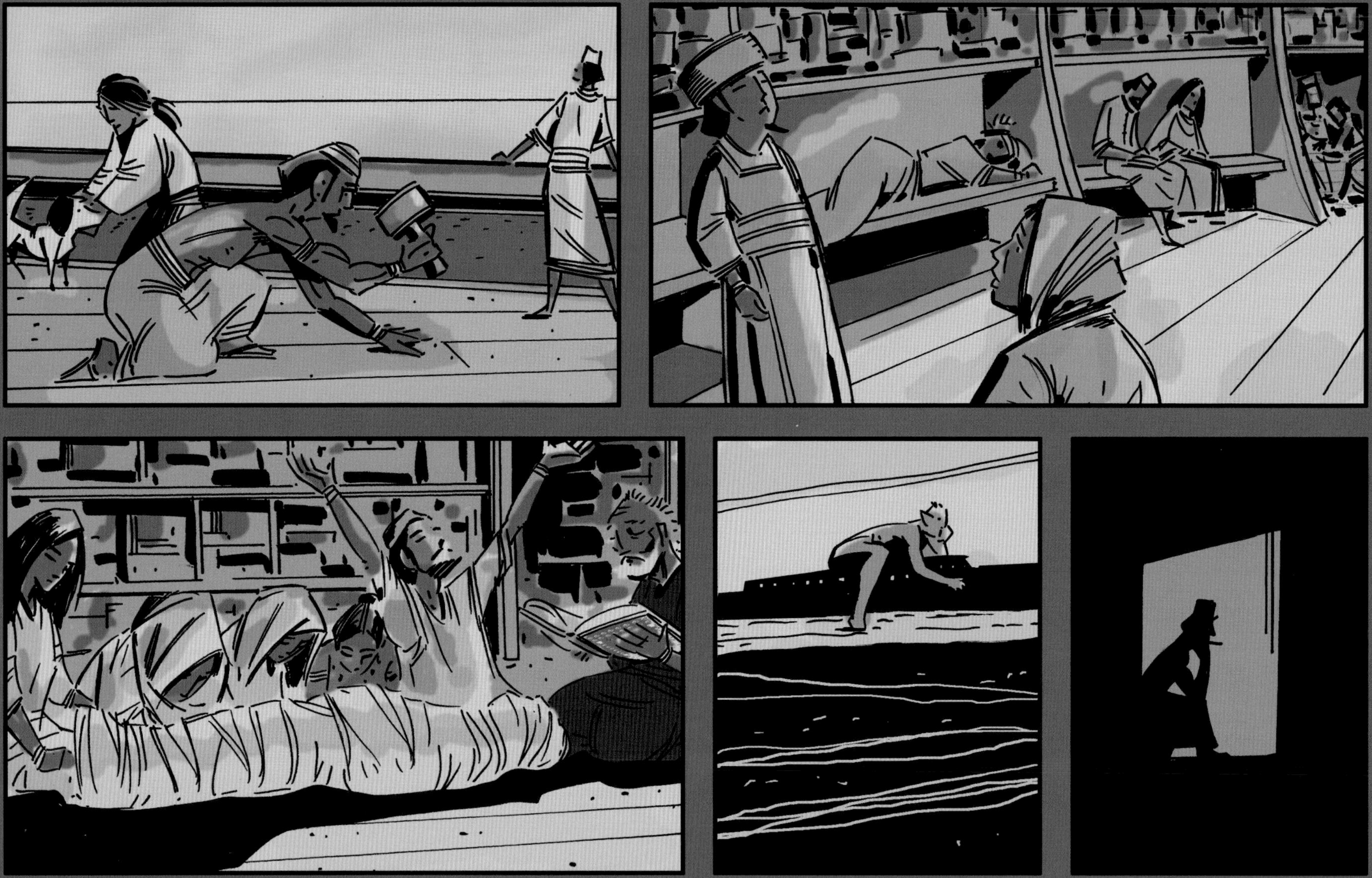

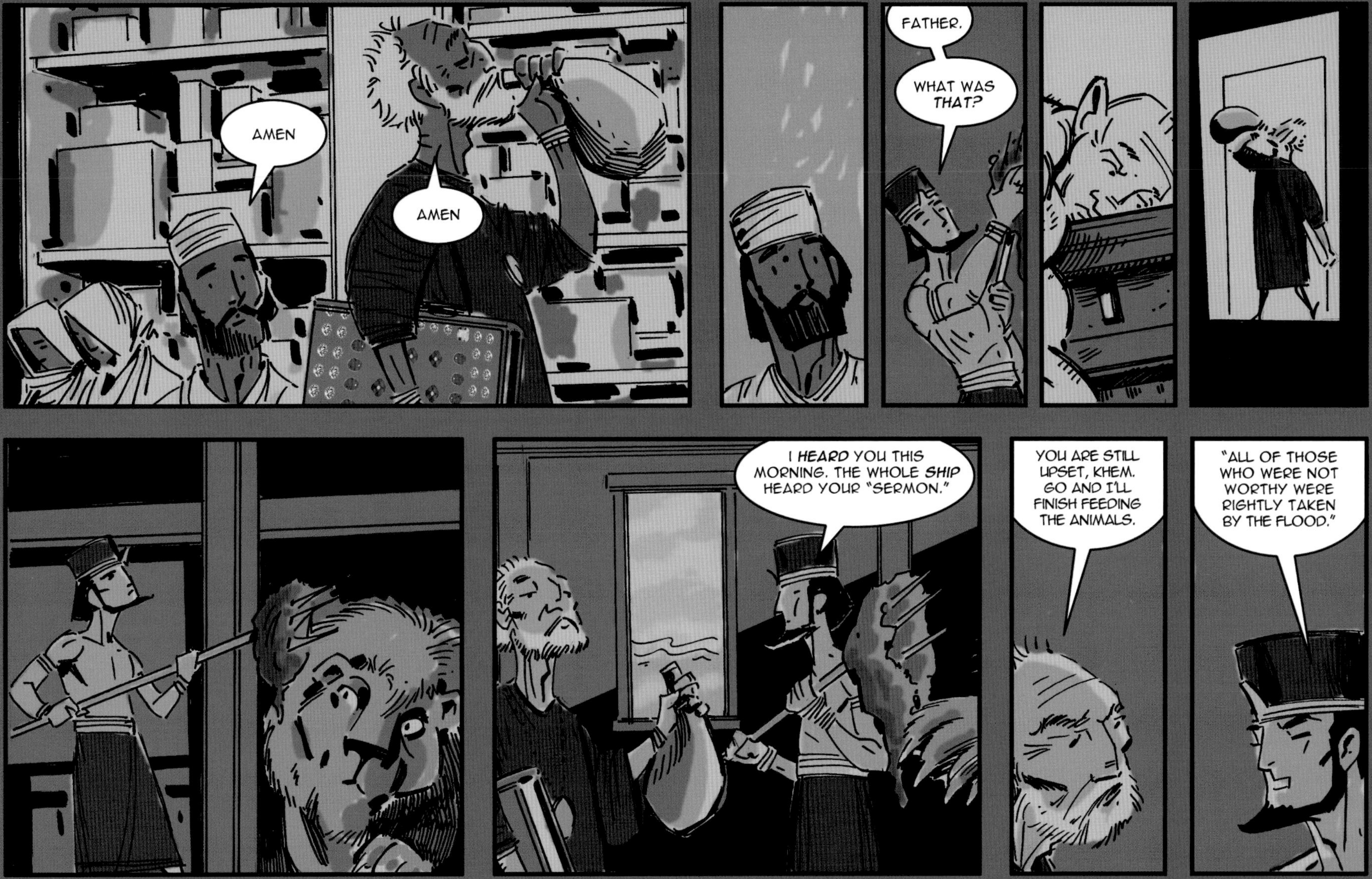
AMEN
AMEN
FATHER.
WHAT WAS THAT?
I HEARD YOU THIS MORNING. THE WHOLE SHIP HEARD YOUR "SERMON."
YOU ARE STILL UPSET, KHEM. GO AND I'LL FINISH FEEDING THE ANIMALS.
"ALL OF THOSE WHO WERE NOT WORTHY WERE RIGHTLY TAKEN BY THE FLOOD."

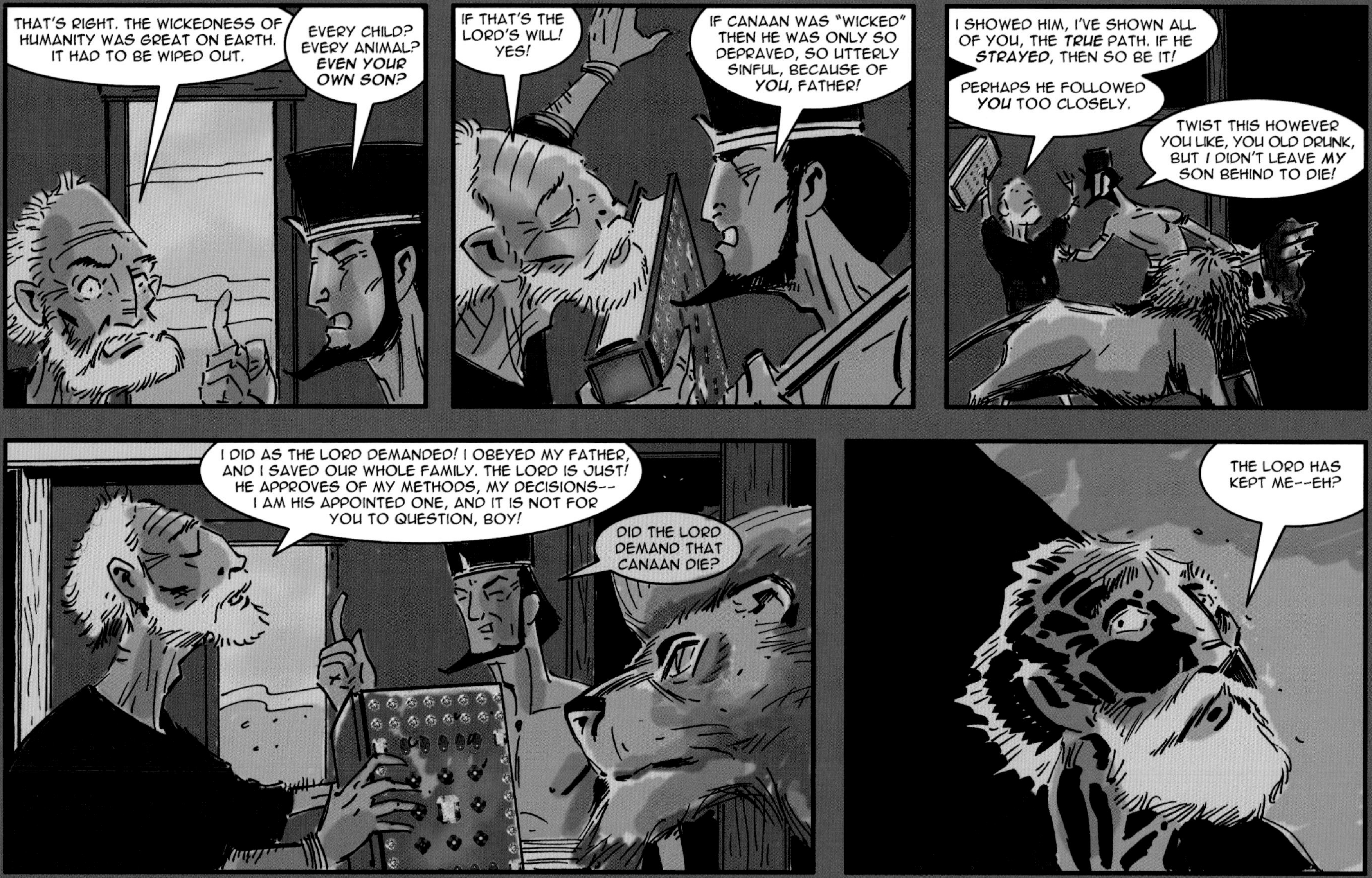

THAT'S RIGHT. THE WICKEDNESS OF HUMANITY WAS GREAT ON EARTH. IT HAD TO BE WIPED OUT.
EVERY CHILD? EVERY ANIMAL? EVEN YOUR OWN SON?
IF THAT'S THE LORD'S WILL! YES!
IF CANAAN WAS "WICKED" THEN HE WAS ONLY SO DEPRAVED, SO UTTERLY SINFUL, BECAUSE OF YOU, FATHER!
I SHOWED HIM, I'VE SHOWN ALL OF YOU, THE TRUE PATH. IF HE STRAYED, THEN SO BE IT!
PERHAPS HE FOLLOWED YOU TOO CLOSELY.
TWIST THIS HOWEVER YOU LIKE, YOU OLD DRUNK, BUT I DIDN'T LEAVE MY SON BEHIND TO DIE!
I DID AS THE LORD DEMANDED! I OBEYED MY FATHER, AND I SAVED OUR WHOLE FAMILY. THE LORD IS JUST! HE APPROVES OF MY METHODS, MY DECISIONS-- I AM HIS APPOINTED ONE, AND IT IS NOT FOR YOU TO QUESTION, BOY!
DID THE LORD DEMAND THAT CANAAN DIE?
THE LORD HAS KEPT ME--EH?

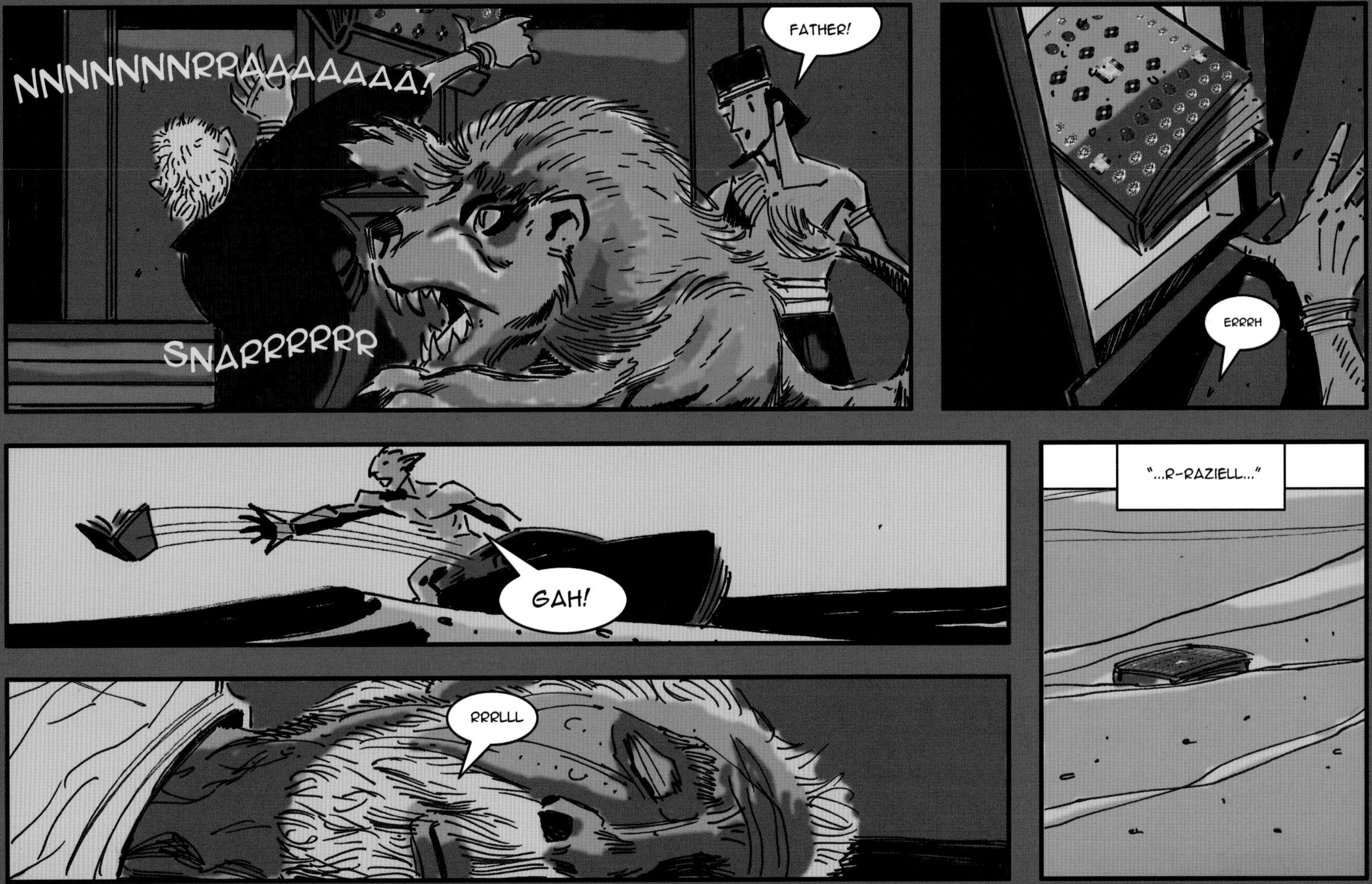
NNNNNNNRRAAAAAAA!
FATHER!
SNARRRRRR
ERRRH
GAH!
"...R-RAZIELL..."
RRRLLL

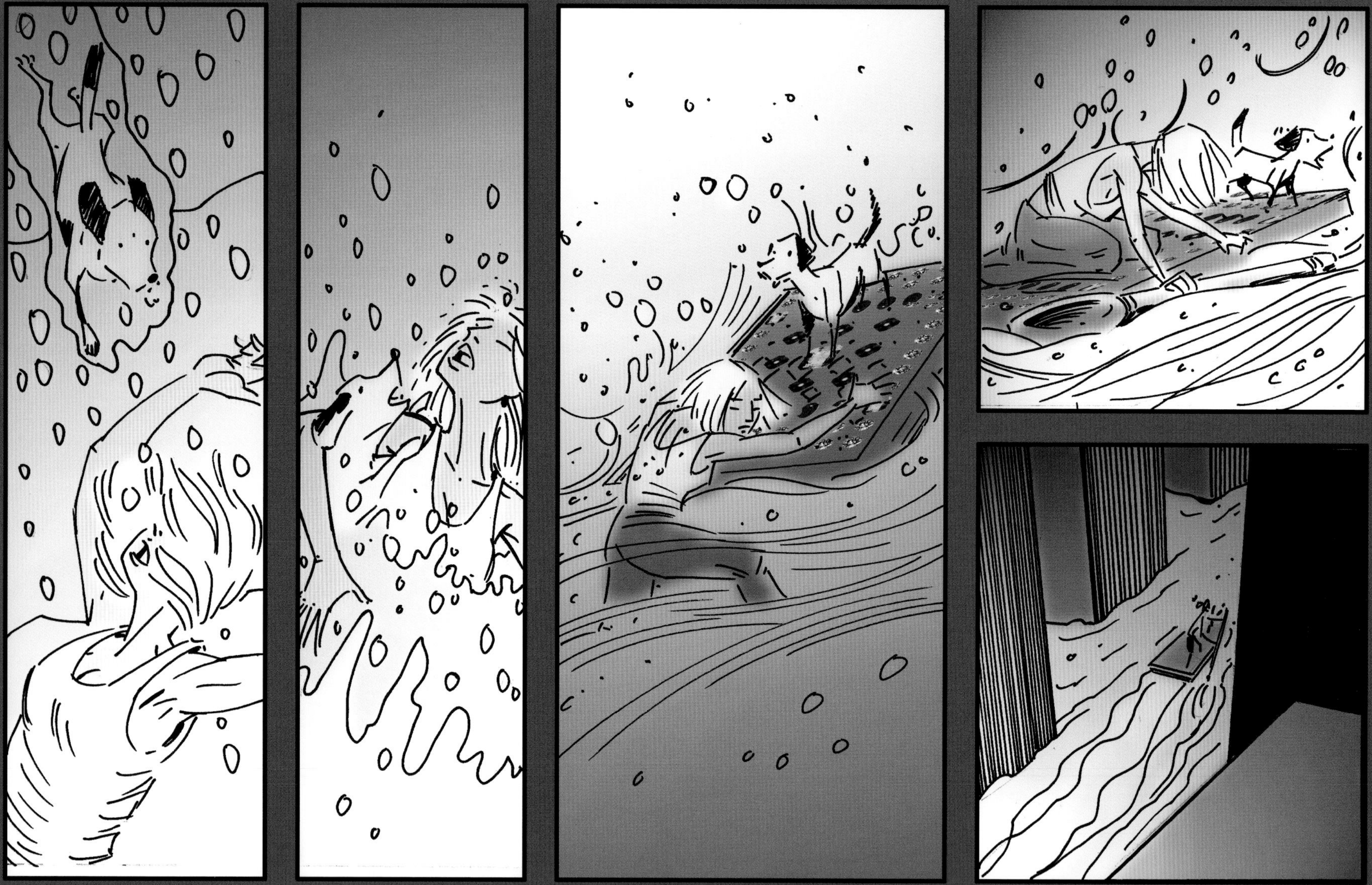

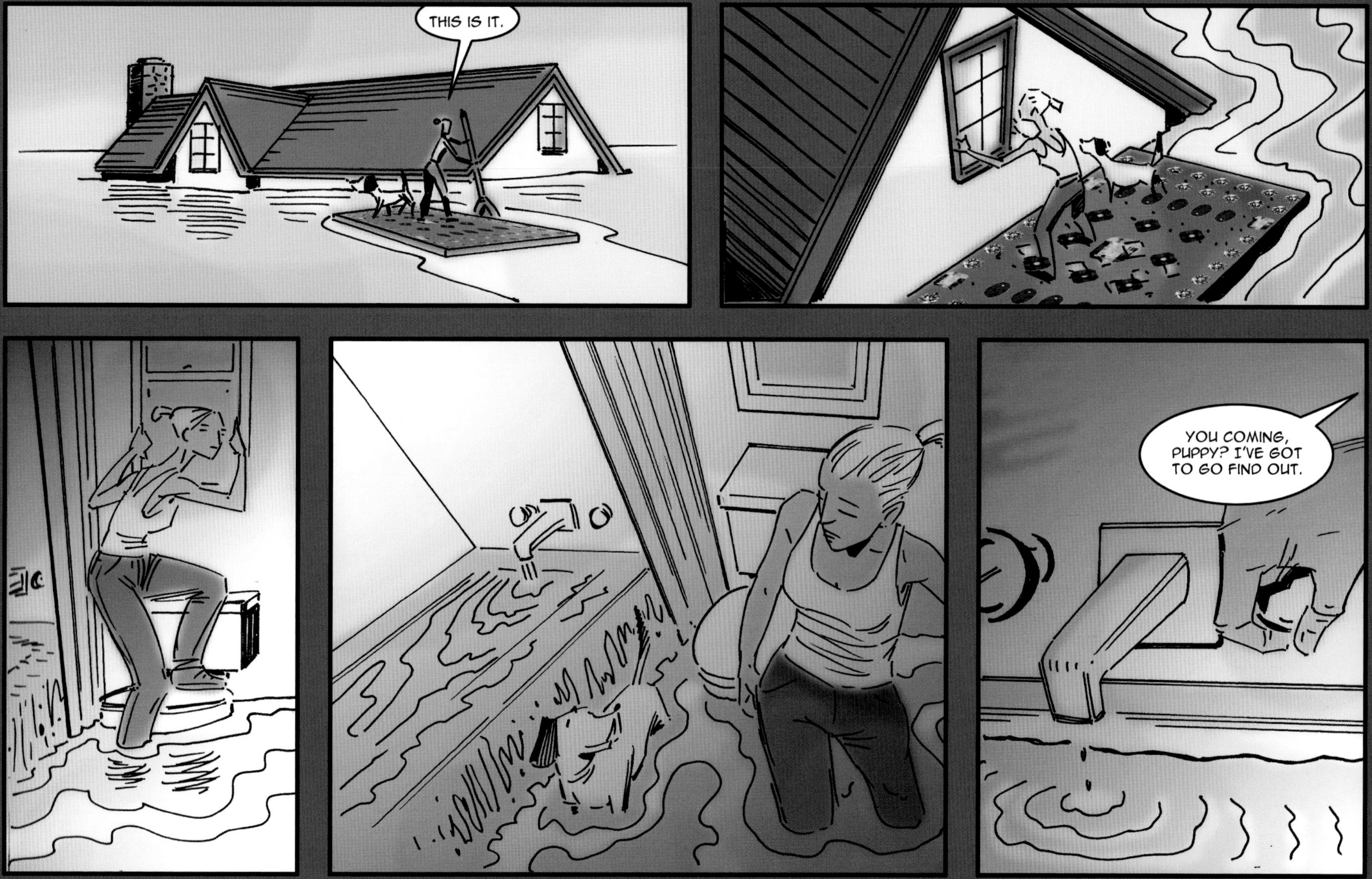
THIS IS IT.
YOU COMING, PUPPY? I'VE GOT TO GO FIND OUT.

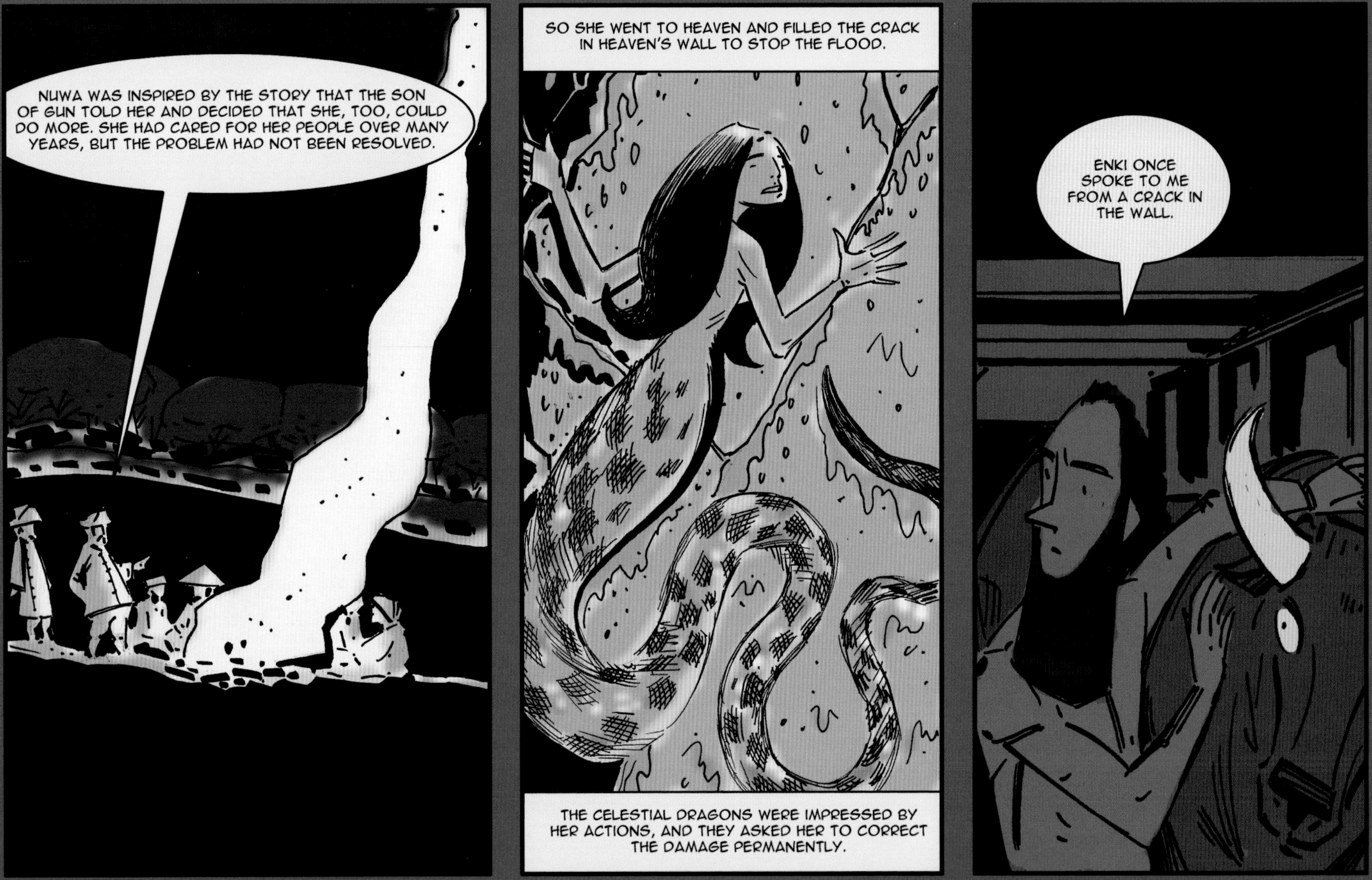
NUWA WAS INSPIRED BY THE STORY THAT THE SON OF GUN TOLD HER AND DECIDED THAT SHE, TOO, COULD DO MORE. SHE HAD CARED FOR HER PEOPLE OVER MANY YEARS, BUT THE PROBLEM HAD NOT BEEN RESOLVED.
SO SHE WENT TO HEAVEN AND FILLED THE CRACK IN HEAVEN'S WALL TO STOP THE FLOOD.
THE CELESTIAL DRAGONS WERE IMPRESSED BY HER ACTIONS, AND THEY ASKED HER TO CORRECT THE DAMAGE PERMANENTLY.
ENKI ONCE SPOKE TO ME FROM A CRACK IN THE WALL.

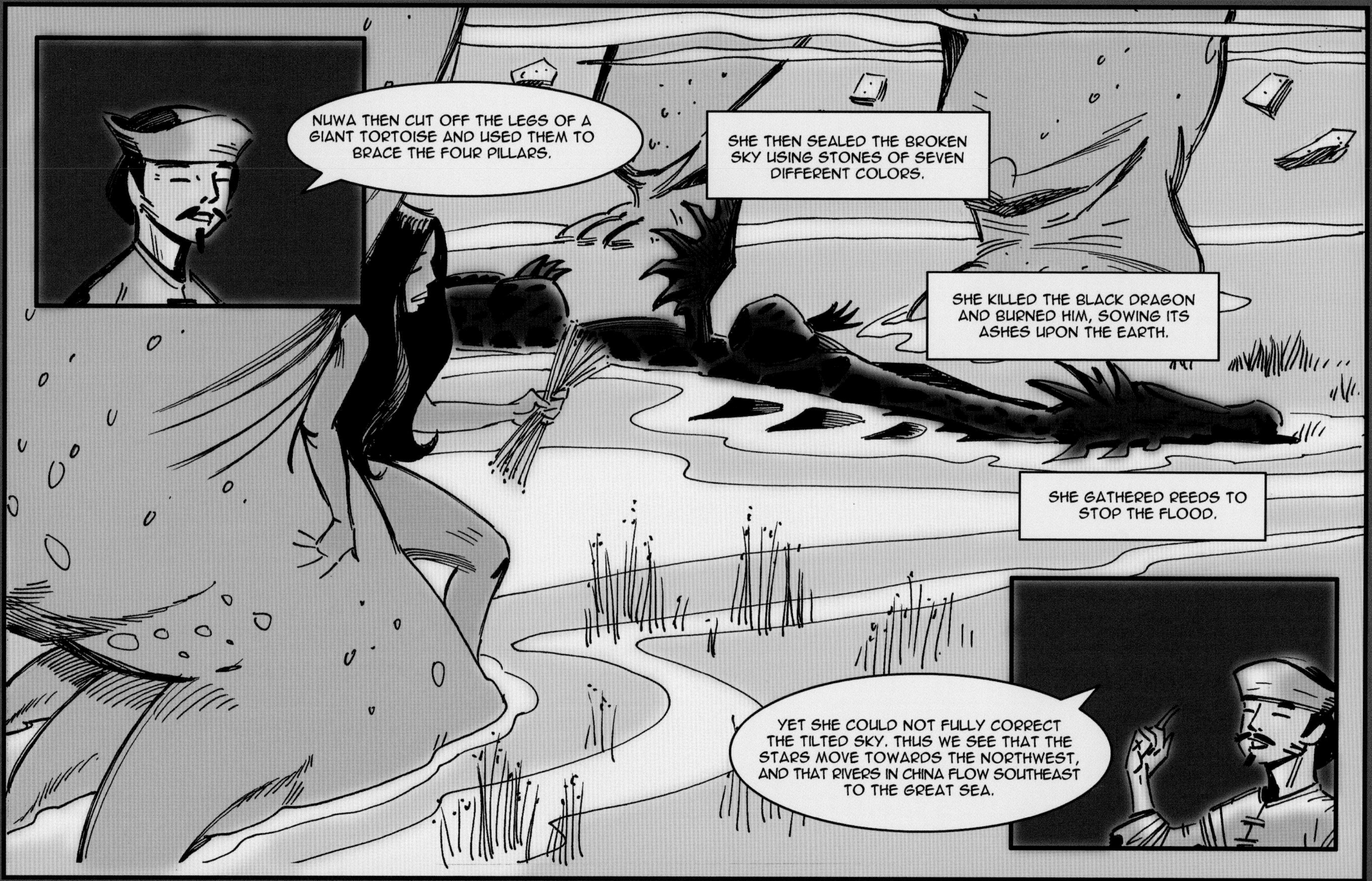
NUWA THEN CUT OFF THE LEGS OF A GIANT TORTOISE AND USED THEM TO BRACE THE FOUR PILLARS.
SHE THEN SEALED THE BROKEN SKY USING STONES OF SEVEN DIFFERENT COLORS.
SHE KILLED THE BLACK DRAGON AND BURNED HIM, SOWING ITS ASHES UPON THE EARTH.
SHE GATHERED REEDS TO STOP THE FLOOD.
YET SHE COULD NOT FULLY CORRECT THE TILTED SKY. THUS WE SEE THAT THE STARS MOVE TOWARDS THE NORTHWEST, AND THAT RIVERS IN CHINA FLOW SOUTHEAST TO THE GREAT SEA.

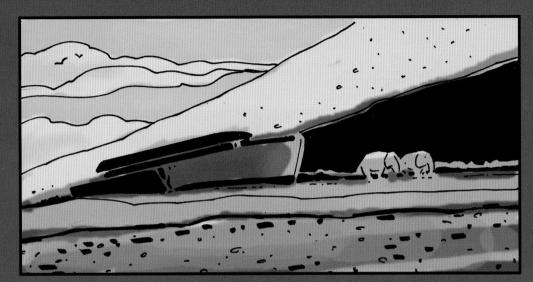

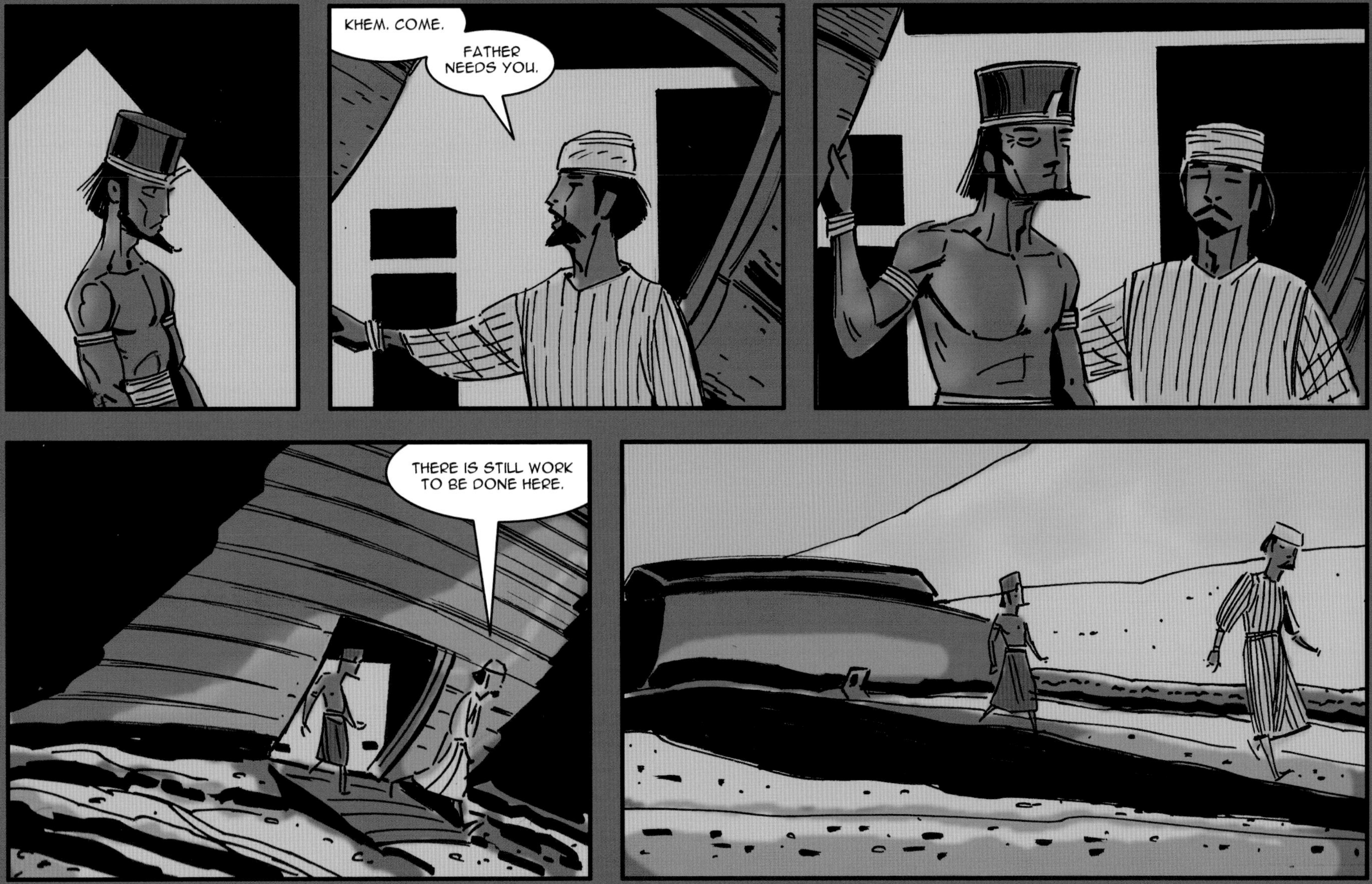
KHEM. COME.
FATHER NEEDS YOU.
THERE IS STILL WORK TO BE DONE HERE.

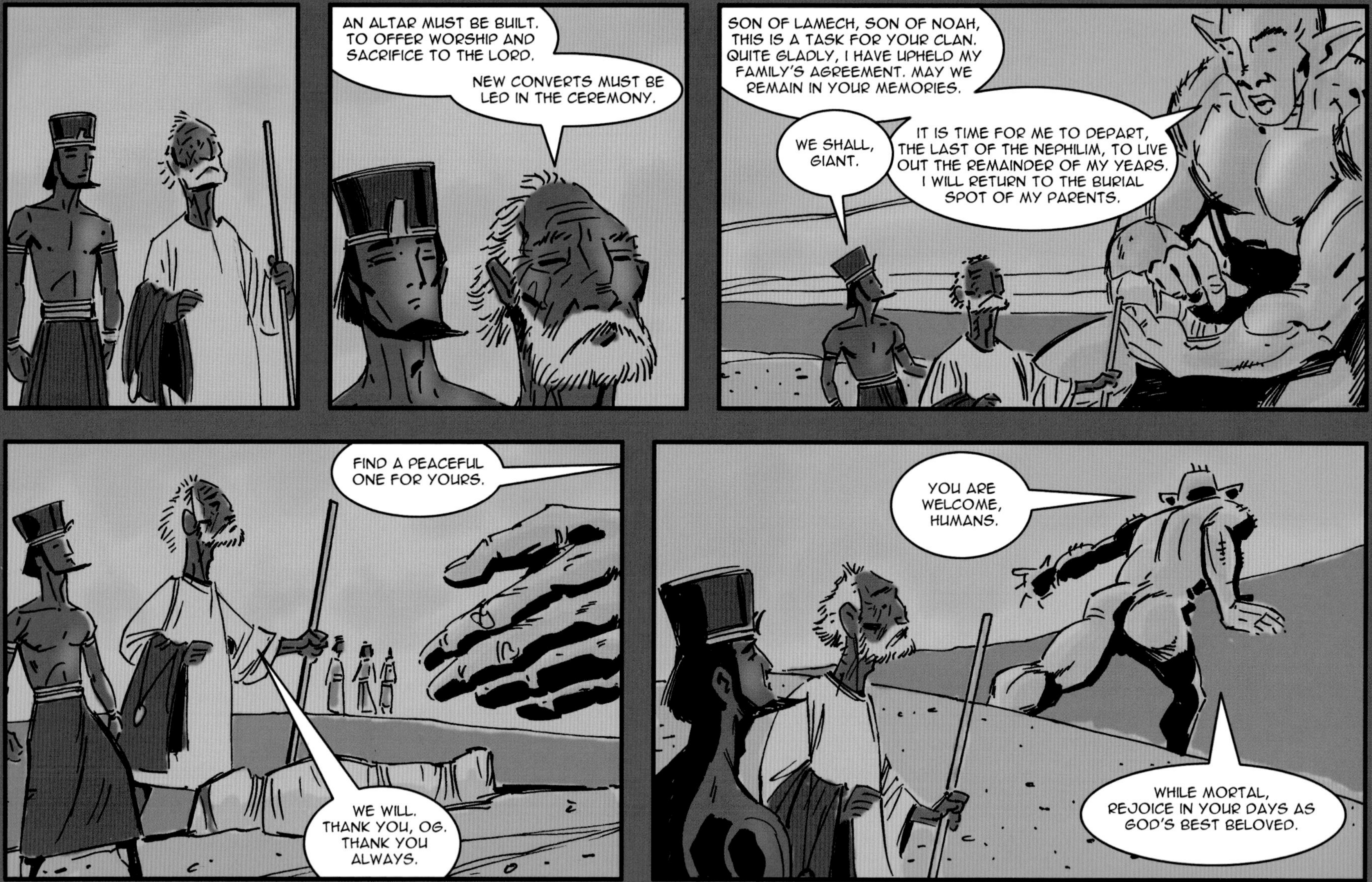
AN ALTAR MUST BE BUILT. TO OFFER WORSHIP AND SACRIFICE TO THE LORD.
NEW CONVERTS MUST BE LED IN THE CEREMONY.
SON OF LAMECH, SON OF NOAH, THIS IS A TASK FOR YOUR CLAN. QUITE GLADLY, I HAVE UPHELD MY FAMILY'S AGREEMENT. MAY WE REMAIN IN YOUR MEMORIES.
WE SHALL, GIANT.
IT IS TIME FOR ME TO DEPART, THE LAST OF THE NEPHILIM, TO LIVE OUT THE REMAINDER OF MY YEARS. I WILL RETURN TO THE BURIAL SPOT OF MY PARENTS.
FIND A PEACEFUL ONE FOR YOURS.
WE WILL. THANK YOU, OG. THANK YOU ALWAYS.
YOU ARE WELCOME, HUMANS.
WHILE MORTAL, REJOICE IN YOUR DAYS AS GOD'S BEST BELOVED.

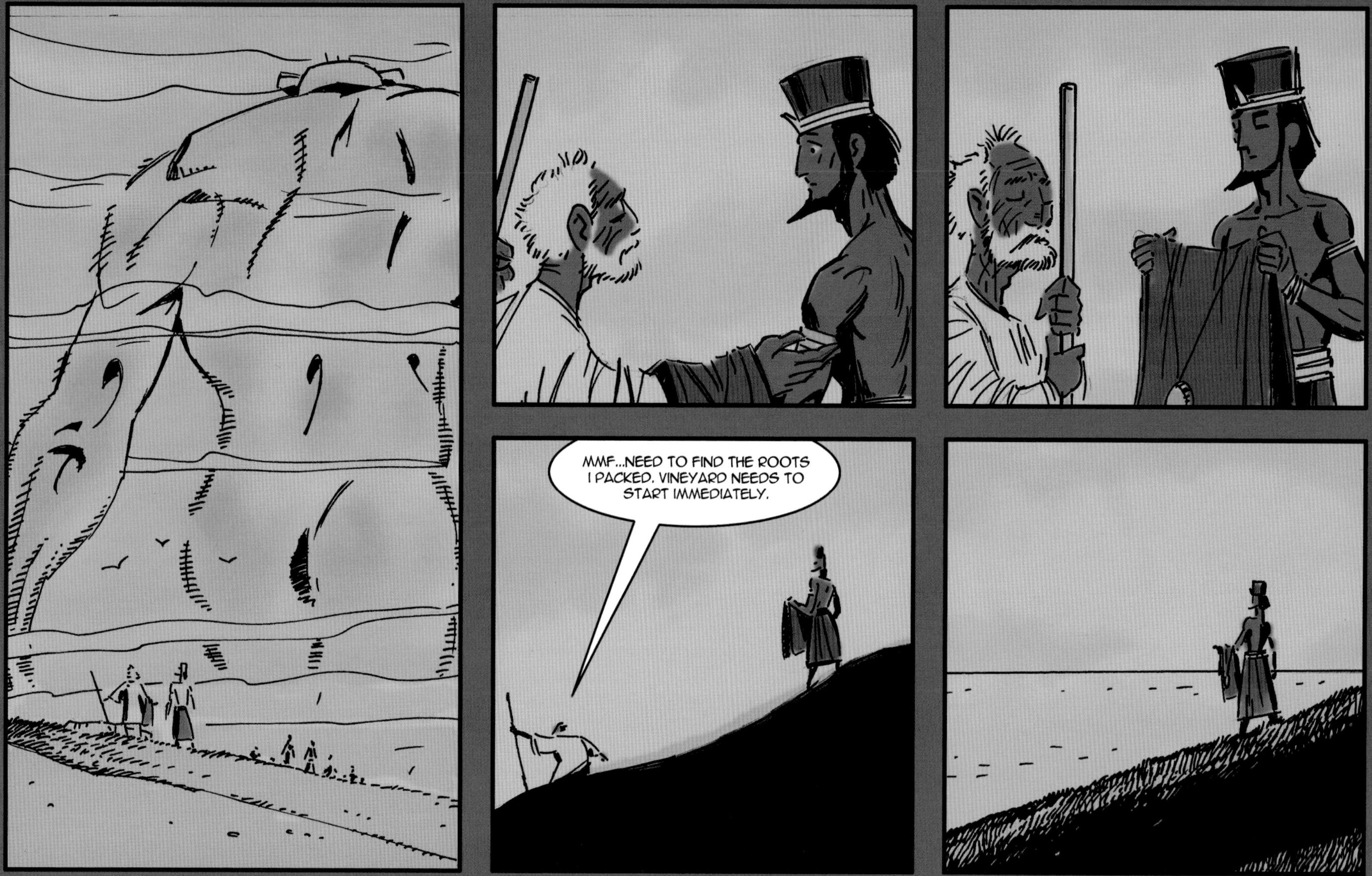
MMF...NEED TO FIND THE ROOTS I PACKED. VINEYARD NEEDS TO START IMMEDIATELY.

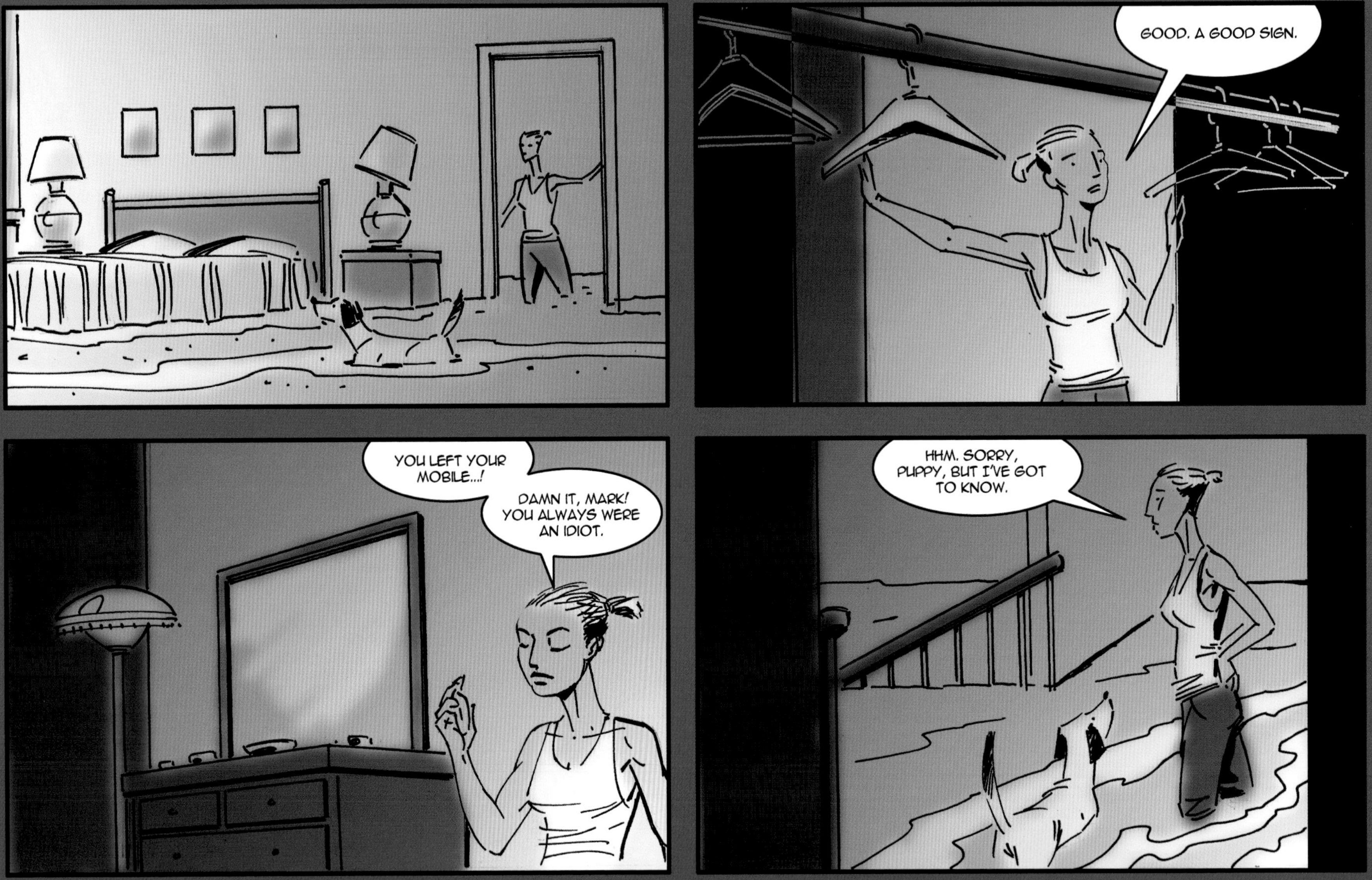
GOOD. A GOOD SIGN.
YOU LEFT YOUR MOBILE...!
DAMN IT, MARK! YOU ALWAYS WERE AN IDIOT.
HHM. SORRY, PUPPY, BUT I'VE GOT TO KNOW.

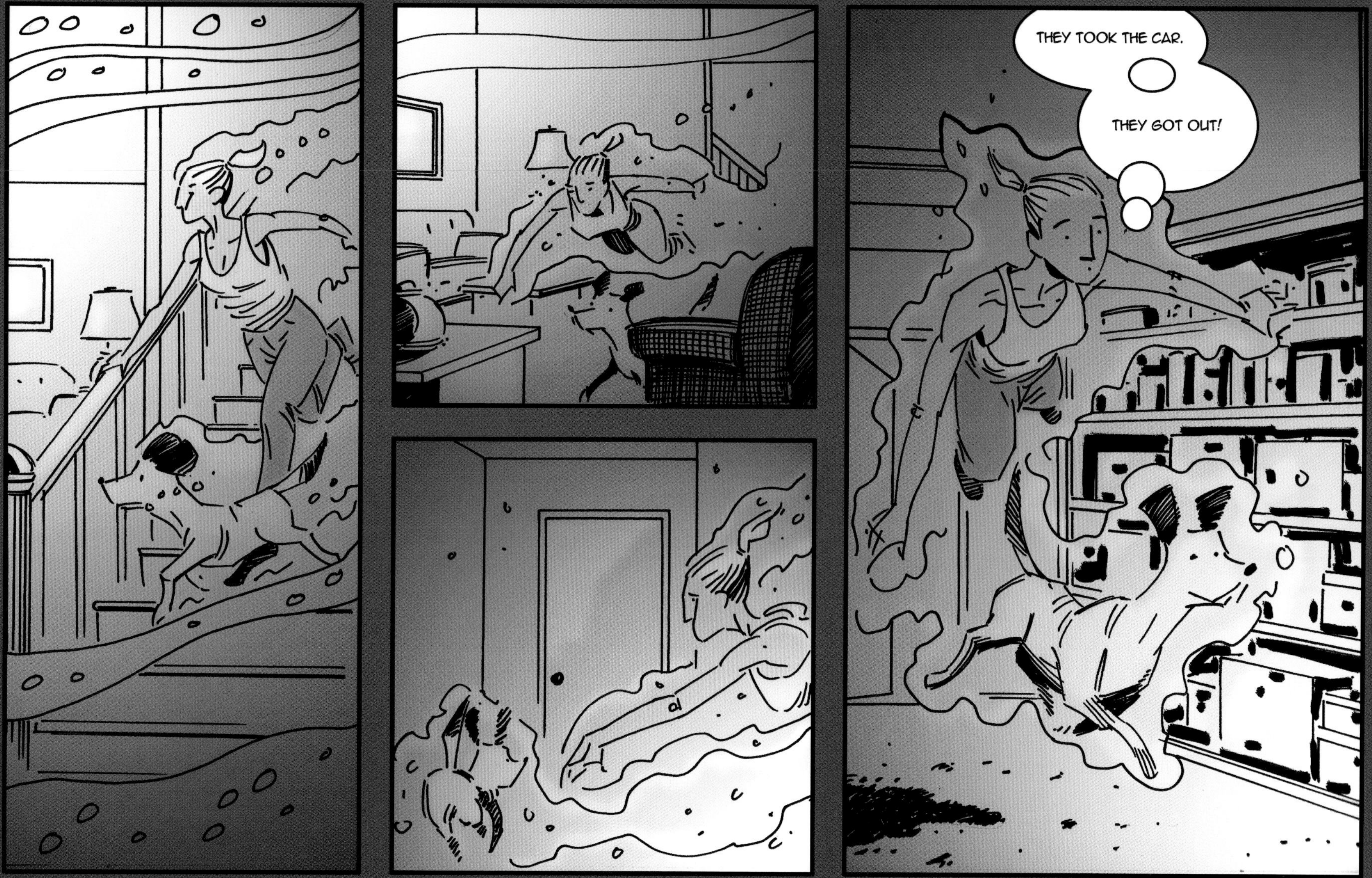
THEY TOOK THE CAR.
THEY GOT OUT!

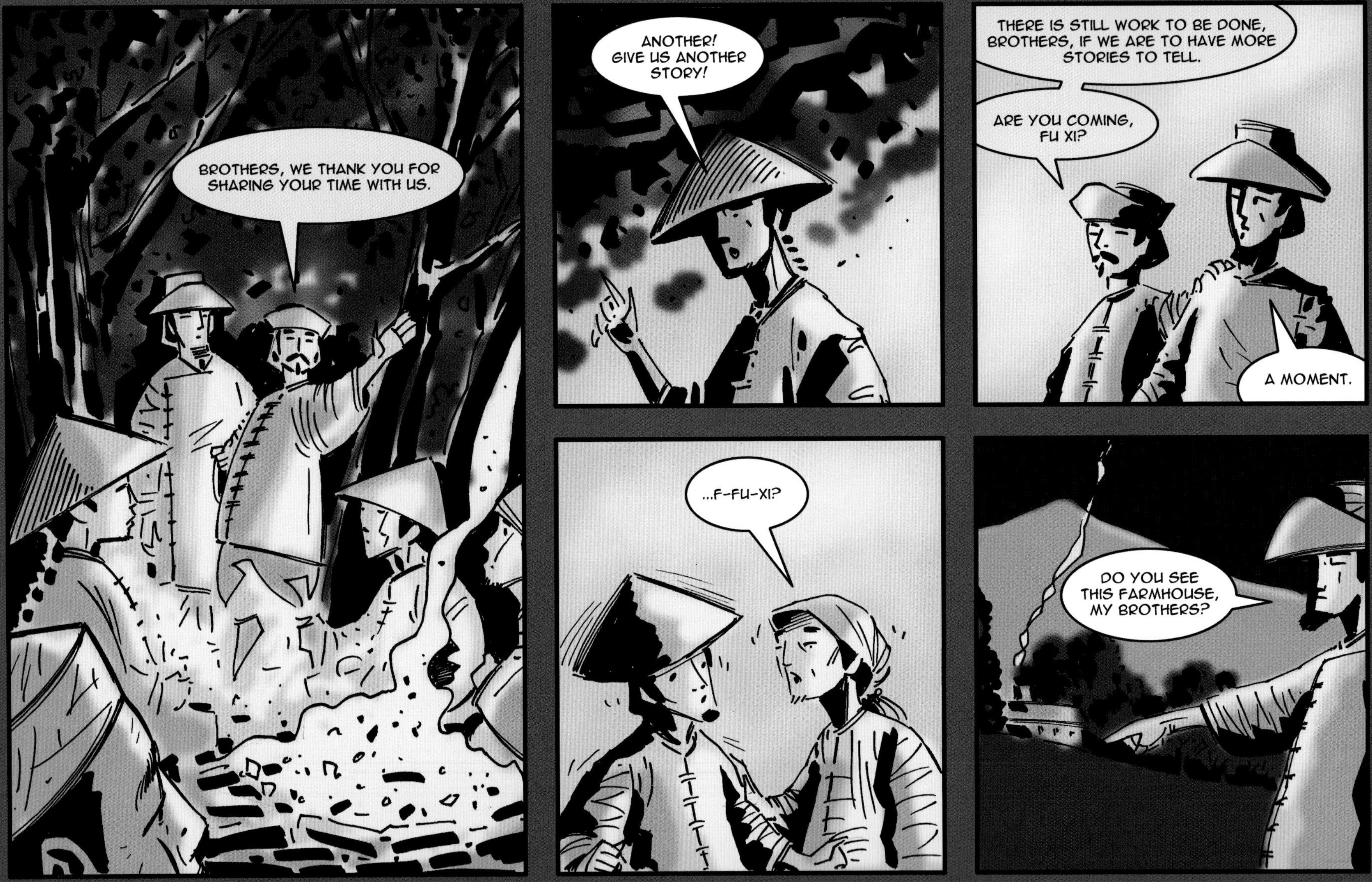
BROTHERS, WE THANK YOU FOR SHARING YOUR TIME WITH US.
ANOTHER! GIVE US ANOTHER STORY!
THERE IS STILL WORK TO BE DONE, BROTHERS, IF WE ARE TO HAVE MORE STORIES TO TELL.
ARE YOU COMING, FU XI?
A MOMENT.
...F-FU-XI?
DO YOU SEE THIS FARMHOUSE, MY BROTHERS?

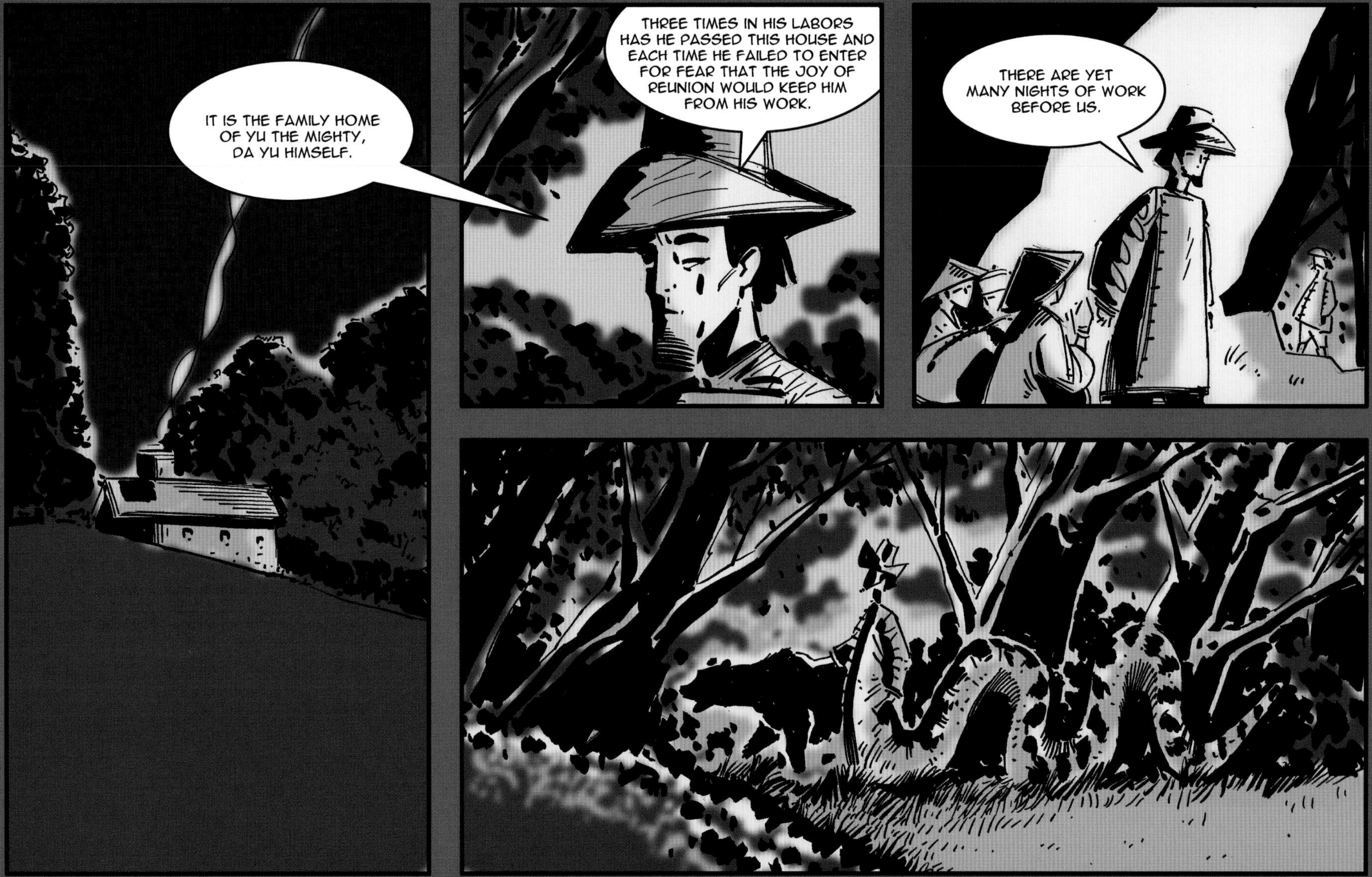
IT IS THE FAMILY HOME OF YU THE MIGHTY, DA YU HIMSELF.
THREE TIMES IN HIS LABORS HAS HE PASSED THIS HOUSE AND EACH TIME HE FAILED TO ENTER FOR FEAR THAT THE JOY OF REUNION WOULD KEEP HIM FROM HIS WORK.
THERE ARE YET MANY NIGHTS OF WORK BEFORE US.

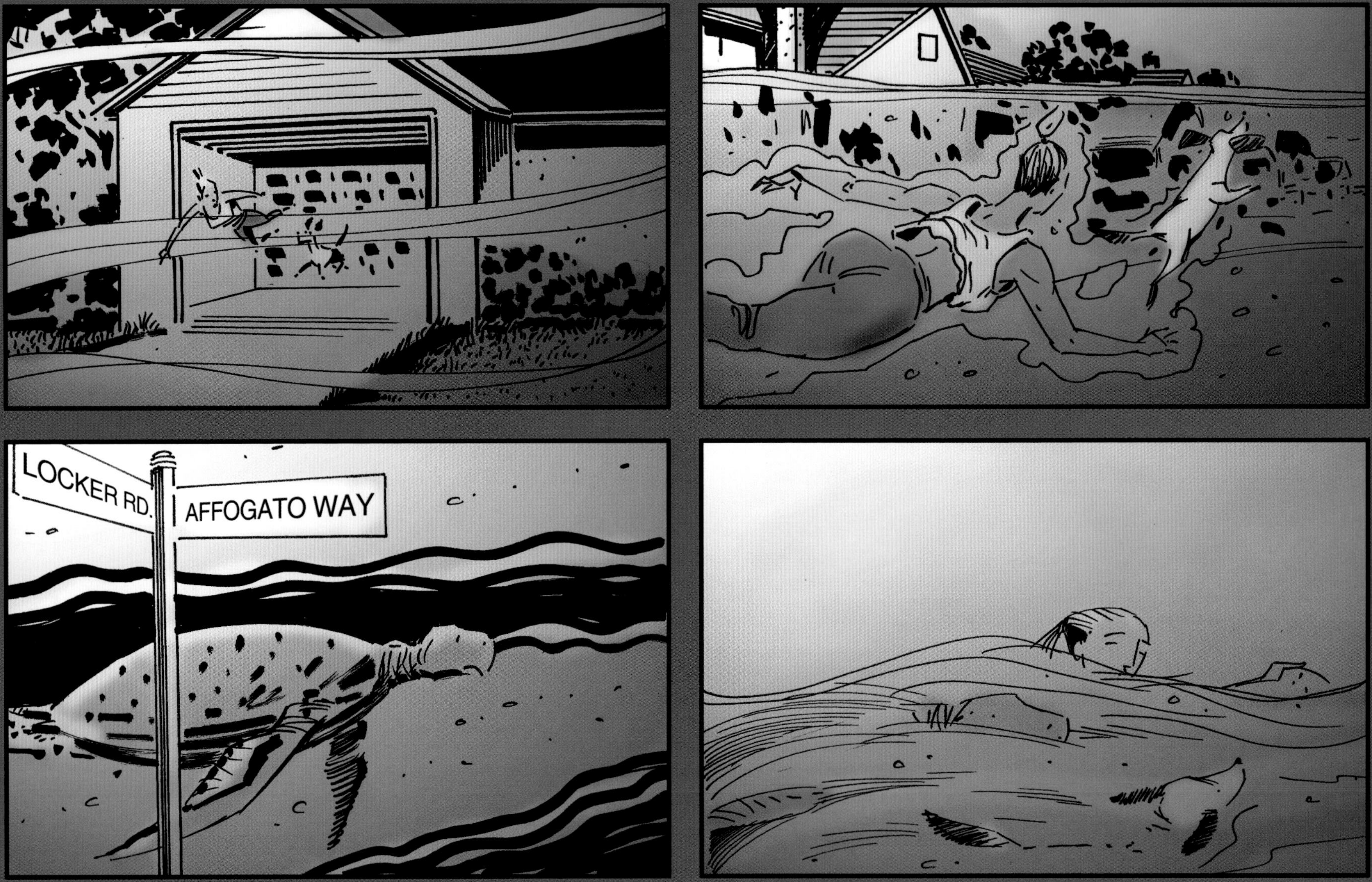
LOCKER RD.
AFFOGATO WAY

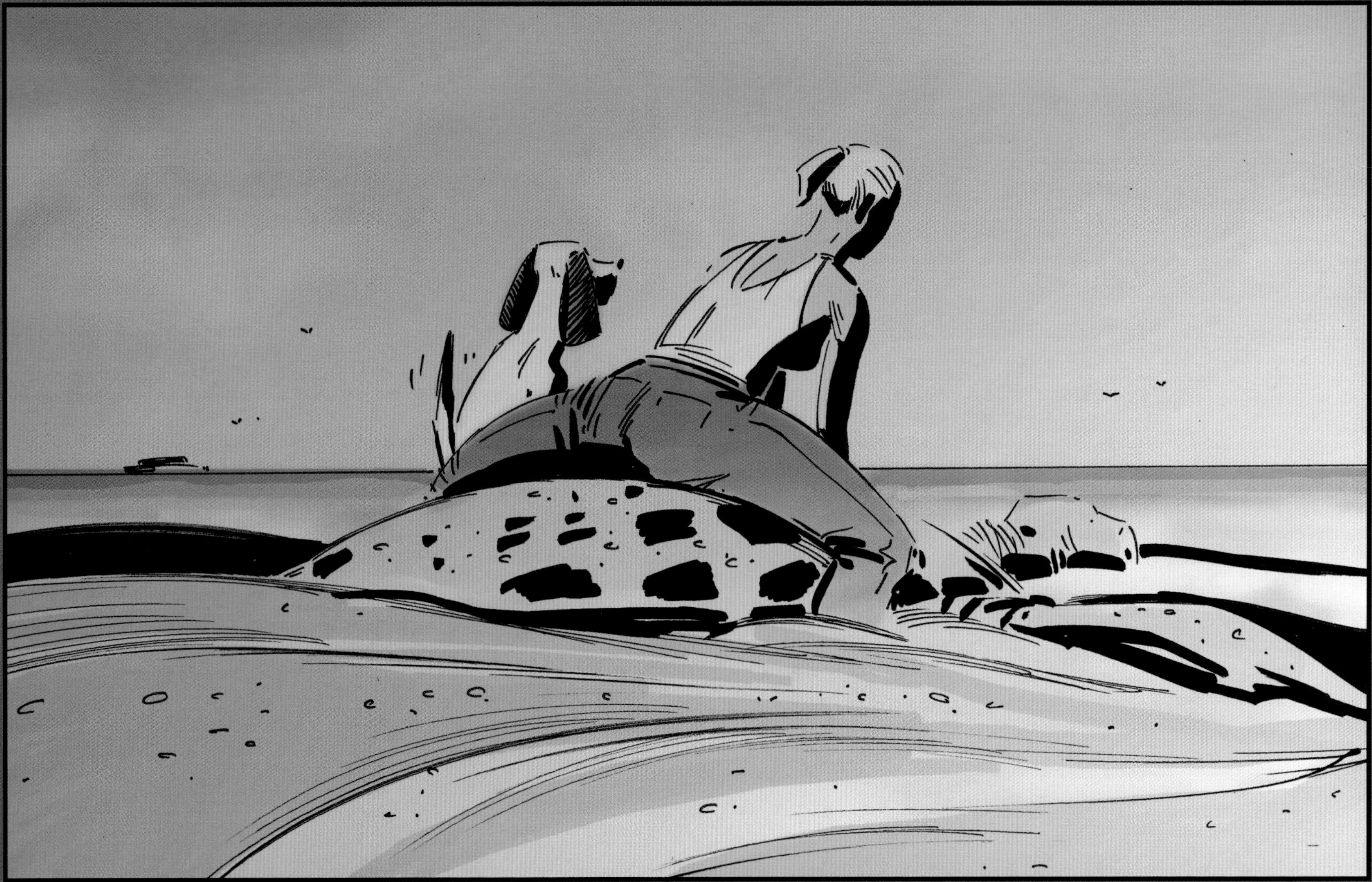

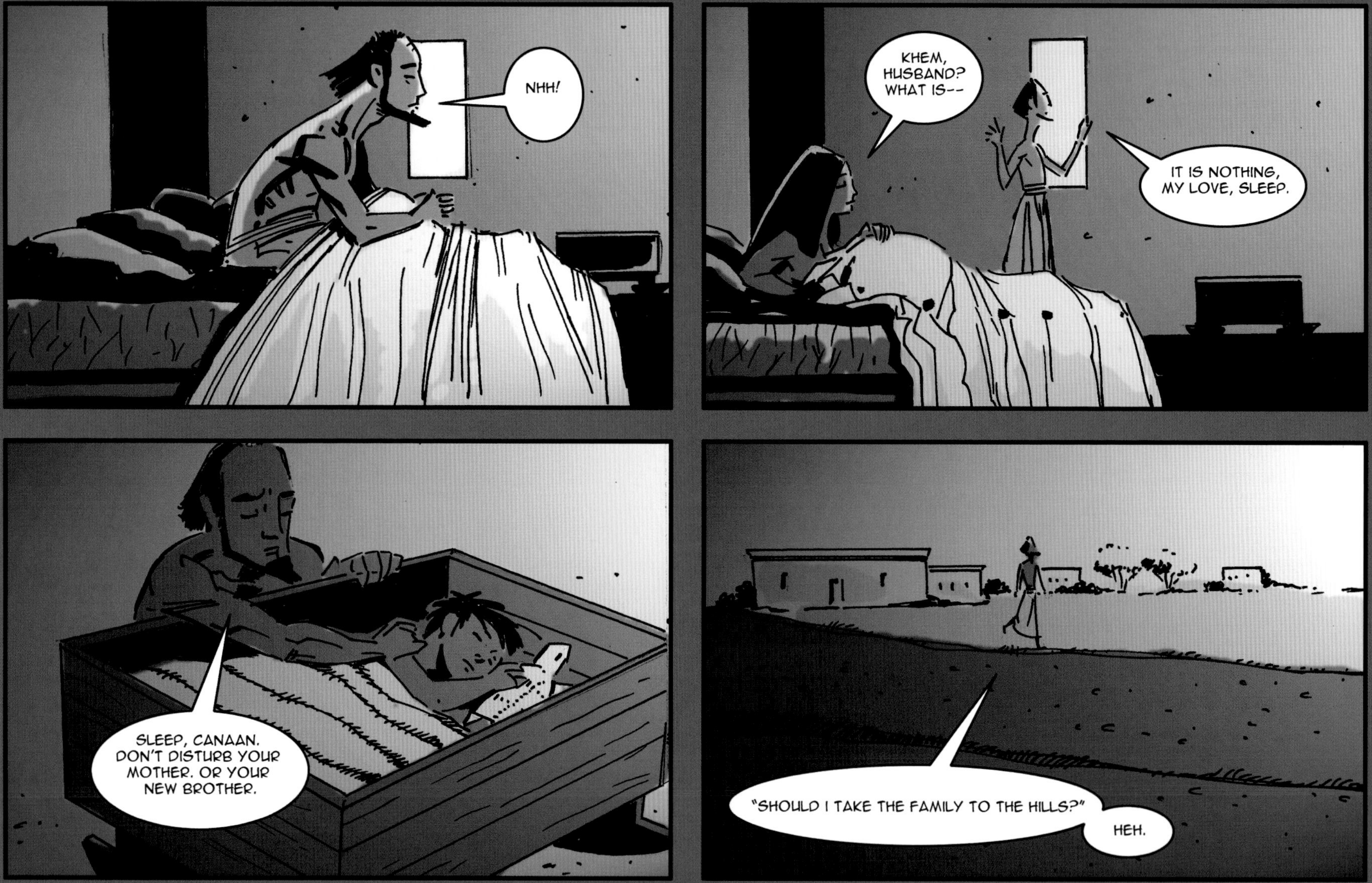
NHH!
KHEM, HUSBAND? WHAT IS--
IT IS NOTHING, MY LOVE, SLEEP.
SLEEP, CANAAN. DON'T DISTURB YOUR MOTHER. OR YOUR NEW BROTHER.
"SHOULD I TAKE THE FAMILY TO THE HILLS?"
HEH.

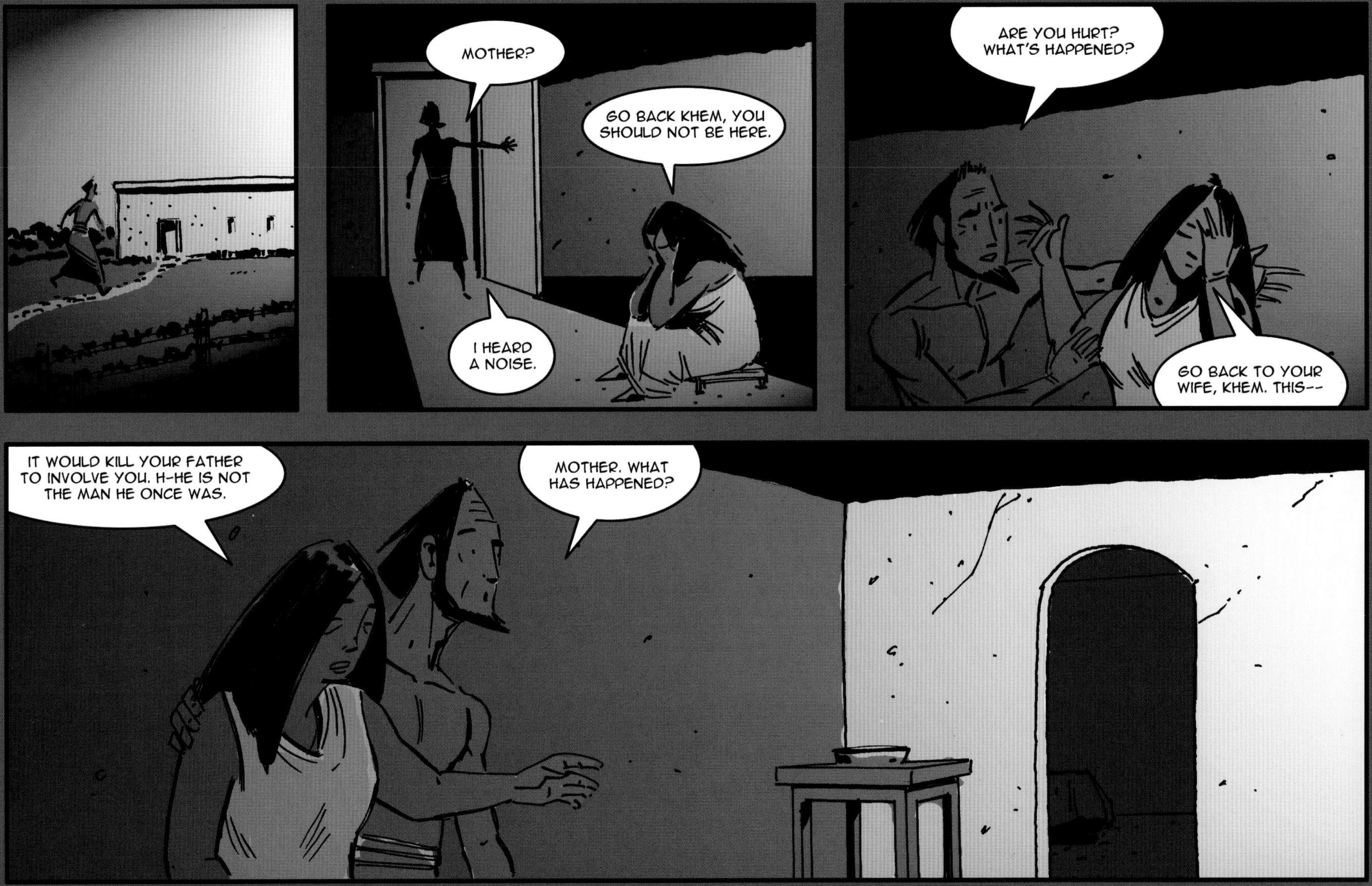
MOTHER?
I HEARD A NOISE.
GO BACK KHEM, YOU SHOULD NOT BE HERE.
ARE YOU HURT? WHAT'S HAPPENED?
GO BACK TO YOUR WIFE, KHEM. THIS--
IT WOULD KILL YOUR FATHER TO INVOLVE YOU. H-HE IS NOT THE MAN HE ONCE WAS.
MOTHER. WHAT HAS HAPPENED?

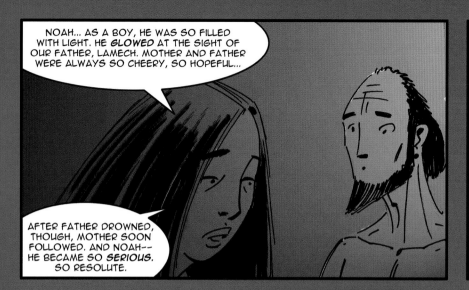

NOAH... AS A BOY, HE WAS SO FILLED WITH LIGHT. HE **GLOWED** AT THE SIGHT OF OUR FATHER, LAMECH. MOTHER AND FATHER WERE ALWAYS SO CHEERY, SO HOPEFUL...

AFTER FATHER DROWNED, THOUGH, MOTHER SOON FOLLOWED. AND NOAH-- HE BECAME SO **SERIOUS.** SO RESOLUTE.

HE, HEH, HE COULD STILL FIND JOY IN ME, I SUPPOSE. AND IN HIS WINE. OVER THE YEARS HE FOUND MORE IN THE LATTER-- BUT I HAD NO COMPLAINTS.

HE BECAME A SPIRITUAL LEADER AND A PATRIARCH. I HAD DOUBTS BUT STILL, I WAS SO PROUD...

NOW... ALL HE DOES IS GO TO HIS VINEYARD AND DRINK HIS WINE. HE CURSES AT ME. HE'S CONSCIOUS JUST LONG ENOUGH TO RAMBLE ON ABOUT AN IMAGINARY MAN WHO TALKS TO HIM ABOUT THE GRAPES.

A-AND...

NOW HE NO LONGER LUSTS FOR ME...!

HE CAN NO LONGER BE AROUSED BY MY FLESH.

120

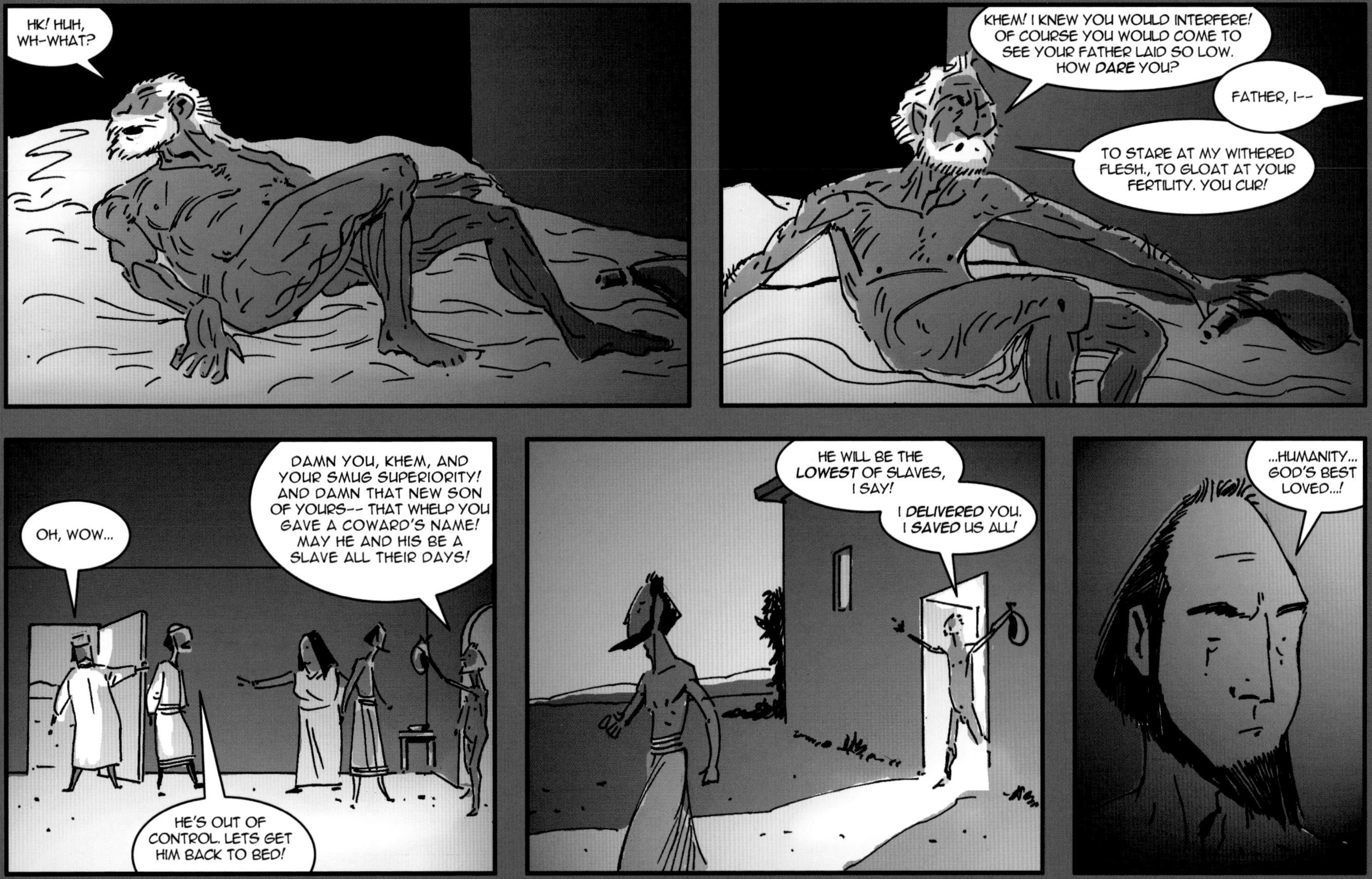
HK! HUH, WH-WHAT?
KHEM! I KNEW YOU WOULD INTERFERE! OF COURSE YOU WOULD COME TO SEE YOUR FATHER LAID SO LOW. HOW DARE YOU?
FATHER, I--
TO STARE AT MY WITHERED FLESH., TO GLOAT AT YOUR FERTILITY. YOU CUR!
OH, WOW...
DAMN YOU, KHEM, AND YOUR SMUG SUPERIORITY! AND DAMN THAT NEW SON OF YOURS-- THAT WHELP YOU GAVE A COWARD'S NAME! MAY HE AND HIS BE A SLAVE ALL THEIR DAYS!
HE'S OUT OF CONTROL. LETS GET HIM BACK TO BED!
HE WILL BE THE LOWEST OF SLAVES, I SAY!
I DELIVERED YOU. I SAVED US ALL!
...HUMANITY... GOD'S BEST LOVED...!

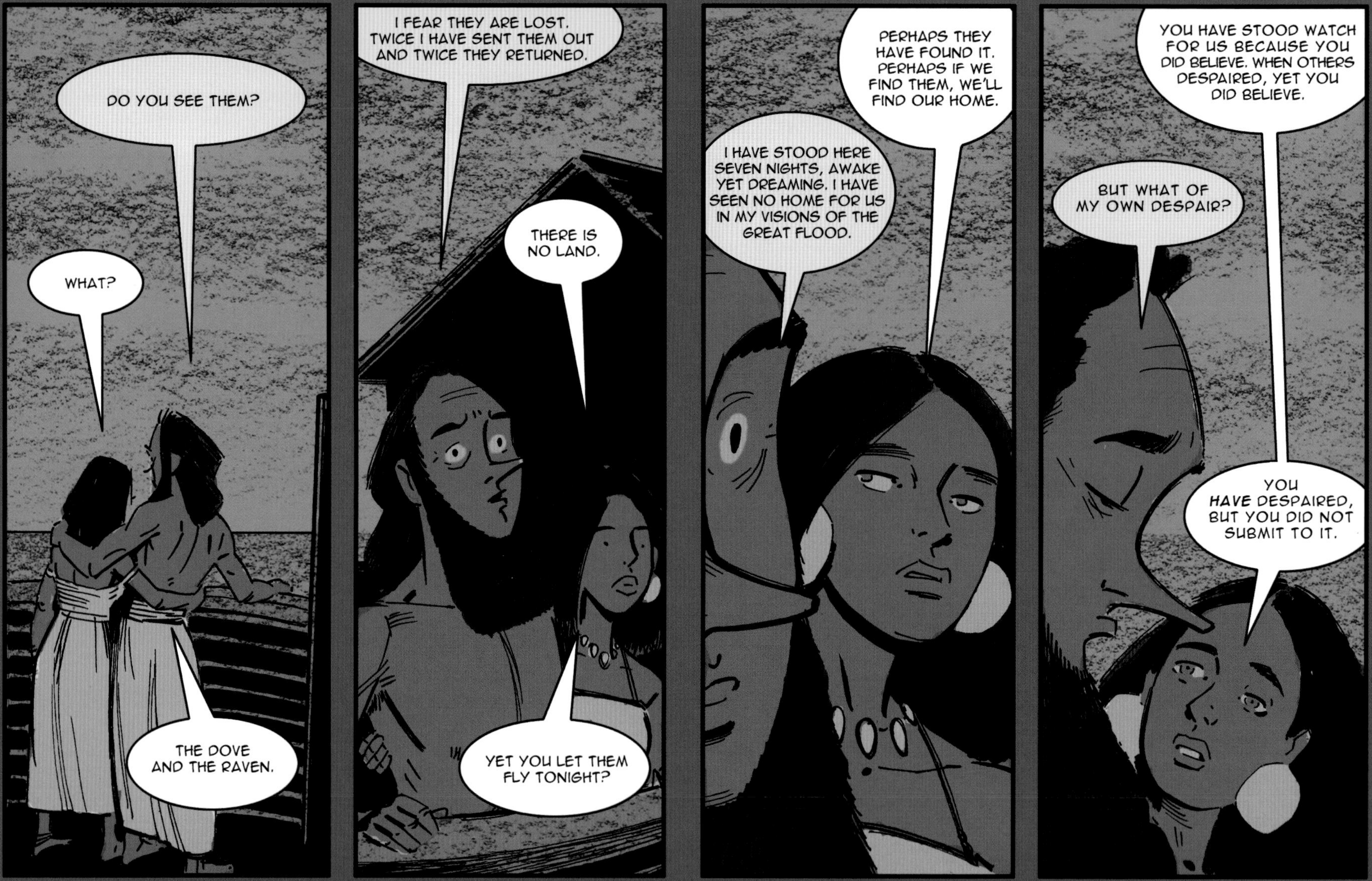
DO YOU SEE THEM?
WHAT?
THE DOVE AND THE RAVEN.
I FEAR THEY ARE LOST. TWICE I HAVE SENT THEM OUT AND TWICE THEY RETURNED.
THERE IS NO LAND.
YET YOU LET THEM FLY TONIGHT?
I HAVE STOOD HERE SEVEN NIGHTS, AWAKE YET DREAMING. I HAVE SEEN NO HOME FOR US IN MY VISIONS OF THE GREAT FLOOD.
PERHAPS THEY HAVE FOUND IT. PERHAPS IF WE FIND THEM, WE'LL FIND OUR HOME.
YOU HAVE STOOD WATCH FOR US BECAUSE YOU DID BELIEVE. WHEN OTHERS DESPAIRED, YET YOU DID BELIEVE.
BUT WHAT OF MY OWN DESPAIR?
YOU **HAVE** DESPAIRED, BUT YOU DID NOT SUBMIT TO IT.

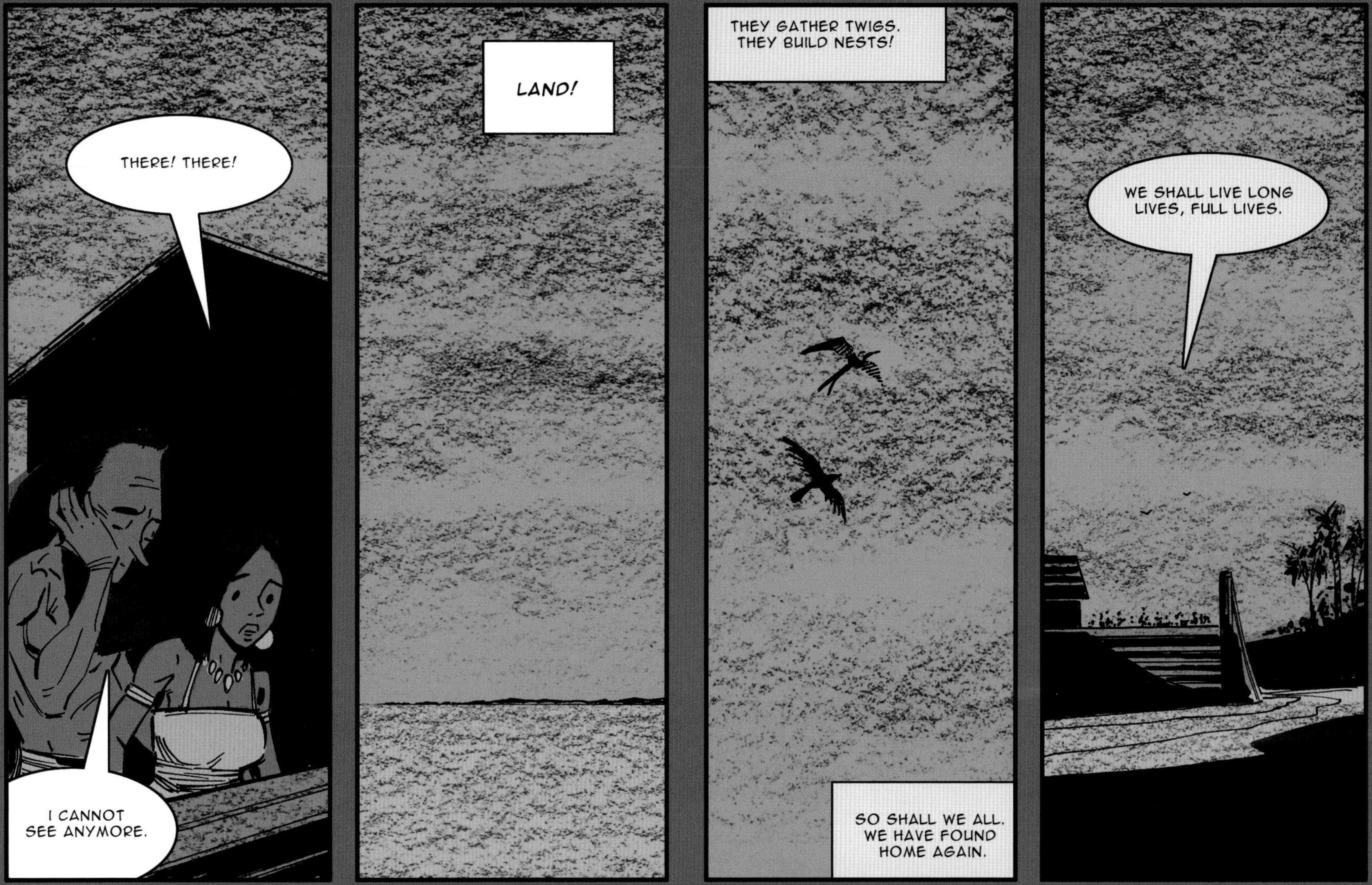
THERE! THERE!
I CANNOT SEE ANYMORE.
LAND!
THEY GATHER TWIGS. THEY BUILD NESTS!
SO SHALL WE ALL. WE HAVE FOUND HOME AGAIN.
WE SHALL LIVE LONG LIVES, FULL LIVES.

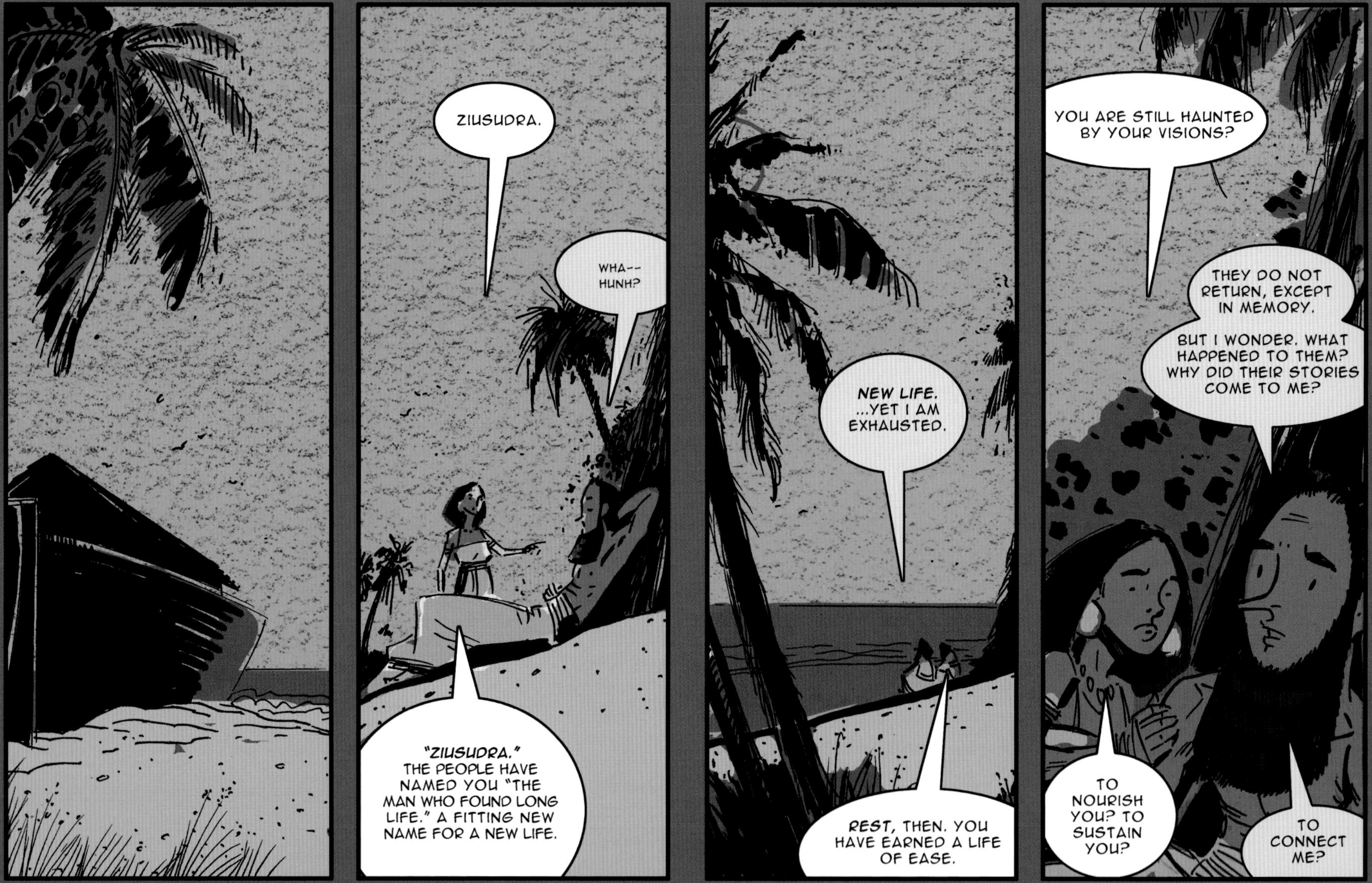
ZIUSUDRA.
WHA-- HUNH?
"ZIUSUDRA." THE PEOPLE HAVE NAMED YOU "THE MAN WHO FOUND LONG LIFE." A FITTING NEW NAME FOR A NEW LIFE.
NEW LIFE. ...YET I AM EXHAUSTED.
REST, THEN. YOU HAVE EARNED A LIFE OF EASE.
YOU ARE STILL HAUNTED BY YOUR VISIONS?
THEY DO NOT RETURN, EXCEPT IN MEMORY.
BUT I WONDER. WHAT HAPPENED TO THEM? WHY DID THEIR STORIES COME TO ME?
TO NOURISH YOU? TO SUSTAIN YOU?
TO CONNECT ME?

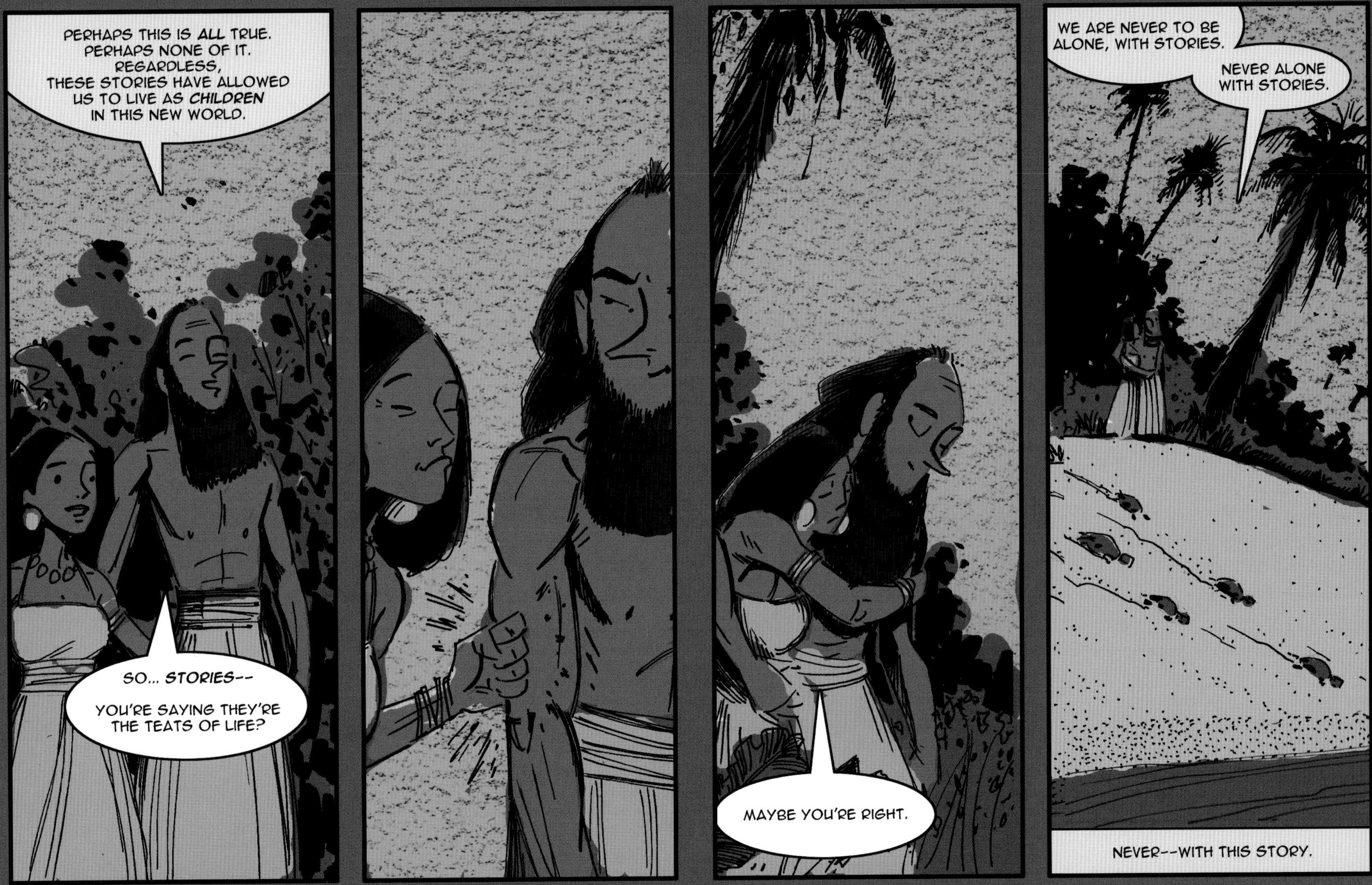
PERHAPS THIS IS ALL TRUE. PERHAPS NONE OF IT. REGARDLESS, THESE STORIES HAVE ALLOWED US TO LIVE AS CHILDREN IN THIS NEW WORLD.
SO... STORIES-- YOU'RE SAYING THEY'RE THE TEATS OF LIFE?
MAYBE YOU'RE RIGHT.
WE ARE NEVER TO BE ALONE, WITH STORIES.
NEVER ALONE WITH STORIES.
NEVER--WITH THIS STORY.

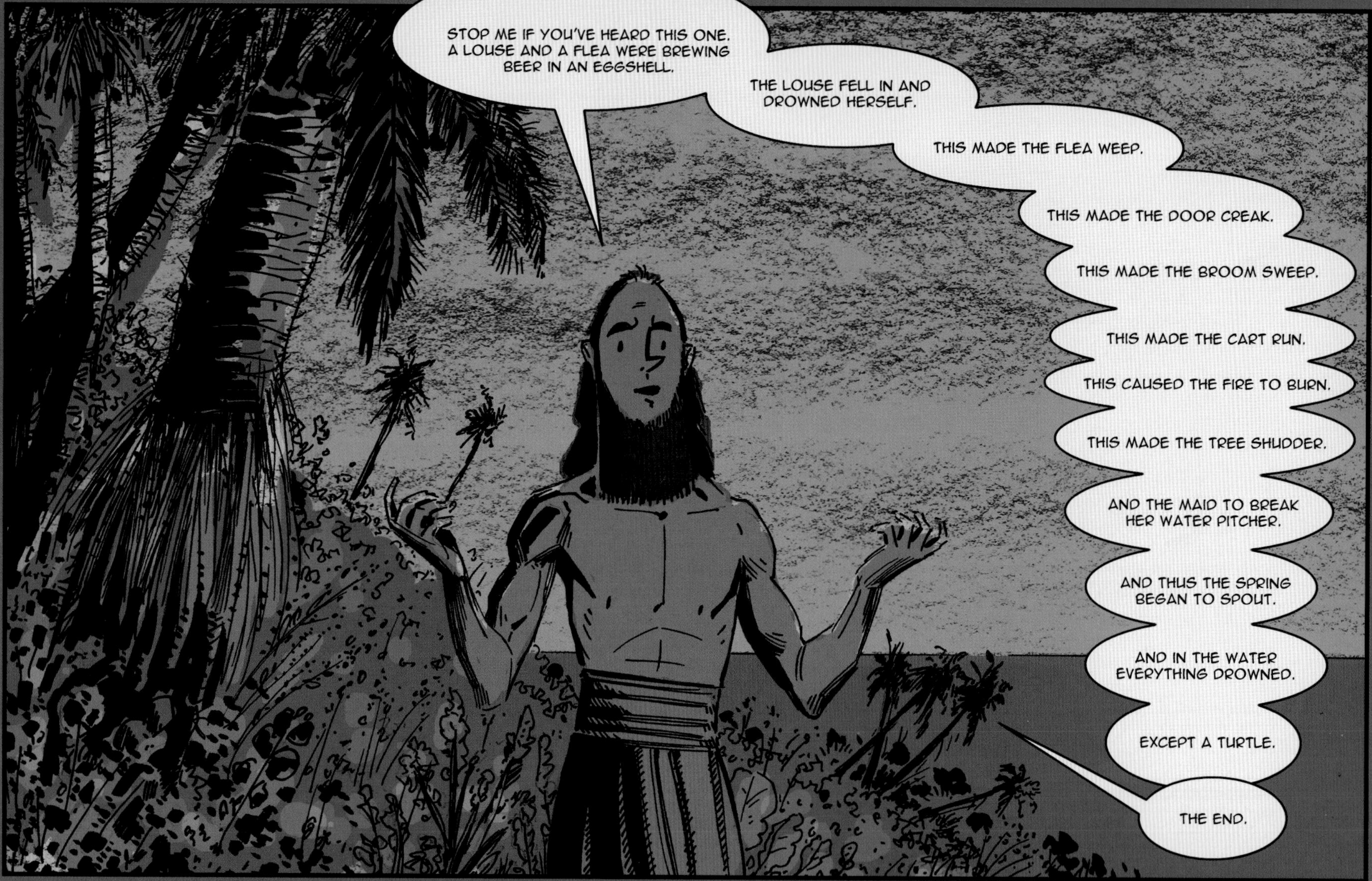
STOP ME IF YOU'VE HEARD THIS ONE. A LOUSE AND A FLEA WERE BREWING BEER IN AN EGGSHELL.
THE LOUSE FELL IN AND DROWNED HERSELF.
THIS MADE THE FLEA WEEP.
THIS MADE THE DOOR CREAK.
THIS MADE THE BROOM SWEEP.
THIS MADE THE CART RUN.
THIS CAUSED THE FIRE TO BURN.
THIS MADE THE TREE SHUDDER.
AND THE MAID TO BREAK HER WATER PITCHER.
AND THUS THE SPRING BEGAN TO SPOUT.
AND IN THE WATER EVERYTHING DROWNED.
EXCEPT A TURTLE.
THE END.

ABOUT THE AUTHORS

A. David Lewis is a Boston educator earning degrees from Brandeis University, Georgetown University, and Boston University. In his academic capacity, he lectures nationally on comics studies, serves as an Editorial Board member for the *International Journal of Comic Art,* founded the Religion and Graphica Collection at B.U., and co-edited *Graven Images: Religion in Comic Books and Graphic Novels* for Continuum International Publishing. Lewis also self-published the award-winning *Mortal Coils* series and *The Lone and Level Sands* graphic novel, later produced by Archaia.

Marvin Mann began his comics career in 1989 inking *The Trouble With Girls* (Malibu Graphics). After a departure into furniture-making and 3d modeling and animation he returned to comics in 2002 by creating a 240 page silent comic strip and two flipbook animations for *Pause and Effect: The Art of Interactive Narrative* (New Riders). He is the artist and co-creator of four original graphic novels to come from Archaia, *The Lone and Levels Sands, Some New Kind of Slaughter, The Grave Doug Freshley* and *Inanna's Tears*. He lives in California.